FRIENDS AND LOVERS
The Phenomenology of Desire in Shakespearean Comedy

FRIENDS AND LOVERS
The Phenomenology of Desire
in Shakespearean Comedy

W. Thomas MacCary

COLUMBIA UNIVERSITY PRESS
NEW YORK   1985

The Andrew W. Mellon Foundation, through a special grant,
has assisted the Press in publishing this volume.

Library of Congress Cataloging in Publication Data

MacCary, W. Thomas.
Friends and lovers.

Includes index.
1. Shakespeare, William, 1564–1616—Comedies.
2. Love in literature.   3. Phenomenology and literature.
4. Psychoanalysis and literature.   I. Title.
PR2981.M28   1985   822.3′3   84-17605
ISBN 0-231-05784-9 (alk. paper)

Columbia University Press
New York   Guildford, Surrey

Printed in the United States of America

This book is dedicated to
MARGARET CHAMBERS MacCARY

CONTENTS

ACKNOWLEDGMENTS

I had been at work on this project for over ten years when in January 1983 Frank Kermode came to Columbia, where I was then teaching. In a series of brief encounters over the next four months, I tested the different points of my thesis upon him, and he alerted me to other opinions I must consider. I completed the manuscript in that time and submitted it to Columbia University Press, whose editor-in-chief, William Germano, had already expressed an interest in its development.

In July 1983 I received the report of a reader, who later identified himself as Murray Schwartz, and I followed his general outline for revision. At this stage the specific suggestions of Richard Abrams were extremely valuable. He had followed and encouraged the evolution of my ideas over the entire period of the book's composition; at this point and later on he gave meticulous attention to both form and content.

It was also at this stage that Madeline Aria went through the manuscript and convinced me to jettison much superfluous material, tighten up my main argument, and in some important respects, change it. For instance, she first pointed out to me that Titania's love for an ass is the fulfillment of Oberon's nightmare fantasy of female sexuality.

In the various revisions I have been fortunate in the attentions of Richard McCoy, James Mirollo and Peter Rudnytsky. Anne McCoy at Columbia University Press unraveled some of my tortuous syntax. Ken Venezio designed the book and its jacket.

I dedicate it to my daughter Margaret. In the spring of 1983, when she was only fourteen, she played Helena in *A Midsummer Night's Dream*, and the next year Olivia in *Twelfth Night*. The productions were sponsored by the Allen-Stevenson School in New York City, and directed by Caroline Berry and David Kersey. To see these plays acted by young people was a revelation to me.

All quotations from Shakespeare are taken from the most recent Arden editions.

Seaman Farm
Stormville, New York
August 1984

FRIENDS AND LOVERS
The Phenomenology of Desire in Shakespearean Comedy

I

INTRODUCTION

I read Shakespearean comedy as a corpus of serious drama in which issues of extreme importance to human happiness are raised and often resolved, where the action itself, though full of coincidence and exotic detail, reveals basic patterns in human experience, and where even the conventions, like disguise, feigned death, and resurrection, suggest the fulfillment of the deepest human desires. I insist that we listen carefully when the young men and women in Shakespearean comedy speak about love, about how they feel toward each other, and about what these feelings mean to their thinking about themselves and their world. I am convinced that the ten comedies I shall discuss here are a consideration of the orientation of desire and its constitution of individual identity—the relation between the erotic and the ontogenetic—comparable in profundity, complexity, and completeness to the dialogues of Plato and the metapsychological essays of Freud.

When I read these comedies I am not most impressed by their celebration of marriage, their validation of social intercourse, or their apology for Christian virtues. They do not resolve themselves into meditations on Grace and Redemption, Mercy, Charity, or any other such "universal" values. Indeed, what most impresses me about these plays is their concreteness, their insistence on the detail of life—especially, but not exclusively, erotic life. Their poetry accomplishes for me not a redemption of my immortal soul, but a redemption of physical reality from the abstraction and hypostatization of other literature—lyric, dramatic, and philosophical—in which such problems are dealt with but where they are taken beyond our experience, so that we finally feel manipulated by their patterns (to the extent that we participate in them at all). Shakespeare always forces his lovers to learn from their own experience of love, to see for the first time with their own eyes, and not to allow their experience of love to be patterned by previously existing forms of love. Indeed, in this and other important respects, Shakespeare has a great deal in common with Cervantes, his near contemporary: both writers take from the vast store of medieval romance those narrative forms which reveal certain constants in human experience, but they force us to see how these can distort our perception of reality, especially the real circumstances of love. Cardenio thinks he sees his betrothed marry another man; Claudio thinks he sees Hero make love to another man.[1] Why do lovers so consistently misread their actual circumstances? For many reasons, of course, but in these cases because of the myth *la donna è mobile*.

If one accepts the argument that Shakespearean comedy is essentially about the modes of love, that love is its real content, then one can begin to appreciate how Shakespeare's treatment of love opens up into an entire worldview. I shall claim for Shakespeare a moral and philosophical relativism which we tend to associate first with Hobbes, his younger contemporary. If we pay attention to all the discussion among Shakespeare's lovers of the importance of seeing and seeming, then we must admit that Shakespeare presents us with a phenomenology of desire. There is no "true" love in Shakespeare in the sense either that, in the Neoplatonic perspective, one claims to love absolute Truth and Beauty in the example of the beloved, or that two particular people are fated to find each other and can only be happy and complete when they do. Rather Shakespeare presents us with young people who feel desire and try to satisfy it first with one object and then with another, a kind of erotic bricolage. We finally appreciate that what these young people are really accomplishing is a mirroring of themselves in the objects of their desire, so the erotic quest is also an ontogenetic quest.

Shakespeare is consistent in this depiction of love throughout his career, and there is a similar consistency in his treatment, in the comedies, of other aspects of human experience. Just as, with Hobbes, he seems to say that every man's appetites and aversions are a law unto that man, but not to other men, i.e., that desire is a purely individual determination and that there can never be universal agreement on its objects, so, too, he seems to say that perception generally is individual, that there are no constant patterns in nature upon which we can depend, but rather, like lovers seeing beauty in a brow of Egypt, we project order upon chaos. In this way we see a close connection between Shakespeare's phenomenology of desire and his phenomenology of art. We must determine, however, the locus of the phenomena: is it the eye or the mind?

Once we have accepted that Shakespeare believes, with Bacon, that we worship idols and insist on fitting actual experience to strange preconceptions, then we must wonder whether Shakespeare thought he was presenting in his plays any model of reality, any actual truth. It is a particularly important concern since, for almost four hundred years, we have been reading Shakespeare as truth. I am convinced that we have established in his texts idols which do not belong there, which are not of his making. I believe that the only constants Shakespeare saw in human experience are desire and creativity, and that these are essentially the same for him—that they are both attempts to find oneself in the world and to impose oneself upon the world, but, by definition, they are functions of, and subject to, change.

The comedies trace a pattern of desire which is originally and even ultimately narcissistic. In most of them we are encouraged to see the action from the point of view of one character, a young man, who must learn to love. At the opening of the play, he is "sick of self-love," in love with love, a scoffer at love, or, in the technical terms of Renaissance psychology, suffering from melancholy, which derives from a double bind; it is desire without an appropriate object because it is uncentered in a self-conscious subject. We compare the opening speeches of Antipholus of Syracuse in *The Comedy of Errors*, and of Antonio in *The Merchant of Venice*:

> He that commends me to my own content
> Commends me to the thing I cannot get.
> I to the world am like a drop of water

That in the ocean seeks another drop,
Who, falling there to find his fellow forth,
(Unseen, inquisitive) confounds himself. (*CE* I.ii.33–38)

Ant. In sooth I know not why I am so sad,
  It wearies me, you say it wearies you;
  But how I caught it, found it, or came by it,
  What stuff 'tis made of, whereof it is born,
  I am to learn:
  And such a want-wit sadness makes of me,
  That I have much ado to know myself.
Sal. Your mind is tossing on the ocean,
  There where your argosies with portly sail
  Like signiors and rich burghers on the flood,
  Or as it were the pageants of the sea,
  Do overpeer the petty traffickers. (*MV* I.i. 1–12)

In the first case, the young man must find his twin brother—and, indeed, reintegrate himself into his whole nuclear family, finding mother and father as well—and only then enter into a satisfying relation with a woman. In the second case, a middle-aged man is so completely involved emotionally with a younger man, his being so completely identified with the younger man—"My purse, my person, my extremest means/ Lie all unlock'd to your occasions." (I.i.138–39)—that he cannot value anything else, anybody else, even his own body and himself. Antonio in this play, as also Antonio in *Twelfth Night*, never learns how to love well, and is left out of the marriages at the end of the play.

Other characters, however, start by not knowing themselves or their appropriate objects of desire and so learn to love; often young women transvestized as young men teach them. Orsino states his dilemma in terms of the sea, the same reference made by Antipholus of Syracuse and by Antonio's friend:

O spirit of love, how quick and fresh art thou,
That notwithstanding thy capacity
Receiveth as the sea, nought enters there,
Of what validity and pitch soe'er,
But falls into abatement and low price,
Even in a minute! So full of shapes is fancy,
That it alone is high fantastical.

(*TN* I.i.9–15)

This is another thematic opening statement by a leading character. Orsino claims great capacity, but his image suggests emptiness; he loves from an insecure center of identity. The narcissist seeks himself in a mirror image of himself, but this makes of the world a void. The imagery of the sea is as descriptive of narcissism as the mirroring of the youth in the pool, and closely related, if not actually derived, therefrom. Viola-Cesario, transvestized to become his mirror, will teach Orsino to love, just as Rosalind-Ganymede will teach Orlando, Julia-Sebastian will teach Proteus, and Portia-Balthasar will teach Bassanio.

We note also in Orsino's speech the emphasis on the visual element in love: "fancy" and "fantasy" are cognate and derive ultimately from the Greek verb *phainō*, "to bring to light," with its middle form *phainesthai*, "to appear." We are reminded again and again in Shakespeare of the phenomenology of love, "the study of the seeming of love:"

> *Tell me where is fancy bred,*
> *Or in the heart or in the head?*
> *How begot, how nourished?*
> *Reply, reply.*
>
> *It is engend'red in the eyes,*
> *With gazing fed, and Fancy dies*
> *In the cradle where it lies:*
> *Let us all ring Fancy's knell.*
> *I'll begin it. Ding, dong, bell.*

(MV III.ii.63–71)

What do lovers learn to look for in their beloved? Shakespeare's answer is clear: the mirror images of themselves. He carefully takes his young men through four stages of object-choice: first, they love themselves (or seek themselves); then, they love mirror images of themselves in twins or friends; after that, they love those same images in transvestized young women; finally they learn to love young women in all their specific, unique, and complex virtues. This is simultaneously a philosophical evolution and a psychological development, as we shall see. Above all, it is Shakespeare's insistence that a lover can love only when he is secure in his own identity; paradoxically, of course, his identity must be a function of the objects he chooses—first parents, then friends, then lovers. There is a tension, then, in Shakespearean comedy between the subject of desire as he constitutes himself as a man capable of loving objects, and the constitution of those objects as he needs them, i.e., the projection of his desires upon friends and lovers. This is all immediately recognizable as the standard pattern of adolescent sexuality, but it is also a recapitulation of the pattern of primary narcissism, the process of introjection through which the infant in his earliest experience of his parents comes into being as a self-conscious subject.

Perhaps the best way to express the further claim that Shakespeare perceived a relation between this way lovers have of seeing themselves in their beloveds and the way men generally see themselves in the world, is to refer to Freud, who relates his "discovery" of men's unconscious minds to Copernicus' discovery of the heliocentric universe, and Darwin's of the origin and evolution of species.

But in thus emphasizing the unconscious in mental life we have conjured up the most evil spirits of criticism against psychoanalysis. Do not be surprised at this, and do not suppose that the resistance to us rests only on the understandable difficulty of the unconscious or the relative inaccessibility of the experiences which provide evidence of it. Its source, I think, lies deeper. In the course of centuries the naive self-love of men has had to submit to two major blows at the hands of science. The first when they learnt that our earth was not the centre of the universe but only a tiny fragment of a cosmic system of scarcely imaginable vastness. This is associated in our minds with the name of Copernicus, though something similar had already been asserted by Alexandrian science. The second blow fell when biological research destroyed man's supposedly privileged place in creation and proved his descent from the animal kingdom and his ineradicable animal nature. This revaluation has been accomplished in our own days by Darwin, Wallace and his predecessors, though not without the most violent contemporary opposition. But human megalomania will have suffered its third and most wounding blow from the psychological research of the present time which seeks to prove to the ego that it is not even master in its own house, but must content itself with scanty information of what is going on unconsciously in its mind (Conclusion of "Introductory Lecture XVIII").

One similarity among the three systems Freud emphasizes is the denial of centrality and control, or focus: if the earth is the center of the universe, and the earth and all that is on it was created for man's benefit, and man rules all this and himself with his reason, then all is as it should be in this best of all possible worlds; but, then, Copernicus decenters the earth in the universe, Darwin decenters man in nature, and Freud decenters the rational element in man himself. There is another similarity among these three revolutionaries, however, and I claim premonition of and participation with them for Shakespeare: there is relativity in all these systems which paradoxically is constant in both its negation and affirmation of all that men need and value.

In thinking through Copernicus's system we are first shocked that sense-impressions are deceptive—the sun does not move around the earth, but rather the earth circles the sun. Even more unsettling is the new kind of thinking which becomes necessary if this circumstance is accepted: as a man on earth one is not a fixed observer of the "wanderers" (*planetai*), but all that one sees must be corrected by the factor of one's own wandering. What one sees, then, depends on where one is at the time and one's rate of movement, or, the experience of the subject is a function of his relation in space and time to the object of his experience. We shall note a number of passages in Shakespeare where human relations are compared to celestial movement, the most difficult and important being Leontes' "mad" speech beginning "Affection, thy intention stabs the centre." What we shall come to appreciate is that just as Shakespeare insists that Leontes learn to see his relations with Polixenes and Hermione differently, to dispel those myths of expectation formed from biblical and other authorities on the nature of women, so he implies that nothing in the human experience of nature can be constant: the center does not hold, and individual identity is only a function of difference from others.

The Darwinian perspective is also characterized by relativity in that not only is man part of the continuum of nature, rather than being a special creation unique and apart, but also that the species themselves are specific in time and space rather than being universal constants. Species differentiation is determined by genetic potential and the actualities of environment. Surely we see all this in *Lear*, when, with the artificial props of courtly and family life pulled out, first Edgar and then the King himself are bestialized, tracing a seemingly infinite regress into the chaos of nature. Shakespeare thus shows that there is no constant pattern of "the Human" which can hold individual examples on a set course, and so a criticism based on a metaphysics of humanism is inadequate for this and the other plays. Indeed, nature iself becomes "nothing," that word which rings down through the plays of Shakespeare's full maturity, not only in *Lear*, but also in *The Winter's*

Tale, wherein, again, all emphasis is on the determining force of seeing, Shakespeare's phenomenology:

> and all eyes
> Blind with the pin and web, but theirs; theirs only.
> That would unseen be wicked? is this nothing?
> Why then the world, and all that's in't, is nothing,
> The covering sky is nothing, Bohemia nothing,
> My wife is nothing, nor nothing have these nothings,
> If this be nothing.

(I.ii.290–96)

This is not idle hyperbole. The "this" Leontes refers to is the sexual relations he has fantasized between Hermione and Polixenes. Here and in the "Affection" speech, the figure is copulation: can something be bred from the union of nothing with nothing? Leontes has created something out of nothing and knows that, if this is possible, then the things we all take for granted could also be our creations. How does Shakespeare finally reconcile this kind of false creation, the stuff of sexual jealousy based on the myths of women's infidelity, with artistic creation, the stuff that dreams are made on?

In Freud, as in those other great shapers of worldview to whom he compares himself, there is both an insistence on the lack of a center in human experience and a search for meaning in relations. We cannot appeal to reason as a universal force in which all men participate in order to validate our experience because we each individually shape our own experience according to the dynamic functions of our unconscious minds: condensing, displacing, transforming. Here too myths, or idols, take over, because as Freud himself acknowledges, the unconscious of an individual can shape his experience into patterns that he has not himself actually known, i.e., the unconscious can be phylogenetic as well as ontogenetic.[2] So, too, in Shakespeare: Leontes fears and mistrusts Hermione, not because she has given him cause, but because she is a woman and he has been prepared unconsciously for women's perfidy.

The extraordinary quality of Shakespeare's drama is, as in all great documents of intellectual subtlety we compare it to, its restitution of some larger and more impressive sense of man's capacity than any it takes from him. Like Copernicus and Darwin and Freud, he decenters man in his physical, natural, and mental worlds, derives him from relations with others rather than from some originary and transcendent model of his own excellence, i.e., God, and yet—or for this very reason—he insists on the creative potential of man to remake himself in his own image, not God's. He even shows us, like Lacan, that men become what they desire, that they enter into "the discourse of the other," and yet speak of themselves as "I." Shakespeare constantly calls to our attention, and to the attention of his characters, actual things, actual situations, and, as a dramatist, he presents action in such a way that all forms and ideals must dissolve: we must see with the eyes and not with the mind. He tells us that we must live in the present, seize each moment, and allow it to contradict any preconceived notion. If it seems that I thus claim for him a peculiarly twentieth-century view of life, one which is derived from Husserl, then I appeal to the principle of recapitulation, which I see as important both in individual development and also in the way intellectual history works: there are cycles in men's thinking about themselves and their circumstances. Shakespeare represents for us one of those peaks in complexity of thinking that occurs before a rationalistic retrenchment, coming as it does at the breaking up of one ordered worldview and before a new one can be erected. It is comparable, perhaps, to the first generation of sophists in fifth century Greece; to Dante, Boccaccio, and Petrarch in fourteenth century Italy; and to those men of our own time who have the courage to demand more than their immediate tradition bequeaths them.

I am in good company making such claims. On the relation generally between philosophy and language and their evolution in history, I appeal to Hermann Fränkel, who writes of Greek intellectual life:

I do not adhere to the doctrine that we have no right to ascribe to a thinker a notion for the unequivocal expression of which he possessed and used no specific tool. Quite to the contrary: It is perfectly normal for this or that concept to have existed in a person's mind in a less definitive form, long before someone else couched it in dry and set philosophical phraseology.[3]

With specific reference to the Renaissance, Ernst Cassirer warns us that the period produced few systematic philosophers, so we must look to general literature for the evolution of ideas; that a *kulturwissenschaftliche* method is successful which finds a unity of direction and does not insist on a unity of actualization; and that the great thrust of Renaissance thought is toward an understanding of the intelligible in and through the sensible, the universal in and through the particular,[4] i.e., a turning away from Plato and toward Aristotle.

My attempt, then, to see Hobbesian relativism in Shakespeare has at least the theoretical support of these great Hegelian historians of ideas. J. F. Danby has made much the same claim for a Shakespearean prestatement of Hobbes, with particular attention to *Lear*.[5] I go beyond Danby, though, in claiming for both Shakespeare and Hobbes a questioning of unity itself. Danby would agree that Shakespeare is similar to Hobbes in seeing simultaneously a lack of universal order and the necessity therefore to impose one. For Hobbes, the imposition of absolute authority in the form of "Leviathan" is the only possible correction to the mutually contradictory demands of individual men; for Shakespeare, there is a similar desire for order arising out of the chaos of the English wars of succession. They also both see the appeal to reason as futile; men cannot agree in their judgments because they are driven in different directions by their own appetites and aversions. Hobbes undoubtedly took his position as a result of reading Galileo, because he began to see men as planets, each driven by its own mysterious force. Galileo had no clearly developed notion of a universal law of gravity; it remained for Newton to postulate such a law, and we should allow its immediate acceptance by and influence on English intellectuals to account for the basic differences between Hobbes and Locke. Just as Galileo's mapping of individual planetary movements was the model for Hobbes' observations on the contradictory needs of individual men, so the law of universal gravity became the model for Locke's appeal to human reason to mediate all political disputes. Without unity of perception can there be formal or efficient unity?[6] It seems that Hobbes' insistence that universals exist only in language and have no reference to any forms or causes outside language makes of language precisely that tool for shaping actual chaos into patterns by which men can live which Shakespeare so clearly defines in all his references to his own craft.

Shakespeare thought and wrote in a period between the decline of one great rationalist system and the emergence of another. Danby accurately describes Hooker's view of man in nature, which he compares to Hobbes', as a rationalism derived from an essentially medieval world picture: Nature is God's instrument by which he makes His mind known. Men, unless they perversely resist, cannot help but be caught up in the forces of Nature, and thus to speak God's plan. Danby traces similarities between Bacon and Hooker in such beliefs. Clearly this is far from Shakespeare's world picture: he consistently presents nature as a pageant made up of illusions which can be interpreted in many ways, and is dependent for its very existence on each man's shaping fantasy.

I cannot claim that Shakespeare's philosophy of love determined his philosophy of nature, but that they mutually influenced one another is certain. They are both indicative of the peculiar intellectual currents of his time and can both be accurately described as phenomenologies. Furthermore, I shall argue that the way Shakespeare presents seeing and seeming in love and nature is best understood as a mirroring, a mutually constitutive activity of subject and object. When this struggle is over, so is life, another essential perception which Shakespeare shares with Hobbes:

The felicity of this life consisteth not in the repose of a mind satisfied. For there is no such *finis ultimus*, utmost aim, nor *summum bonum*, greatest good, as is spoken of in the books of the old moral philosophers. Nor can a man anymore live, whose desires are at an end, than he whose senses and imaginations are at a stand. Felicity is a continual progress of the desire, from one object to another, the attaining of the former being still but the way to the latter (*Leviathan*, chapter XI).

Life is by definition an active struggle between self and object, not a passive acceptance by the subject of the object's "reality." This suggests a distinction between philosophy and religion, or within philosophy, between phenomenological and metaphysical currents. With its similarity to Hegel, this probably accounts for the seeming appropriateness of Lacanian psychoanalysis to a reading of Shakespeare's accounts of erotic relations, since Lacan's is essentially a Hegelian reading of Freud. The great question which keeps heaving in and out of focus in reading Shakespearean comedy is, that once we have defined the dynamics of his love relationships as a series of assimilations and differentiations between self and other, based on a refusal to accept preexisting patterns of such relationships (the "myths" or "idols" of romance and Neoplatonism), and we have suggested that the appeal men finally find in women is their lack of men's determination for ceaseless struggle with each other, then are we not identifying the love of women in marriage with death, the end of the struggle, the end of desire, the end of the drive to define the self in terms of the self? Freud has dealt with this problem in his essay on *The Merchant of Venice*, "The Theme of the Three Caskets," and it well might prove impossible for us to move beyond his identification of the woman in her three functions as mother, wife, and grave. Certainly, in the late romances, Shakespeare's every third thought is on the grave, and he also reconciles men in those plays with the women from whom they have been long estranged, women who are "so much wrinkled," and these women have more of the priestess about them than the wife or lover. Is this some kind of palinode to Neoplatonizing, a return at the end of his career to that form of erotic adoration he so convincingly disparages in the early comedies? Acquiescence in the peaceful pattern of existence which Hermione and Thaisa offer—without tension, without struggle—is a correction to the narcissistic agitation of the early comedies, where men constantly invest, libidinally and aggressively, their own self-images, a pattern which Shakespeare also shows there to be death-directed.

Shakespeare's comedies, then, are not only about marriage. They are also about the beginnings of desire in the search for the self in mirror-images of the self and the gradual acceptance of difference and independence in the other ("the object is as much subject as object"). Finally the erotic and creative urges—the shaping fantasies of desire and art[7]—are both expended, and though our central characters show some satisfaction in the momentum with which life will go on without them, under the impetus they have given things for the sake of their children, their own particular prospect is death, which is seen as both a negation of the self in the absence of struggle and an assimilation of the self to the other. In neither case is there any intimation of immortality, in nature or in art. The comedies do not offer the solace of gloried memory as the tragedies do. There is nothing left of Prospero: he dies with the applause.

II

A DIFFERENT KIND
OF COMEDY

hroughout this study I distinguish three different determinants of Shakespeare's accomplishment in comedy: his participation in intellectual history, his place in the history of comedy, and his portrayal of the actual experience of love. In this section I therefore divide my observations on Shakespeare and his traditions into three essays. First, I consider Shakespeare's accurate presentation of the complex relations between erotic orientation and identity. Here I take Lacan as the most complete statement of Freudian and post-Freudian theories on the way we first come into consciousness of ourselves as distinct from others and then recapitulate this process in our choice of lovers, so that every erotic relation is both a mirroring of the self and a repetition of previous choices of others.

Second, I show how Shakespeare combines the two major patterns of ancient comedy in his manipulation of plot and character. I distinguish, in the Greek originals and in their Roman adaptations, between the Persephone pattern, wherein a young girl is freed from infertile bondage to an unchosen lover to fulfill her own and her "true" lover's expectations of her and life generally, and the kind of comedy where attention is not focused on one young girl but on various objects of desire which all enable the hero to see and express himself more clearly. In the Greek material this distinction is not only formal but chrono- logical, since in the first major period of Greek comedy, the Old Com- edy, which is represented for us by the eleven surviving plays of Ar- istophanes, the hero seeks sexual satisfaction with a bewildering variety of aims and objects. Only with Menander, in the period of New Com- edy a century later, is all erotic interest concentrated in the figure of the young girl. I thus distinguish between narcissistic and "anaclitic" orientation of desire in comedy, which suggests either choice of self as object, or "attachment" to another. In more conventional terms, the distinction is between Aristophanes' heroic comedy and Menander's romantic comedy.

I do not intend to displace Shakespeare from the center of attention in these opening essays. I cannot always insist on actual and immedi- ate influence between the texts I compare, so my project is not *Quel- lenforschungen*. Shakespeare did not know Aristophanes and Menander firsthand. It is only through the adaptations of Menandrean comedies by Plautus and Terence that he could have known Menander, and there is no sure sign that either one of them knew Aristophanes firsthand. I argue instead for the determinism of the tradition, that Shakespeare spontaneously recreates those comic patterns which always appeal, be- cause comedy always has one function to fulfill: the gratification of de- sire.

I make similar claims in the case of general intellectual history, which is the subject of my third essay. Shakespeare probably never read a Platonic dialogue, but in his use of Neoplatonic thought on the nature of love, he seems to have spontaneously restored the original patterns of the dialogues. In Neoplatonism reality is figured in the lady, and the lover worships her from afar; in Plato himself, the relation be- tween the older male lover and his younger male beloved is crucial for the philosophical progress that leads finally to the Forms. In both cases, then, the comic and the philosophical, I distinguish between narcissis- tic and romantic inclinations, and marvel when Shakespeare combines these in his comedy in a complexity unmatched by any ancient or modern poet.

The most salutary effect of such an approach is the correction of conventional expectations for comic resolution. We expect marriage not

only as a consummation of the lovers' desires and as a promise of social integration, but as a philosophical affirmation that seeming contradictions can be resolved and as a fertile example for all nature to
follow. Shakespeare, however, in company with other great comic poets,
ancient and modern, does not allow us to equate his individual heroes'
happiness with holistic renewal and reunion. At least equally important with marriage in Shakespearean comedy—and all it represents—
is the continued demand of the particular characters to be unque and
perfect in and of themselves. We shall find that Shakespeare causes us
to see the action of each comedy through the eyes of one character,
and this character has peculiar needs and desires. The sublety and
complexity of his comedy is largely due to the contradictions these create
with the integrative patterns of the action.

The Psychoanalytic Tradition

My purpose here is to establish the appropriateness of psycho-analytic theories on the origin and evolution of self-consciousness to our reading of Shakespeare. We begin with the mirror and consider Hamlet's use of it to define the function of art. He addresses the players:

Suit the action to the word, the word to the action, with this special obser-vance, that you o'erstep not the modesty of nature. For anything so o'erdone is from the purpose of playing, whose end, both at the first and now, was and is to hold as 'twere the mirror up to nature; to show virtue her feature, scorn her own image, and the very age and body of the time his form and pressure. Now this overdone or come tardy off, though it make the unskillful laugh, cannot but make the judicious grieve, the censure of the which one must in your allowance o'erweigh a whole theater of others (III.ii.17–28).

The pleonastic quality of this speech makes us think of Polonius and his speeches on art, marriage, and courtly behavior. Can we detect here a parody of contemporary literary criticism, such as Sidney's, just as in the players' speeches we see parody of contemporary drama, such as Kyd's? If "playing" should indeed hold the mirror up to Nature, then its most important quality would be verisimilitude and that is not what we generally claim for Shakespeare. Superficially his plots and characterizations are outrageous, in no way constrained by that moderation which Hamlet demands. Hamlet claims that playing, by seeming natural, can instruct and improve. Again, unless we are all to become kings or clowns, there is little of immediate application to ourselves in Shakespeare.

Our overwhelming assurance is that Shakespeare holds the mirror up, not to Nature, but to ourselves: we see there not the surface reality of manners and mores—for this we turn to Ben Jonson—but our deepest fears and desires. So, too, with Shakespeare's characters: in almost all of his plays there is a specific point of view, a perspective on the action through the eyes of one character, so that we see ourselves in him as he seeks himself in others. This particular character is more easily identified in the tragedies and histories, where his is usually the title role, than in the comedies. The comedies often present a more masquelike or pageant effect; we seem to be caught up in the action, whirled about as in a dance, and set down with a rather blurred impression of what has happened, and to whom. On closer study, though, we shall find that in each comedy there is a single character who constantly asks, "Who am I, and what does all this mean to me?" Usually it is a young man who appeals for help in identifying himself first to a male companion, then to a young woman disguised as a young man, and finally to that young woman fully revealed.

The youth of these characters is extremely important. We have been warned not to think of Romeo and Juliet as mature, well-adjusted adults in their thirties, as they always used to be played: she is fourteen, and he is not much older. In the comedies it is equally important to appreciate that the lovers are young; Shakespeare gives us a fairly accurate depiction of adolescent sexuality, which is characterized, on the one hand, by sexual ambiguity and ambivalence (confusion about one's own sex and the sex of the object of one's desire), and, on the other, by an obsession about love that equates it with death. Both the young men and the young women turn first to their childhood companions of the same sex before they risk involving themselves with new acquaintances of the opposite sex. There is an absoluteness about their demands of friends and lovers: love or death, sex or violence, all or nothing. This intensity makes them the appropriate subjects for serious comedy, which we have defined as that struggle through desire to identity—in adolescence we must reestablish the goals of primary narcissism and attain them all over again.

What we need to know is how Shakespeare's plots and characters, seemingly so alien to our own experience, present us with precisely the dilemmas we have always felt ourselves faced with. We do not all have twins; we have not all been separated from our parents by shipwreck and raised in exotic places; we have not all fallen in love with members of the opposite sex while they were disguised as members of our own sex. Psychoanalysis is uniquely suited to answer the question, "What is profoundly familiar about these situations which seem superficially so strange?" Our main focus of attention will be on the psychoanalytic theory of narcissism; we shall consider briefly the contributions of Freud and Lacan in this opening essay, and introduce those of Kernberg in the analysis of the individual plays. Our perspective will then be developmental: we shall see how situations which are the common experience of us all in our earliest years recapitulate themselves in later life and how the drama of primary narcissism (the experience of the infant in his demands to be fed, to be kept warm, and to be loved) is replayed at puberty and other turning points in life, those crucial times when we need, through the "mirroring" provided by others, to reassure ourselves of our own existence.

We should appreciate, then, in Shakespearean comedy a tension between two kinds of desire: for friends who are like ourselves and for lovers who are different. Most critics have stresssed only the social integration celebrated in the marriages that end most of the comedies, but some have been sensitive to the deprivation which some characters feel as a consequence: "Love is the source of integration and disintegration, the promise of immortality and the loss of the self."[1] Our greatest mistake is to consider marriage the only goal of Shakespearean comedy, and to be dissatisfied with those plays, especially the early ones, which do not lead directly there. If we once admit that problems of self-definition are persistent in Shakespearean comedy—from *The Comedy of Errors* to *The Tempest*—then we can better appreciate how Shakespeare varies his treatment from play to play and how some are more successful than others. It is clear, for instance, that the valuation of friendship over love is a theme explored among the main characters in *The Two Gentlemen of Verona* and *Love's Labor's Lost,* but only among secondary characters in *The Merchant of Venice* and *Twelfth Night.*

C.L. Barber's work on the comedies has probably been the most influential in this half of the century. He began by showing how Shakespeare, in his "festive comedies," fulfilled the needs of the urban population in Elizabethan England for regeneration and social integration that the various fertility rites had traditionally satisfied for rural people.[2] He went on to examine, with reference to psychoanalytic studies, the ways in which Shakespeare shows attractions and aversions within the nuclear family.[3] In Salangar, who has written revealingly on the traditions of comedy and romance behind Shakespeare, we find the social function of marriage stressed: "His comedies, then, are essentially celebrations of marriage. . . . Marriage appears as the resolution of the broader tensions, as the type or focus of harmony in society as a whole."[4] R. Wheeler, using a psychoanalytic approach, stresses the experience of the individual, but also marriage as the main telos: "In the festive comedies the main action moves away from ties of family and friendship to new relationships in marriage."[5]

Our task, in presenting the psychoanalytic theory of narcissism as an aid to the reading of Shakespearean comedy, is to distinguish between its appeal to individuals because it presents a pattern of the fulfillment of desire, and its social function of making the community of men and women attractive and capable of fulfilling individual desires. We must come to see marriage as a socializing force, an institution into which the individual moves at maturity. We must be sensitive, however, to the ways in which Shakespeare shows us that society and maturity are not the answers to all individual problems, that men and women continue to make demands which institutions by their very nature cannot satisfy.

C. Kahn has shown that men in Shakespeare define themselves primarily against women in the comedies and older men in the histories and tragedies. She recognizes, though, that men in the comedies, especially in the early ones, use women for "narcissistic mirroring," for "ontological reassurance,"[6] i.e, that women as lovers are made to fill the place of other men as friends. It remains for me to show the varieties of narcissistic object-choice in the early and middle comedies and to trace these through to the late romances. We begin with the friends of the early comedies, proceed to the transvestized lovers of the middle comedies, and finally examine in the late romances the young daughters of middle-aged fathers. All of these are "self-objects" rather than "true" objects, desirable for their reflection of the subject rather than for their own independent virtues.

Kahn's explication of the Shakespearean corpus in terms of misogyny is also valuable, since it demonstrates the pattern of simultaneous fears and desires, of resentment and need, that characterizes men's relations with women. Nevertheless, Shakespearean comedy remains finally unappreciated if we do not understand how it poses the problems of man's search for himself in his own terms, i.e., identity in similarity rather than identity in difference.

In the history of psychoanalysis, as in the history of the criticism of Shakespearean comedy, desire for the other—first the mother and then, for men, some other woman—stands at the beginning. Narcissism, the desire for the self, only comes later, as a kind of correction. Chronologically, though, in individual development and in the history of comedy (as we shall see in the next chapter), narcissistic orientation comes first, and oedipal orientation develops out of that. Freud's first statement of this sequence comes in the 1914 essay "On Narcissism: An Introduction":

The sexual instincts are at the outset attached *[anlehnen]* to the satisfaction of the ego-instincts; only later do they become independent of these, and even then we have an indication of that original attachment *[Anlehnung]* in the fact that the persons who are concerned with a child's feeding, care, and protection, become his earliest sexual objects; that is to say, in the first instance his mother or a substitute for her. Side by side, however, with this type and source of object-choice, which may be called the "anaclitic" or "attachment" type *[Anlehnungstypus]* psychoanalytic research has revealed a second type which we were not prepared for finding. We have discovered, especially clearly in people whose libidinal development has suffered some disturbance, such as perverts and homosexuals, that in their later choice of love-objects they have taken as a model not their mother but their own selves. They are plainly seeking themselves as a love-object, and are exhibiting a type of object-choice which must be termed "narcissistic." In this observation we have the strongest of reasons which have led us to adopt the hypothesis of narcissism.[7]

The human being has originally two sexual objects: himself and the woman who tends him, and thereby we postulate a primary narcissism in everyone, which may in the long run manifest itself as dominating his object-choice.[8]

The reasoning here is typical of Freud: we can come to know the normal through our study of the abnormal; what is normal in one phase of development becomes abnormal when extended into later phases. Like Darwin, to whom Freud compared himself in other respects, Freud did not believe in constant and exclusive categories. He depicted all sorts of human behavior as being on a continuum. Thus we should all be able to see ourselves in both Shylock and Antonio, and not regard them as freaks held up for our ridicule or pity. Though Shylock shows traits we associate with the anal retentive character and Antonio is recognizable as a pathic homosexual, we should nevertheless respond to their dilemmas. The proper and complete response is one which arouses in us memory traces of our own early development—when we were all narcissistic and polymorphously perverse—and lets us see that we are not yet free from the repetitive patterns in which that experience set us. I claim, indeed, for Shakespearean comedy, what Aristotle claims for tragedy: the power to arouse in us pity and fear and lead us through the character's change in fortune to some recognition of our own. I also claim for serious comedy the force of psychoanalysis: we come to see ourselves in its characters just as we come to know ourselves in analysis.

Freud's use of *Anlehnung* to define the choice of the mother as object of desire is significant; he does not mean by this that we "lean up against" the mother and thus derive our identity from her, but rather that our choice of her "leans up against" our choice of ourselves. Freud seems to avoid claiming priority for the narcissistic choice of object, but it is clearly implied: "the sexual instincts are at the outset attached [*anlehnen*] to the satisfaction of the ego-instincts." Desire for the mother, then, which in a later stage will be called oedipal, is not always already there. The child's early love for the mother works like a reflection in a mirror; indeed the English analyst D.W. Winnicott claims in reference to what the French analyst J. Lacan calls *le stade du miroir*, "the precursor of the mirror is the mother's eyes."[9] The child loves the mother for caring for him, for giving him reassurance of his own existence, and for responding to his demands—not because she is, in and of herself, attractive to him.

Indeed there is a strain of psychoanalytic theory about the early months of life, which we trace from Melanie Klein to Otto Kernberg, that insists on the existence, almost from the beginning of life, of fear and resentment on the part of the child of the mother's power.[10] We must consider this in dealing with some of the clearly misogynistic passages in Shakespeare's comedies. We need only point out here that the Oedipus complex—the male child's desire to kill the father and take his place in the mother's bed—is not the only pattern of human experience to which psychoanalysis has called our attention, nor should we expect it to be the only pattern in Shakespearean comedy. Oedipal orientation is a later development, which is commonly thought to be prevalent from the third to the sixth years. It is even possible to consider it a compromise formation following upon the disappointment of the child's earlier demands for a world centered solely in himself.

One of the most famous passages in all of Freud's writing comes at the beginning of his treatise *Beyond the Pleasure Principle* (1920). He describes how he sat with his eighteen-month-old grandson during the absence of the child's mother. In his crib the child had a spool attached to a string. Throwing the spool out of the crib, the child exclaimed something Freud construed to be *Fort!* ("gone"), and reeling it back in, he said *Da!* ("there"). Freud thought this remarkable because he interpreted the child's play to be a repetition of the painful moment of the mother's departure; this repetition compulsion then goes "beyond the pleasure principle." There is a footnote, however, to this assessment of the situation, which again draws our attention to the persistence of narcissism, the paradox that the child requires the mother to meet his needs but loves himself first and her only for tending him:

One day the child's mother had been away for several hours and on her return was met with the words "Baby oo-o-o!" which was at first incomprehensible. It soon turned out, however, that during this long period of solitude the child had found a method of making *himself* disappear. He had discovered his reflection in a full-length mirror which did not quite reach to the ground, so that by crouching down he could make his mirror-image "gone."[11]

The child creates himself in his mother's absence: where she was, there must he become.

Now I have already suggested that we see situations in Shakespearean comedy and hear characters describe themselves in such a way that we feel the operation of some sort of wish for death. If this were said about Hamlet—"To be or not to be"—no one would think it strange: everyone can recognize the anxiety that drives the prince to question the need for his own continued existence. Most would allow that this is due not only to the fact that his oedipal desires have been fulfilled by his uncle, so that this role having been thus usurped he sees no other recourse for himself, but also to the fact that he feels overpowered by his mother (hence the misogyny that engulfs even the innocent, young Ophelia,) and that he feels she has deprived him of his identity by conspiring with his uncle to deprive his father of his life.[12] There are similar situations in comedy, however, and similar characters who voice similar doubts about their own authentic being. Once we recognize that serious comedy is about identity, then it should not surprise us to learn that the other side of desire is death:[13] comic patterns might move toward marriage as one way of fulfilling desire, but desire is originally for the self, and some comedy insists that the object of desire assimilate to the subject before marriage is possible. Comedy can also trace the persistence of such narcissistic choice of object so that it makes marriage impossible. Finally, comedy can show that marriage itself figures death for the male subject who accepts marriage but feels diminished and alienated from himself in the process.

What is there about narcissism that suggests a desire for death? Why does Antonio, the merchant of Venice, yield himself so readily to the knife? The absoluteness of narcissism demands all or nothing, complete fulfillment of the desire for the "self-object" or no desire for any object, either the capture of the idealized self in the other, or the loss of the self in death. For Antonio this means either holding on to Bassanio, keeping him in childlike dependence upon him, or wishing for death without him. Thus the seeming contradiction that the individual concerned only for validation of his own existence should contemplate an end to his existence is resolved in Shakespeare: he shows not only that the man caught in narcissistic patterns of desire actually desires death, but also that those patterns themselves are death-directed since the narcissist deprives himself of the sustenance of others, beginning with the mother. There is something maternal about Portia, and her competition with Antonio for the possession of Bassanio seems appropriate on three levels: she competes with the father for the possession of the son; she competes with the male lover for the possession of the beloved; she competes with her own son for the possession of that perfect image of himself which she first projected.

Freud never tried to resolve dialectically the contradictions inherent in his theories of narcissism, both because his mind seemed to work in terms of bipolar opposition and because he became preoccupied with oedipal concerns. In *Beyond the Pleasure Principle* and *Civilization and Its Discontents*, however, he insists that our first aggression, like our first libidinal investment, is against the self; only later do we learn to choose other objects for these forces. The process of individuation is, then, characterized by both libidinal and aggressive investment in self-objects: this accounts for the transvestism of heroines in Shakespeare's comedy—objects are chosen first for their similarity to the subject and only then allowed to differ—and for the indistinguishability of his rivals—Proteus and Valentine, Demetrius and Lysander, Leontes and Polixenes are all like twinned lambs.[14]

Perhaps Lacan, who does think dialectically, can explicate the dynamics of this pattern for us. The passages we have cited from Freud are among those Lacan made the foundation of his own psychoanalytic philosophy. He first defined *le stade du miroir* in 1936:

The mirror stage is a drama whose internal thrust is precipitated from insufficiency to anticipation—and which manufactures for the subject, caught up in the lure of spatial identification, the succession of phantasies that extends from a fragmented body-image to a form of its totality that I shall call orthopaedic—and, lastly, to the assumption of the armor of an alienating identity which will mark with its rigid structure the subject's entire mental development.[15]

Le corps morcelé is the child's image of himself: he sees himself fragmented because his existence is still determined by the bits and pieces of information he receives from his mother and from others. Until eighteen months he lacks the integrated ego which can consolidate his sense of his own reality. Where will this come from? Lacan gives us a clear notion of the difference between the child before and after the acquisition of language: we see that during the mirror stage the child exists in the realm of the imagistic, but when he learns language he enters the realm of the symbolic, where he must remake himself according to the patterns set by his culture:

The jubilant assumption of his specular image by the child at the *infans* stage, still sunk in his motor incapacity and nursling dependence, would seem to exhibit in an exemplary situation the symbolic matrix in which the *I* is pre-

cipitated in a primordial form, before it is objectified in the dialectic of identification with the other, and before language restores to it, in the universal,
its function as object.[16]

So completely does Lacan believe in the formation of the individual's
sense of self out of the material of the other that he can claim, "the
unconscious of the subject is the discourse of the other."[17]

The dissatisfaction consequent upon such a derivation is the distinction between *demande* and *désir*. Lacan defines *désir* as the difference between the child's actual somatic needs and the demands which
he can express in language, an indication of the radical inadequacy the
individual finds in language, and the society it represents, to provide
him with a recognizable reflection of himself. For Freud this was the
generating force behind repetition compulsion: "It is the difference in
amount between the pleasure of satisfaction which is demanded and
that which is actually achieved that provides the driving factor which
will permit of no halting at any position attained."[18] If we can think
for a moment of all erotic activity as essentially narcissistic—the drive
to find in others a mirror for the self—then we can see here, in the
inevitable dissatisfaction of the constantly repeated search for the perfect object, some indication of the void that was there to begin with.
The self is a function of its difference from the other; the only chance
one has for finding satisfaction in the choice of a love-object lies in
one's ability to see more in that object than one sees in oneself, more,
that is, than one is looking for. This is the lesson that Rosalind as
Ganymede teaches Orlando and that Orsino learns from Viola-Cessa-
rio: preconceived notions of perfection in the object of desire denote
only arrogance and ignorance of love in the subject.

When N. Holland, in his 1957 survey of the first fifty years of psychoanalytic criticism of Shakespeare, claimed that the plots and major
characters of all the plays are motivated by primarily oedipal concerns,
although oral and anal obsessions are evident in the incidental imagery,[19] he was speaking before the research of Kohut and Kernberg
on narcissism, before Winnicott in England and Mahler in America
directed psychoanalytic attention to the very young child, and before
Lacan's impact began to be felt in international circles. He was certainly speaking before any of this research and theory began to be as-
sembled as a model for the reading of Shakespeare. It becomes a mat-

ter of the phenomenology of reading: before we were concerned with narcissism, we did not see it in the plays; now that we are concerned with it, we are perhaps blind to all else. Only our readings of the individual plays will show whether the new perspective reveals more than it distorts. We should, however, be aware that much of this concern is already there in Freud, that Lacan is an impressively good reader of Freud. On the question of the priority of narcissistic orientation to oedipal orientation and its constitutive influence thereupon, we need only compare Freud, "On Narcissism," when he describes how the entirely positive self-image of the young child turns negative in the oedipal stage, with the result that an intra-psychic admonitory agency is set up:

This ideal ego is now the target of the self-love which was enjoyed in childhood by the actual ego. The subject's narcissism makes its appearance displaced onto this new ideal ego, which like the infantile ego, finds itself possessed of every perfection that is of value. As always, where the libido is concerned, man has here again shown himself incapable of giving up a satisfaction he has once enjoyed. He is not willing to forego the narcissistic perfection of his childhood; and when, as he grows up, he is disturbed by the admonitions of others and by the awakening of his own critical judgement, so that he can no longer retain that perfection, he seeks to recover it in this new form of an ego ideal. What he projects before him as his ideal is the substitute for the lost narcissism of his childhood in which he was his own ideal.[20]

There is the subtle shift from the "ideal ego" as the vestige of the narcissistic image of perfection in early childhood to the "ego ideal," which is the image of someone else—in the oedipal male's case, the father—whose perfection he can never hope to approach. Indeed, the ego ideal will, in Freud's later writings after 1923, become the superego. How does love of the self turn into hatred and fear of the other? Lacan explains:

The Oedipus complex is a secondary identification by introjection of the imago of the parent of the same sex. The energy for that identification is provided by the first biological upsurge of genital libido. But it is clear that the structural effect of identification with the rival is not self-evident, except at the level of fable, and can only be conceived of if the way is prepared for it by a primary identification that structures the subject as a rival with himself.[21]

The term primary narcissism . . . throws light on the dynamic opposition between this libido and the sexual libido, which the first analysts tried to define when they invoked destructive and, indeed, death instincts, in order to explain the evident connection between narcissistic libido and the alienating function of the *I*, the aggressivity it releases in any relation to the *Other*, even in a relation involving the most Samaritan of aid.[22]

All of those pairs of doubles, the twins and friends of *The Comedy of Errors, The Two Gentlemen of Verona, A Midsummer Night's Dream* and *The Winter's Tale*, are in this way bound by libidinal and aggressive energy. It is then this confrontation with libidinally and aggressively invested self-objects that both creates and destroys their separate identities. Shakespeare suggests that these connections can be short-curcuited, that woman can neutralize male phallic aggression and deflect interest onto themselves, the women. The plays show that this is at least temporarily successful. That same mirrored rivalry comes back, however, in *The Winter's Tale*, and, of course, if we consider *The Two Noble Kinsmen* as Shakespeare's last attempt at the problem,[23] then he has returned, full circle, to Palamon and Arcite of "The Knight's Tale," where he began in *The Two Gentlemen of Verona* and continued in *A Midsummer Night's Dream*. Love, like life, must be a struggle, and if the struggle ends, there is death. There is no struggle in the anaclitic relation of the child to the mother or of the Neoplatonic lover to his idealized mistress. There is struggle in all narcissistic orientations of desire, but if these are not corrected by a recognition that the object is as much subject as object—an idependent, aging, changing human being—then that relationship, too, can degenerate, deprived of energy created in and by the other.[24] These are love's enunchs, the acolytes at their own altars, the narcissi around the reflecting pool—hypostatizations of youth and beauty lost to life and its variety.

II.2

The Comic Tradition

II.2.A THE WOMAN IN BONDAGE

Northrop Frye traces in Greek New Comedy a "comic Oedipus situation":

New Comedy unfolds from what may be described as a comic Oedipus situation. Its main theme is the successful effort of the young man to outwit an opponent and possess the girl of his choice. The opponent is usually the father (*senex*), and the psychological descent of the heroine from the mother is also sometimes hinted at. The father frequently wants the same girl, and is cheated out of her by the son, the mother thus becoming the son's ally. The girl is usually a slave or courtesan, and the plot turns on a *cognitio* or discovery of birth which makes her marriageable.[1]

Two of Plautus' plays follow this pattern exactly: the *Casina*, based on an original by Diphilos, and the *Mercator*, based on an original by Philemon. Even here the comic energy is centered not in the son, but in the father; generally we feel the appropriateness of the victory of younger over older and the new beginning which comedy conventionally requires, but in both these plays where the father is the barrier, he is nevertheless the focus of attention. Frye is, of course, not insensitive to this kind of effect. He cites *The Merry Wives of Windsor*, in which the young man's role is negligible and we only care about Falstaff.[2] If we distinguish three patterns of comedy according to the type of regeneration which takes place, each is determined by the perspective from which the action is seen: in the Persephone pattern a young girl is held in infertile bondage to an older man who is usually recognizable as her father; in the Dionysos pattern an old man is resurrected and rejuvenated; in the scapegoat pattern the barrier figure is dispatched, but in a kind of reversal, we feel more sympathy for him than joy for his dispatcher, though we know he must go. In Shakespearean comedy, too, these three patterns seem more descriptive of the actual tensions and releases than Frye's "comic Oedipus." Where, in Shakespeare, do young male lovers really take control of their circumstances? They tend to be weak and ineffective, more the accidental beneficiaries of comic good fortune than its active engineers. (Petruchio is the exception, but *The Taming of the Shrew* is exceptional in many respects.) If we insist on seeing something oedipal in Shakespearean comedy, then we must qualify our use of the term by invoking the Bergson law that comedy tends to mechanize nature.[3] We know that it is somehow right for Bassanio and Ferdinand to win their young women from the paternal bondage in which they are held, but other forces than theirs accomplish this for them: the young women themselves take control; their old fathers finally relent; the whole order of things changes. Menander saves his heaviest irony, in the *Dyskolos* (which we shall discuss in the next section), for the young man Sostratos, who speaks at great length about his perseverance and how it has paid off, but we know that it is the gods who have arranged his marriage.

The only thing that comedy insists upon is that the object of desire be young and beautiful and innocent. This, of course, fits well with our general assumption that serious comedy tends more toward the fulfillment of central characters' erotic wishes than toward social organization. Why, we might ask, do we tend to think only of the young and beautiful, in comedy as in life, when we think of desirable objects? Because they are easily thought of as "objects"—smooth, fresh, physically unwrinkled, and emotionally uncomplicated, like dolls. They are tabula rasa for the inscription of a lover's image of his ideal object of desire. This kind of object-choice fits better with the theory of narcissism than with oedipal orientation: we seek the younger, more beautiful images of ourselves when we choose narcissistically, rather than the powerful, sustaining, all-knowing oedipal figure. This explains why in comedy we are often more interested ethically in the crusty

old barrier figure—he has a past, and reasons for his actions and perversions—but our erotic interest remains with the young people, driven
though they may be (like automata) by passions beyond their control
and comprehension. It also explains why such interest can upset the
balance in comedy, so that at the end of *The Misanthrope* or *Tartuffe*
we are more concerned about those who do not marry than about those
who do. Clearly, Shakespeare tries to correct this, or rather he pushes
the conventions almost to the point of parody. At the end of *The Winter's Tale,* Leontes is erotically attracted to his daughter Perdita, and
here the counteroedipal pattern of the father claiming a sexual prerogative over his daughter combines with the narcissistic pattern of an
aging lover seeking in his beloved the younger, more beautiful image
of himself. But he is finally reconciled to his wife Hermione, whom he
first discovers as a statue, and complains that she was not so wrinkled
when he last saw her. Had the statue been like the young Hermione,
this would have confirmed Leontes' choice of Perdita, the younger,
more beautiful image of both parents.

If we pursue these distinctions in pre-Shakespearean comedy, we shall
find in Greek Old Comedy, the comedy of Aristophanes, that women
either take complete control of the plays, or are reduced to personified
abstractions, like Peace and Harvest. In Greek New Comedy, the
comedy of Menander, Diphilos and Philemon—which was adapted for
the Roman stage by Plautus and Terence and thus indirectly known
by Shakespeare—though the basic pattern is to free the young woman
from bondage to an unchosen, infertile old lover (father, soldier, or
pimp), there is always the insistence that she enter a new form of bondage, a highly restrictive form of marriage, which seems engineered to
control her fertility. Here, again, there is separation between the young,
marriageable girls, who often do not even speak, and the ethically involved, older women, who tend to be courtesans. Shakespeare continues on this course, but adds to it the narcissistic interest so characteristic of Aristophanes, whose comedy he could not have known even
indirectly. Of course, the essential difference between the two Greek
forms, which we shall explore in the next part of this essay, is that in
Old Comedy men pursue total freedom and self-expression whereas in
New Comedy they pursue only the young woman.

Though the basic oedipal pattern of father and son competing for the sexual possession of the mother (or some replacement for her) is not strong in Shakespearean comedy of any period, there is from the beginning a central concern with the sexual prerogative of the father over the daughter. As Kahn has shown,[4] this concern increases as we approach the late romances, where the focus of interest shifts from the young lovers to the father figure, and the whole movement of the plays tends toward his renunciation of incestuous demands upon the young girl, along with all that her youth and beauty represent: creativity, political power, knowledge, and potency generally. Thus we do see in Shakespeare the bare outline of the "barrier play," where young lovers must admit to their union parental impediment. It appears in its most primitive form in the "Pyramus and Thisbe" of *A Midsummer Night's Dream*, where there is an actual wall rather than just the psychological barrier of parents forbidding the young people's marriage. If we examine briefly how this basic problem of possession is adapted by Shakespeare, and compare his treatment with that in the earlier comic tradition, we can better appreciate his departure from it to create a different kind of comedy, one which is narcissistic in its orientation of desire and absolute in its demand for gratification.

Frye has distinguished between the real world of the court and city, where individual desires are bound by society, and the "green world" of the forest, where lovers are free to pursue their true objects.[5] Such is the case in *A Midsummer Night's Dream*, whose action moves sonata-like from court to forest to court, and at the end we already see the alliances formed away from the court failing to withstand its pressures. Parental prerogative in sexual matters is the original barrier in the play, driving the young lovers into the forest, and though it might seem insignificant beside the central concern of the play—the phenomenology of desire—it casts its spell over all subsequent proceedings. Two points are made in the opening scene: first, Egeus himself claims that his daughter Hermia has been bewitched by Lysander, and only thus would prefer him to Demetrius, her father's choice of suitor for her:

> This hath bewitch'd the bosom of my child.
> Thou, thou, Lysander, thou hast given her rhymes,
> And interchang'd love-tokens with my child:
> Thou hast by moonlight at her window sung

> With faining voice verses of feigning love,
> And stol'n the impression of her fantasy
> With bracelets of thy hair, rings, gauds, conceits,
> Knacks, trifles, nosegays, sweetmeats (messengers
> Of strong prevailment in unharden'd youth):
> With cunning hast thou filch'd my daughter's heart,
> Turn'd her obedience (which is due me)
> To stubborn harshness.
>
>   (I.i.27–38)

This puts one in mind of Brabantio's claim against Othello that he bewitched Desdemona and only so could have won her affection:

> She is abused, stol'n from me and corrupted
> By spells and medicines bought of mountebanks.
> For nature so preposterously to err,
> Being not deficient, blind, or lame of sense,
> Sans witchcraft could not.
>
>   (I.iii.60–64)

This father is as much concerned with racial and social difference as with the child's "natural" obedience to him, but the latter underlies his protest, just as it does Lear's complaint against Cordelia, "a wretch whom Nature is ashamed/ Almost to acknowledge hers" (I.i.215–16). This introduces a second point: What punishment is appropriate to a daughter who refuses her father's choice of a suitor for her? In *A Midsummer Night's Dream* Theseus responds to Hermia's request to know the worst that may befall her if she refuses to wed Demetrius:

> Either to die the death, or to abjure
> For ever the society of men.
> Therefore, fair Hermia, question your desires,
> Know of your youth, examine well your blood,
> Whether, if you yield not to your father's choice,
> You can endure the livery of a nun,
> For aye to be in shady cloister mew'd,
> To live a barren sister all your life,
> Chanting faint hymns to the cold fruitless moon.
>
>   (I.i.65–73)

Egeus had assumed that he had the power of life and death over his daughter, that either she must do as he says (marry Demetrius) or die

(I.i.38–45). He claims this is the law of Athens; we associate it more closely with the Roman institution of patria potestas, which did in fact consist of such a prerogative, though in practice it was seldom exercised.[6] Theseus, then, either abridges or interprets the law to fit the present circumstance, adding a third alternative: Hermia can marry no man at all but instead live her life in a nunnery. Indeed the alternatives fall out in pairs: marry Demetrius or no man; marry Demetrius or die; marry no man or die. The last choice is no choice at all, and therefore represents the essential identity: chastity is death. Thus we can speak of the father holding his daughter in infertile bondage, a deathlike state from which her chosen suitor alone can free her. The pattern is that of Persephone.

Kahn has considered this kind of Shakespearean situation from the perspective of the father and offers a number of insights. In the romances, she feels, fathers who insist on the chastity of their daughters are denying their own sexuality. This is particularly convincing in her discussion of *The Winter's Tale*,[7] where Leontes' attack upon Hermione reveals not only his complex of misogyny and homosexuality but also his nostalgia for a sexually undifferentiated past, the garden before Eve, whose real threat to man is not so much sexual difference from him, in and of itself, as that she reveals difference itself and thus introduces desire into his world, through the recognition that man himself is incomplete. In the tragedy *Romeo and Juliet*, so close to *A Midsummer Night's Dream* in basic situation and date, Kahn sees the father's sexual prerogative over the daughter as one manifestation of the overwhelming force of patriarchy in Shakespeare.[8] In *Othello* she finds that Iago can appeal to Brabantio's worst fears, in the level of his dreams, because Brabantio had dreamed prophetically of losing his daughter, and the father sees the seduction of his daughter by a lover not of his choosing as cuckoldry. She cites the villain's cry, "Look to your house, your daughter and your bags" (I.i.79–80).[9] Elsewhere she cites in a similar argument Page's fear in *The Merry Wives of Windsor*: "My bed shall be abused, my coffers ransacked, my reputation gnawn at" (II.ii.305–6).[10]

These passages must remind us in turn of Shylock's anxiety over leaving his daughter Jessica at home in his absence, and the later report of his lament at her elopement:

There is some ill a-brewing towards my rest,
For I did dream of money-bags to-night.

(II.v.17–18)

Lock up my doors, and when you hear the drum
And the vile squealing of the wry-neck'd fife
Clamber not you up to the casements then
Nor thrust your head into the public street
To gaze on Christian fools with varnish'd faces:
But stop up my house's ears, I mean my casements,
Let not the sound of shallow fopp'ry enter
My sober house.

(II.v.29–36)

"My daughter! O my ducats! O my daughter!
Fled with a Christian! O my Christian ducats!
Justice, the law, my ducats, and my daughter!
A sealed bag, two sealed bags of ducats,
Of double ducats, stol'n from me by my daughter!
And jewels, two stones, two rich and precious stones,
Stol'n by my daughter! Justice!—find the girl,
She hath the stones upon her, and the ducats!"

(II.viii.15–22).

The father's anxiety that his daughter will be stolen is persistently identified by Shakespeare with anxiety over money, and, ultimately, the integrity of his own body: the rape of the daughter is the theft of the gold, but it is also castration and anal penetration. Shylock shares the Rat Man's fantasy that rats will enter his body through the anus and feed on his innards. Rats are first mentioned as a threat to goods in a ship's hold, as well as to goods on dry land: "—but ships are but boards, sailors but men, there be land-rats, and water-rats, water-thieves, and land-thieves, (I mean pirates)" (I.iii.19–22). The identification between house and body is clear in his warning to Jessica—"But stop up my house's ears—I mean my casements"; thus we are prepared for the example of his obsession he chooses to explain to the court.

What if my house be troubled with a rat,
And I be pleas'd to give ten thousand ducats
To have it ban'd? what, are you answer'd yet?
Some men there are love not a gaping pig!
Some that are mad if they behold a cat!

And others when the bagpipe sings i' th' nose
Cannot contain their urine . . . .

(IV.i.44–50)

We easily see in Shylock the triad of traits which Freud and Jones associated with overstimulation during the anal phase of childhood development and described as "the anal-retentive character": orderliness, parsimony, and stubbornness.[11] What we must understand, however, in order to appreciate its importance in the comic tradition, and its particular importance in Shakespeare, is the twofold identification: not only is gold identified with the body's product, excrement, but also with the miser's daughter. The pattern is easily traced back into New Comedy.

In Plautus' *Aulularia (The Pot of Gold)*, based on a lost original by Menander, the miser Euclio confuses his daughter Phaedria with his gold. When the young man Lyconides comes to confess that he has gotten Phaedria pregnant—"I have robbed you of your dearest possession"—Euclio thinks the crime he admits to is the theft of the gold. Other similarities with *The Merchant of Venice* include a long "lock-up-my-house" speech, and the claim by a slave that Euclio not only stops up his chimney to prevent smoke from escaping, but also his mouth and anus lest anything escape through those openings.[12]

Jessica is part of the father's body in other ways as well. When Shylock freely associates—"My daughter! Oh, my ducats! Oh, my daughter!/ . . . / . . . A sealed bag, two sealed bags of ducats,/ . . . / And jewels, two stones, two rich and precious stones"—he is following Marlowe, who has Barabas, the Jew of Malta, cry out as his daughter Abigail tosses him his money from the window of their house, now expropriated by Christians as a monastery:

> O, my girl,
> My gold, my fortune, my felicity;
> Strength to my soul, death to mine enemy;
> Welcome, the first beginner of my bliss!
> O, Abigail, that I had thee here too,
> Then my desires were fully satisfied;
> But I will practice thy enlargement hence.
> O girl, o gold, o beauty, o my bliss!

(*The Jew of Malta*, II.i.47–54)

Shylock, however, specifies castration—two sealed bags, double du-cats, two stones, two rich and precious stones—and this fits into the central pattern of the plot, his bond with Antonio. We must appreci-ate that his wrath against Antonio, the free-spending Christian mer-chant of Venice, though long-lasting and general, is deepened and specified by the seduction of his daughter. To take the pound of flesh from Antonio, then, becomes talion punishment, as he explains:

> My own flesh and blood to rebel!
> . . . .
> I say my daughter is my flesh and my blood.
> . . . .
> let him look to his bond! . . . let him look to his bond!
> . . . let him look to his bond!
>
> (III.i.31–44)

Fiedler has shown that the main plot of the play, Portia's choice of a husband, is based on the folktale pattern of the ogre's daughter.[13] Por-tia's father's control of the sexual life of his daughter and her money is posthumous, and this makes the similarities between him and Shy-lock all that much more arresting.

For Shylock Jessica is "money in the bank" and his keeping her bound in his house, out of circulation, is an example of his oft ex-pressed attitude toward money generally: he wants it to increase and reproduce itself, but he does not want to run risks with it.[14] Hence, his double antipathy to Antonio:

he hath an argosy bound to Tripolis, another to the Indies, I understand moreover upon the Rialto, he hath a third at Mexico, a fourth for England, and other ventures he hath squand'red abroad. (I.iii.15–19)

> How like a fawning publican he looks!
> I hate him for he is a Christian:
> But more, for that in low simplicity
> He lends out money gratis, and brings down
> The rate of usance here with us in Venice.
>
> (I.iii.36–40)

The argument of the play is complex in tracing the relations between loving and giving. When Bassanio learns "to give and hazard all he hath," he seems to have learned a class-specific lesson, to live like a lord. Perhaps the clearest, harshest statement of this theme elsewhere in Shakespeare is in *Timon of Athens,* where the hero gives lavishly as long as he has wealth, but then turns misanthrope when those he gave to do not give to him in his need.[15] Do we not see in the contrast between Antonio and Shylock the two phases of Timon's behavior?

If so, we must admit that there are many levels on which the question of giving and keeping can be asked and answered, and that Shakespeare usually asks it on one level and answers it on another. He asks what Shylock's attitude toward money is and answers by having Shylock tell us how he feels about his daughter. He shows us that Shylock feels castrated when Jessica is taken from him, and that he will have a pound of flesh off Antonio. Bassanio must swear, with all Portia's suitors, never "To woo a maid in way of marriage" if he fail to choose right, which means, of course, that he swears himself to celibacy, a kind of castration. The suitor and the father then see their potency determined by the daughter, or the possession of the daughter, but the suitor would "use" her sexually, while the father, unless he is as shameless as Antiochus in *Pericles,* would only keep her chaste and barren. The father thinks of his daughter as part of his body, an extension of himself. The suitor, as husband, will come to think of her that way, too. She will be his "external soul," that part of himself which makes him vulnerable to attacks by other men.[16]

The *archetypus archetypi* of this material must be the pattern of death and rebirth ritualized in the mystery cults and best known to us from the cult at Eleusis, mythologized as the rape of Persephone by Hades (who is death personified), and dramatized throughout the history of Greek comedy, tragedy, and satyr-play. Though we can trace this pattern back through the plays of Aristophanes—the heroes of the *Peace* must free the female figure Peace from bondage and bring her back to Athens—it does not come to dominate comedy until Menander begins to write at the end of the fourth century. In our best and earliest source for the myth of Persephone's rape by Hades, the *Homeric Hymn to Demeter* (ca. 650 B.C.), we see the action from the young girl's point of view, or at least sympathize with her since she is the focus of attention. Floral imagery is used not only to identify her with all that is fresh and young and virginal, but also to suggest her awakening of sexual interest. The sequence is rape by the father's brother (with the father's connivance), lament by the mother, threat by the mother that the earth will remain infertile until her daughter is returned, capitulation by the father, and final compromise: the daughter will spend part of the year (Winter) with her "husband" in the underworld, the other part with her mother upon the earth (Spring). It is remarkable that there is no young lover; unlike Shakespeare's comedies where the perspective is usually that of the young lover or the father or some combination of the two, the point of view in the *Hymn* is determined by the shared concerns of the mother and daughter, with their resistance to male violence and possessiveness.

It is possible to see in the *Hymn* a basic ambiguity common to all such erotic material: is the object of desire valued in and of herself, or only artificially or symbolically, as a prize in a contest or as a means of glorifying the subject, or, in the vulgar sense, as a "sex-object," someone who arouses desire in someone else but not feelings of compassion? The same questions then arise about Persephone in the *Homeric Hymn* as they do about Hermia, Jessica, Hero, Desdemona, Perdita, Imogen, Marina and Miranda: what are the feelings between fathers and daughters? We have suggested how complex Shylock's feelings toward Jessica are; we cannot deny the *Hymn's* insistence that Hades is a father-figure to Persephone—Zeus and Hades are brothers, and the *Hymn* calls them both "Son of Cronos"—and that he comes to her as both sexual threat and forbidden but (or therefore) desired lover. The whole episode is an incestuous rape fantasy, though whose is not quite clear:

Apart from Demeter, lady of the golden sword and glorious fruits, Persephone was playing with the deep-bosomed daughters of Oceanus and gathering flowers over a soft meadow, roses and crocuses and beautiful violets, irises also and hyacinths and the narcissus, which Earth made to grow at the will of Zeus and to please the Host of Many, to be a snare for the bloomlike girl—a wondrous, radiant flower. It was a thing of awe whether for deathless gods or mortal men to see: from its root grew a hundred blooms and it smelled most sweetly, so that all wide heaven above and the whole earth and the sea's salt swell laughed for joy. And the girl was amazed and reached out with both hands to take the lovely toy; but the wide-pathed earth yawned there in the plain of Nysa, and the Lord, Host of Many, with his immortal horses sprang out upon her—the Son of Cronos, He who has many names.
He caught her up reluctant on his golden car and bore her away lamenting.

Then she cried out shrilly with her voice, calling upon her father, the Son of Cronos, who is most high and excellent. But no one, either of the deathless gods or of mortal men, heard her voice, nor yet the olive trees bearing rich fruit.[17]

We do not compare the rape of Persephone with the rape of Jessica; rather it is the final release of Persephone from bondage to Hades that we compare to the situation in *The Merchant of Venice* and to many other Shakespearean plays: *A Midsummer Night's Dream, As You Like It, Pericles, Cymbeline, The Winter's Tale, The Tempest, Romeo and Juliet, Othello, Lear.* Whereas Persephone is engulfed in flowers, the imagery surrounding Jessica is money,[18] but Perdita calls upon her prototype:

> O Proserpina,
> For the flowers now that, frighted, thou let'st fall
> From Dis's wagon!
>
> (*WT* IV.iv.116–18)

Perdita elicits a straightforward admission of desire from her father. Before Leontes knows her to be his daughter, her youth and beauty remind him of her mother, whose death he thinks he caused, and this then leads to her resurrection and Leontes' reconciliation with her, his friends, and all cyclical nature. Her young lover Florizel begs Leontes' protection, and Paulina scolds Leontes for forgetting his wife:

Flo.   Beseech you, sir,
  Remember since you ow'd no more to time
  Than I do now: with thought of such affections,
  Step forth mine advocate: at your request,
  My father will grant precious things as trifles.
Leon. Would he do so, I'd beg your precious mistress,
  Which he counts but a trifle.
                        Sir, my liege,
Paul. Your eye hath too much youth in 't; not a month
  'Fore your queen died, she was more worth such gazes
  Than what you look on now.
Leon.   I thought of her,
  Even as these looks I made. (V.i.217–27)

Hermione has been "killed" by her husband's perverse notion of her sexuality and bound below the earth for a winter's season, while her daughter, also "killed," reaches the bloom of maidenhood. Like Persephone, then, Hermione has returned a young virgin in her daughter Perdita, contradicting once more her husband's false accusation that she had been unchaste. In the statue scene we hear from Leontes the final statement of the myth, and we need only ask its significance:

> Her natural posture!
> Chide me, dear stone, that I may say indeed
> Thou art Hermione; or rather, thou art she
> In thy not chiding; for she was tender
> As infancy and grace. But yet, Paulina,
> Hermione was not so much wrinkled, nothing
> So aged as this seems.
>
> (V.iii.23–29)

Whose fantasy is this? Is it the fulfillment of the man's desire that his wife be replaced by a younger, more beautiful image of herself, a virgin, a statue, or a daughter, or is it the woman's wish to escape the sexual demands and jealousies of men? The myth itself is without perspective, but individual renderings of it have definite points of view. In the *Hymn to Demeter* we see and feel the action from the woman's point of view, and mother and daughter are inextricably bound. Indeed in cult they were both called *korē*, virgin or daughter, a seeming denial not only of woman's sexual need of man, but even of his role in the reproductive process: Persephone is Demeter, or a child parthenogenetically produced by Demeter.[19]

Where are the mothers in Shakespearean comedy? Thaisa makes a brief appearance at the end of *Pericles* very much as Emelia does at the end of *The Comedy of Errors*: both are priestesses of Diana and therefore living virginal lives, cloistered, as it were, like Hermione in her underground hideaway during the sixteen years of Leontes' discontent. Hermia would have had to live her life "Chanting faint hymns to the cold fruitless moon." Enforced chastity for the woman seems to be Shakespeare's answer to all the problems created by sexual difference and therefore desire: it is what a father enforces upon his wayward daughter; it is what estranged wives of middle age take upon themselves; it disproves accusations of infidelity against young wives. The paradox with which comedies of the Persephone pattern present us is that men desire young women for their fertility and then, by means of marriage, walls, or underground chambers, attempt to control that mysterious force.[20]

In Greek myth and ritual, and in the comic tradition, the woman is freed from infertile bondage to her father, but she enters into a new bondage, marriage, wherein her sexual energy is channeled toward a productive goal, legitimate offspring. Freud said that marriage was a compromise formation for women, that they get children instead of penises. I think the Demeter myth shows us something much more profound in women's suffering than penis envy: women recreate themselves in their children, but then men steal their children from them. Comedy certainly calls attention to men's jealousy and their fear of women's ability to reproduce themselves. Fathers feel the potential of their daughters to shame and ruin them because of their sexual appetites; the father responds to the sexual promise of his daughter, but feels he cannot control it (or satisfy it). Desdemona's choice of Othello is the fulfillment of a father's nightmare—that his daughter is so sexually rapacious that she, like Pasiphaë or Catherine the Great, requires a beast to satisfy her. If unrestrained her sexual capacity is inhuman. Control is then the crucial consideration: by definition the sexually attractive young girl is under the control of her father, and the independent mature woman is sexually insatiable. With reference to the figures of primary narcissism and its recapitulation in adolescence, the former is identified with the friend, or image of the self, and the latter with the overwhelming mother.[21] Titania's choice of an ass, that most irrational and sexually incontinent of beasts—and her name suggests her concern for size as much as her identification with Diana-Artemis—is what all men expect of women uncontrolled by male authority. This, too, has a long history in comedy; Aristophanes, while presenting women as the creative force and salvation of the state from war, ridicules them for being sexually insatiable and bibulous. All Lysistrata's companions on the Acropolis can think about is the wineskin and the phallos.[22]

We have discovered, then, yet another paradox: in the comic tradition there is a strain which presents a pattern of freeing the woman from bondage to an infertile (incestuous) lover, but these very comedies insist that the woman must always be bound, and only then is she sexually attractive and acceptable. This kind of comedy represents a conspiracy against women, passing them from father to father's choice of lover and never allowing them their own free choice for fear they would choose every man—or no man, but a beast, instead. Imagine Portia without her father's restraint; look at the difficulty Bertram has with Helena, Troilus with Cressida, Antony with Cleopatra. Perhaps the finest example of this in all of Shakespeare is Hamlet's abuse of Ophelia. He accuses her of being a whore because his mother has overwhelmed him with her sexuality and there is no father there to neutralize that corrosive force. The Dark Lady of the *Sonnets* rises up before us, blasting us with her lust and the disease incident upon her promiscuity. What Shakespeare has done in following the comic tradition that sees the pattern of action in the Persephone myth from the male point of view, is, while continuing to associate the young girl with freshness, fertility, and innocence (she is herself a flower), to emphasize her fascination with the penis (the hyacinth or narcissus) and therefore to see in her the potential for the insatiable sexual demands of mature women, i.e., mothers.

I must argue at greater length in the next part of this essay the large and important differences between Greek Old Comedy and New Comedy. I say here simply that between Aristophanes and Menander the locus of desire shifted from the hero himself and his restored potency—what I called above the Dionysos pattern—to the young girl in the Persephone pattern, a displacement we might characterize as a shift of attention not only from one object to another (from himself to her), but also from one aim to another (from using and experiencing to binding and keeping). By the time we reach Menander in the late fourth century, comedy no longer focuses upon the operation of desire in the lover, but upon the stimulating force. In both cases, of course, the young girl is not a major character; often she is nameless, simply *korē*, a term of double significance which encourages us to claim that much of the comic tradition validates the sexual and social control of women: they must be sexually inexperienced and still under a father's authority. In Aristophanes the flute girl or the personified abstraction Harvest is a nonspeaking part, a role assigned either to a male in a body stocking or to some female nonactor, and the lack of development in the character emphasizes the fact that she is purely symbolic. If we identify with the hero, then, like an adolescent who has just discovered that he can achieve orgasm, we are more concerned with the erotic process as manifested in our own bodies than we are with the occasion for that arousal. We ask, then, who is this young girl, and why is she suddenly so attractive? How does she establish herself at the center of comedy in the late fourth century in Athens and remain there through the rest of the tradition, essentially unchanged until Shakespeare?

A number of Menander's plays depict a young woman in flight from an unchosen lover, one who has taken her into his bed, but, because of irregularities in her background, has not wed her. Invariably this lover is a soldier, and we expect of him violent behavior, not only because that is the way soldiers are generally, but because that is how the comic tradition, reaching back to Lamachos in Aristophanes' *Acharnians*, portrays them and names them: Polemon ("Battle"), Thrason ("Violence"), Stratophanes ("Army-Brilliance"). Early scenes show that the soldier has so abused the girl—by shaving her head, for instance, and thus marking her as a whore—that she has fled from him and taken refuge at an altar. In the *Sikyonian*, Philoumene ("Girl Beloved") has managed to situate herself at the very altar of Demeter and Persephone at Eleusis during one of the festivals in their honor. The issue of such action is always the same: the girl is recognized as a freeborn citizen and thus legally marriageable. She finds her father so that he can pronounce the standard Greek engagement formula: "I give her to you for the propagation of legitimate offspring." The father thus relinquishes his sexual prerogative over his daughter, and she becomes suddenly content, now seeing only love in that soldier where formerly she saw violence.

What we find most affecting in Menander's plays is the total commitment which the young man makes to the young girl: his happiness depends upon his possession of her. Even when Menander allows a lover to doubt his beloved's fidelity to him, this does not, as often in Shakespeare (e.g., *Much Ado* and *The Winter's Tale*) turn the whole play dark. This is due to the greater subtlety in Shakespeare's characterization, of course, and also to the whole complex of disbeliefs he weaves about his lovers. He never allows, as Menander does, that a young man is quite capable of tying his sense of well-being to the sexual possession of one young girl. Shakespeare deals with desire in such a way that he is dealing with identity, and no Shakespearean male character is ever satisfied with the identity mere possession of a female can bring him.

Menander's young women are uncomplicated and therefore unthreatening to their male lovers; Menander's young men do not require male friends to prepare them for their love of young women. The same is generally true of the young women in Plautus and Terence, and in English, French, and Italian comedy until the late sixteenth century. Hunter credits Lyly with the first complications in young women, with first assimilating them to the male type of the witty, young lover.[23] Shakespeare further complicates the situation by developing the ambivalence of the young men when faced with such young women. He takes the convention established in late medieval romance—his major source is Chaucer's "Knight's Tale," though he knows it from Boccaccio, de Montemayor, and others—of estimating male friendship over the love of a lady, and makes this a preliminary stage in a young male's erotic development.

Shakespeare's comedy is not romantic the way Menander's is, but insists, as Aristophanes' does, that men need mirrors for themselves in the world outside as well as women safe inside the home. In other words, Shakespeare presents us with the comic tradition entire within each comedy, so that in looking at life through a male protagonist's eyes, we realize that no satisfaction can be found, certainly not exclusively with a young girl. No satisfaction is to be found either in the larger world, because the mirrors it holds up are distorting and effacing. Nevertheless men are more comfortable in the company of other men. Valentine wants Proteus' company abroad, but Proteus, because of Julia, will live "dully sluggardis'd at home." The young noblemen of *Love's Labor's Lost* feel that women distract them from their studies, and their argument seems almost Platonic rather than Neoplatonic, that is, that truth is a function of self-reflection in the Forms, whereas women are only gross matter. In later plays such sexist pretentiousness is parodied in Jaques and pilloried in Vincentio. There is certainly change over the sequence of the comedies, but strangely when men are always alone in the company of women they remember nostalgically their intimacy with other men, as do Leontes and Polixenes in *The Winter's Tale*.

Men's relations with men are no less problematic than their relations with women in Shakespeare's comedies: these friends who are mirror-images of each other compete in love and threaten one another with violence. Men's struggles with other men are for identity, and these become displaced upon the young women newly equipped with swords (in their transvestism) and sharp tongues (in their wit). Can the tension which is formative of the self persist in marriage with a woman who has become like the self for the man? The early comedies do not always end in marriage, the mature comedies are aporetic, and the late romances return to the old problems. The young daughters of middle-aged fathers recall Rosalind and Olivia; Imogen is transvestized; Marina and Perdita and Miranda are all desired for their youthful potential. Hermione, though, is blamed for blasting the young innocence of Leontes' relations with Polixenes. At the end of the play she is briefly a statue, and Leontes is briefly attracted erotically to his daughter; we are reminded of the old patterns of Menandrean comedy and medieval romance. Shakespeare makes a significant change in the Menandrean pattern, however: Leontes' lesson is to accept age and change in the object of his desire. When Shakespeare seems most to follow an old tale, he then reveals a brilliant new synthesis. All the types of object-choice he had previously examined come together in Hermione-Perdita, even, finally, in the priestess-mother of *The Comedy of Errors*. If we decide that all the friends and transvestized lovers in Shakespearean comedy represent protection against male fears of an overwhelming maternal figure, then the beatification of this figure is the only reasonable resolution of the whole dialectic.

II.2.B THE MAN IN THE MIRROR

We have seen in Shakespeare and other makers of the comic tradition a pattern of action in which erotic interest is focused on a young girl who must be freed from infertile bondage to an unchosen lover. We have identified this "lover" as her father, who insists on his sexual prerogative over her—if not to have sex with her himself, then to determine who will. We call this pattern after Persephone, who was raped by her father's brother Hades, with her father Zeus' assistance. This doubling, or splitting, of the father figure is important in many comedies of several periods and national schools. It suggests the daughter's ambivalence toward the father, her seeing him both as the desirable, mysterious stranger, and as the threatening, violent rapist. In Plautus' *Casina*, for instance, Lysidamus claims ius primae noctis over his slave-girl, who has been raised like a daughter in his house; he is thus the false father, the unchosen lover. But then she is recognized as the true daughter of Alcesimus, the man next door, so she can marry the young lover of her choice, who is, of course, Lysidamus' son Euthynicus. In *The Magic Flute*, too, there are two father figures: the kindly, protective, true father Sarastro and the violent, threatening, false father Monostatos.[24]

The doubling, or splitting, that takes place in Shakespeare is of the girl herself into a fresh, completely innocent young girl and into a mature woman with a sexual appetite. This can be done by means of the convention of reserved lady and candid lady's maid, as in the later French tradition of ingenue and soubrette: e.g., Hero and Margaret in *Much Ado About Nothing*, where already there is a phantom Hero. Or it can be done without another woman and consist of a blatant misreading of a faithful wife as profligate, as Leontes misreads Hermione in *The Winter's Tale*.

The Persephone pattern, then, can be developed to express the young woman's—or even the mature woman's—fear and resentment of male sexuality, but generally Shakespeare uses it to represent male fears of female sexuality, and we recognize the man's attempt whether he be young lover or old father, to lock up the woman as his reaction against the phantom image of a sexually insatiable, mature woman (his infantile fantasy of his own mother), which he projects upon even the most unthreatening, sexually undemanding young girl. We shall now see that the comic tradition also presents a different pattern, one in which the man chooses not a woman who, because she might remind him of his mother, would overwhelm him, but rather chooses narcissistically an image of himself: first, himself, indeed; then, the image of himself in a twin or male friend; and then the image of himself in a young girl transvestized as a young man. This last step is Shakespeare's great advance over previous comedy, and indeed all other forms of romance. He combines male and female, narcissistic and anaclitic choices of object, in one witty and attractive hermaphroditic figure, who then takes control of the action and instructs her male lover in how to love. In

the later comic tradition we see such a figure in Beaumarchais' Chér-
ubin (Mozart's Cherubino), a descendant not only of Shakespeare's
Rosalind-Ganymede but also of the Greek Eros, who was originally
depicted as a sexually ambiguous adolescent, not as the cuddly toddler
of baroque art.

This extraordinary erotic evolution, which we can trace not only from
the beginning to the end of Shakespeare's career, but can also find recapitulated in many individual comedies, is itself a recapitulation of
the entire history of comedy, which began as narcissistic, became romanticized in its celebration of the innocent young *korē*, and occasionally produced exemplary tendencies toward fusion, though nothing on
the scale of the individual Shakespearean masterpieces. This erotic argument is developed by Shakespeare in line with straightforward philosophical speculation. Men are taught to love in their mistresses what
they admire in themselves, to dismiss preconceived notions (myths) of
what women are, and to watch as women change, become many things,
all those things, indeed, which men admire in other men. Simultaneously men are taught not to read nature as a predictable pattern (metaphysical reality) but rather as a constantly changing sequence of unique
moments (phenomenological actuality).

We should now analyze more completely that first phase of comedy,
the narcissistic Old Comedy of Aristophanes (productive life 427–388
B.C.), and for this purpose we compare what we have called the anaclitic or oedipal New Comedy of Menander (productive life 321–280
B.C.). We can then appreciate how Shakespeare spontaneously recreates a kind of narcissistic comedy against the essentially Menandrean
tradition which was his heritage. In eight of Aristophanes' plays—
Acharnians, Birds, Clouds, Frogs, Knights, Peace, Ploutos and *Wasps*—
the focus of attention is on an old man who behaves like a child, demanding immediate gratification of all his desires, which show the full
range of polymorphous perversity. Much of his energy is aggressively
invested at the opening of the play, but after a kind of victory over his
enemies, and a different kind of rejuvenation, this same energy seems
to be concentrated in the libidinal investment of some female figure.
The parallelism with the Persephone pattern of comedy should be clear:
both move from the binding of some fertility figure to its release, from
destruction (death and aggression) to creation (sexual union); in Aris-

tophanes we identify the pattern with Dionysos, the male fertility god, who suffered cycles of death and resurrection.

One could claim that Aristophanes' old men achieve a kind of "genital organization," which is where Menandrean heroes begin by deciding that their whole happiness will be determined by the sexual possession of one young girl. In Aristophanes, however, no such simple solution is possible. The girl whom the old hero gets is likely to be some symbolic figure, or a flute-girl, i.e., an object of purely sexual interest. Indeed one of the great distortions in conventional readings of Aristophanes has been the insistence on finding there some redeeming social value in spite of the overwhelmingly individualistic outlook of his protagonists. His heroes might be immediately concerned with political, philosophical, even literary problems, but their deep concern is only with their own desires and identity, with finding some outlet for their aggression and sexual energy. To illustrate how completely things change between Old Comedy and New Comedy, we can compare the *Wasps* of Aristophanes and the *Dyskolos* of Menander, a necessary exercise since the particular differences we are interested in have not been seen before; indeed it is Shakespeare who makes us see them.

Aristophanes uses the term *dyskolia* ("bad temper") for his old hero's aggression, even when the context is erotic, and Menander calls his barrier figure *dyskolos* ("bad-tempered"). Philokleon in the *Wasps* and Knemon in the *Dyskolos* attack both family and strangers who stand in their way, but whereas Knemon's erotic and aggressive energy is focused on his daughter—he would keep her safe at home for himself, and therefore reminds us of Euclio and Shylock—Philokleon's focus is only himself, and his energy is used getting away from home to the courts, where he can harm greater numbers of people.

In the opening scene of the *Wasps*, the slaves Xanthias and Sosias try to restrain Philokleon within the house, but he threatens to become a mouse and nibble his way out, or to become smoke and escape through the chimney. They describe his mania as an erotic perversion—playing on his name "Lover of Kleon"—considering first that he might be *philokubos* ("dice-lover") or *philopotēs* ("wine-lover") or *philothutēs* ("lover of sacrificing") or *philoxenos* ("lover of foreigners"). Here their consideration ends, since Philoxenos was a famous catamite of the day, and they are sure that is not their master's problem. They finally decide he is *philēliastēs* ("lover of litigation") and that this perversion, like all others, "breaks out all the more virulently the more it is repressed." (This passage alludes to the *Sthenoboia* of Euripides, where the nurse describes her mistress's passion for a young friend of her husband's.)

The old jurors who come to fetch Philokleon to court wear the traditional leather phalluses of comedy, but they serve a double function in this play, for they are stingers as well.[25] There is a clear movement in the action from the *dyskolia* of the opening scenes to the sexual orgy of the closing scene. There is a change in direction for the application of Philokleon's energy, but this energy itself is a constant quantity. Originally it is his animosity in the courtroom, a purely negative, destructive, aggressive tendency to work out his frustrations at being kept out of the mainstream of political life on those who come before him for judgement. Later this energy is still destructive, in part, as shown by his misbehavior at the symposium. The implication is that finally, with the flute-girl he rescues from that gathering, there has been a definite change, and his immediate aim is intercourse with her.[26] His rage to assert himself, then, transfers from a political to a more overtly sexual expression.

Even early on Philokleon takes pleasure in aspects of his occupation other than the condemning of defendants. These pleasures are all physical. He prays to Lykos, whose statue stands near the court:

> Save thy neighbor, preserve him intact,
> And nevermore, from this day hence
> Will I piss on thy precinct or fart on thy fence.
>
> (393–94)[27]

When his son, to keep him at home, promises to hold court for him there, he also promises to supply him with a chamber pot, to be hung on his erect penis (the leather phallos attached to his costume), so it will be ready when he is (ll. 807–8). While the domestic court is actually in session, Philokleon eats vast amounts of bean porridge and relieves himself on stage (ll. 891–940). Toward the end of the play, Sosias reports on his behavior at the symposium:

> When he had filled himself up
> With all the best dishes

> He leapt and he jumped,
> And then right in their faces
> He farted and harumphed
> Like a donkey out of traces.
>
> (1304–6)

Philokleon speaks early on of an ass passing gas in a pun on *onos* ("wine bottle" and "donkey") (ll. 618–19). We also hear that he is prone to incontinence (ll. 1127–28). All this toilet talk is summed up by Bdelykleon when he refers to the old man as an "ass-hole that defies washing" (l. 604). This is not gratuitous scurrility but an integral part of the play: Philokleon is being associated with the unrestricted delight in bodily functions which is characteristic of young children. It is not only excrement, of course, but aliment that delights him: we hear often of eating and drinking, belching and regurgitation, not only in the bean scene (ll. 891–940) and in the description of the symposium (ll. 1299–1312), but throughout the play, e.g., ll. 510–11.

Then, too, his early pleasures are not entirely nongenital; he has interests in both boys and girls, as we hear, in legal contexts. He boasts that he and his fellow jurors can break the will which leaves property to a young girl (ll. 583–89); with a pun on *kogchē*, this can also mean that they deflower her. He also boasts that his jury gives physical examinations to the young men who are being presented for citizenship, to ascertain that they really are men (l. 578). There is even the suggestion of incestuous attraction when Philokleon describes as his greatest pleasure being kissed in the French style by his daughter: she probes with her tongue in his mouth for the coins he has been paid for jury duty (ll. 605–9).

The great satisfaction of Aristophanic comedy comes from the control which the hero gains over his world; the female figure at the end is simply one aspect of that world. Freud tells us that control is the great discovery of the anal period, when the child first realizes that his body can be mastered, and, because of the interest which those who tend him take in his bodily habits, he can control them by controlling or refusing to control himself. Freud associates all the obsessional neuroses with the anal phase:[28] what is appropriate as a developmental stage—and we feel this is the case with Philokleon—becomes a perversion if maintained later on. This is how we consider Knemon in

Menander's *Dyskolos,* and a whole series of misers named Smikrines, who appear in his other plays.[29] Knemon's major characteristic is *dyskolia* (hatred and distrust of his fellow man), but an important auxiliary trait is his parsimony. Not only does he refuse to spend money as a man of his means should—and the proper spending of money is a social grace, as Sostratos explains to his father Kallipides at the beginning of the fifth act—but he also holds on to his daughter as if she were a possession of monetary value. She has, of course, erotic value to him as well, but it is specifically anal erotism which causes him to lock her up in the house (symbolic of his own body) and to prevent her from moving freely in the world, even to the extent that a young girl of her class was allowed normally to do. Knemon's misanthropic character is the barrier in the way of a good marriage for his daughter, and the action of the play moves toward his removal. Nevertheless this attitude develops into a positive virtue by the end of the play, with the turning point coming in his great apologia speech (ll. 703–47). A very close relationship exists between Knemon and his daughter, and it is clear throughout that she has profited by her removal from society, that his severe standards have made her virtuous (ll. 34–39, 201–2). We should think of surly old Prospero in his address to the virtuous young Miranda. In all of these comedies where fathers begrudgingly relinquish dutiful daughters, there is the clear indication that the father's valuation of the daughter, though falsely based on a monetary standard or some other notion of possession, is accurate. Miserly, misanthropic fathers tend to raise beautiful, dutiful daughters. When this is not true, as in *The Merchant of Venice* and *Othello,* the results are tragic, or at least melodramatic.

The superficial differences between Aristophanic and Menandrean comedy are easy to catalogue. The plays of Aristophanes are elaborate musical comedies with spectacular settings and costumes, dealing with fantastic exploits which involve politics, poetry, philosophy, and religion. The plays of Menander are exclusively domestic in their setting and are almost totally realistic; music is reduced to inorganic interludes between the acts. Whereas Aristophanes' language is rich in all conceivable variants of human communication (and of animal communication in such tours de force as the hoopoe's song in the *Birds* and the frogs' chorus in the *Frogs*), ranging from obscenity to the hymns of the mysteries, from the broken Greek of Persians to the high diction of tragedy, Menander's language is consistently that used by educated Athenians in normal conversation. The most profound difference, though, is in erotic interest and general worldview. The Aristophanic hero takes the world as his mirror, forcing all aspects of his life to meet his extravagant demands. Some of these demands are still made by the old fathers in Menander, but the fathers are forced aside, and the innocuous young lovers gain their sole demands, the fathers' daughters. In dynamic terms, then, Menander has created his blocking figure out of those very perversions—Frye speaks of comic action as the "removal of neuroses"[30]—which characterize the Aristophanic hero.

Such distinctions can reveal different perspectives on human potential. If a society indulges and even encourages the ostentation of a few privileged men, promotes them to heroic stature, and treats them as outside the bounds of common humanity, then these aristocrats are fulfilling the wishes of the masses and somehow lifting up the thoughts of all men, though the vast majority can never hope to attain to such pleasures. The society which promotes trade and believes in a certain equality among men, whether or not that belief is a political program, disavows such aspirations and constantly insists on limits. The most important of these limits for comedy is marriage itself. Men are shown to be content with one sexual partner all their lives in Menander, whereas in Aristophanes marriage is an institution that has nothing to do with sexual life; that goes on wildly in other people's houses, in public buildings, in the streets.

Men regard women differently in Menander from the way they do in Aristophanes. Dover claims that up through the middle of the fourth century, if a young man spoke of romantic involvement, of being passionately in love, his companions would have taken it for granted that the object of his desire was an even younger man.[31] All of this changed by the end of the century. Indeed, Plato's description of the erotic behavior of Athenian aristocrats, which we shall consider in the next essay, signifies the end of that long tradition. This change in erotic attitudes can be linked with the change in Athens' political fortunes: she came under Macedonian domination, and so her young men lost their opportunity to participate in her government. Political life in the full, rich sense peculiar to Athens was over, so all that had turned a young man's attention outside, to the agora, the pnyx, the various stoas, to the acropolis itself, was gone, and he turned his attention inside, to the domestic sphere, and to the woman he would choose to share that with him. For the first time in Greek literature women are spoken of, in Menander, as objects of desire, and are romanticized, idealized, celebrated. They are still in bondage, but it is a different kind of bondage, and it will not change again, nor will comedy, for another two thousand years. Only sporadically, in Shakespeare and Molière and a few other contributers to the tradition, do we find some suggestion of that different kind of comedy that Aristophanes wrote.

In spite of a seeming absence of anything of a truly philosophical nature in either Aristophanes or Menander, both deal with the problems of identity. In Aristophanes, of course, identity is political: the old heroes insist on directing the state toward its traditional virtues. Disguise or masquerade is used by Aristophanes to suggest true confusion of identity much the same way transvestism and twinning is used by Shakespeare. Dikaiopolis puts on the rags of Telephos, Euripides' beggar-hero, to plead his case before the Acharnians; women transvestize in the *Ekklesiazusai* to take over the assembly, and men transvestize in the *Thesmophoriazusai* to spy on the women's ritual; most significantly, Dionysos in the *Frogs* disguises himself first as Herakles and then as his own slave when he goes to Hades to bring back Euripides, clearly a journey of self-discovery both for the god and for Athens.

In Greek Middle Comedy (ca. 388–321 B.C.) we see emerge those patterns of action suggesting the problems of identity which Shakespeare adapts, plays dealing with those episodes in Greek mythology where twins and doubles cause confusion, such as the seduction of Alkmene by Zeus disguised as her husband Amphitryo.[32] Several plays of the period deal with the exchange of clothes between Herakles and Queen Omphale of Lydia.[33] In both Middle and New Comedy there were many plays dealing with confusions, some sexual: titles of lost Menandrean plays include *Didumai* ("Female Twins"), *Androgynos*, *Homopatrioi* ("Sons of the Same Father"), *Philadelphoi* ("Brothers Who Love Each Other").[34] Even though the Greek comic poets did not develop these concerns as explicitly as did Shakespeare—*The Comedy of*

Errors is based on Plautus' *Menaechmi* and *Amphitryo*, which were in turn based on Greek originals of the Middle or New Comedy—they are inherent in the patterns of action. Indeed functions of identity are specific to time and place; we cannot expect exactly the same demands for self-definition in fourth-century B.C. Athens and in second-century B.C. Rome as we find in sixteenth-century London.[35]

How do we associate the oral and anal preoccupations of early childhood, so emphasized in Old Comedy and early psychoanalytic theory, with the "mirroring" effect we are now tracing there? I suggested above that the fragmentation, *le corps morcelé*, that Lacan thinks the child sees in himself during *le stade du miroir* is attributable in part to the eroticization first of one part of his body and then of another, so that he sees himself as a collection of parts rather than as an integrated whole. Developmentally, these periods are simultaneous, not sequential, so that the mirror stage runs parallel with the oral and the beginning of the anal stage. Otherwise we could claim a neat correlation between polymorphous perversity and Old Comedy, the mirror stage and Middle Comedy, oedipal orientation and New Comedy. More loosely, we see simply that all serious comedy is concerned with identity, that identity is a function of the orientation of desire, that comedy of different periods satisfies men's demand for identity through different orientations of desire. No period of comedy can be claimed to be based purely on one phase of psychosexual development; obviously pre-oedipal concerns are overlaid and interpreted by oedipal concerns. I do claim, though, that the most satisfying comedy is that which raises memory traces in the audience of the earliest stages of development, so that Aristophanic comedy, dealing so explicitly with pre-oedipal material, is more deeply satisfying than the predominantly oedipal comedy of Menander. For Shakespeare I claim a combination of the two, an intricate interweaving of references to different stages of individual development with their appropriate or perverse orientations of desire and determinations of identity.

II.3

The Philosophical Tradition

y title suggests that there is something consistent in the kinds of thinking men do about their relations with the world; since what I shall in large part focus my discussion on here is psychosexuality, I also suggest that there is some consistency between the way men think about themselves in their relations with other men and women—their libidinal and aggressive investments in others—and in the way they see truth. This is easier to demonstrate with the Greek material. There have been recent studies of the patterns of Greek sexuality, especially in the period covered by the evolution of the comic form—from the early fifth century through the early third century B.C.— to which we can refer in constructing the complicated case that men think about life and love in particular ways in particular times and places. Their serious comedy reflects these patterns as much as does "pure philosophy."

The English material is perhaps equally abundant, but not so well studied. It is arguable that cultural differences between the two periods are responsible and not the failure of Elizabethan scholars to make connections. We do not discern so clear and persistent a pattern of sexual fantasy and activity in fourteenth, fifteenth, and sixteenth century London as we do in sixth, fifth, and fourth century Athens. Nevertheless, I think the intellectual and emotional life of the small group of Athenian aristocrats represented for us so vividly in the *Sym-*

posium of Plato might be usefully compared with the society in which we know Shakespeare moved during the early years of his career: almost exclusively male, openly expressive (if not actually physical) in their erotic interest in each other, philosophically speculative, not as politically active as they would have wished to have been. This rarefied and introspective social situation I associate with narcissism in individual development. I therefore find once again the mirror to be the definitive image for both the age and the stage. I will consider the ways in which the elite of late classical Athens and Renaissance London sought their idealized images of themselves in their world, mirrored themselves in their reality, and refused to see beyond themselves to any persistent patterns or verities in nature.

Plato is, of course, a response against this kind of thinking: he sought absolute truth and despised the things of this world. His dialectic is, however, dependent upon the kinds of erotic relations we are trying to determine. Indeed everything in Plato—who wrote during the early and middle years of the fourth century, precisely between the careers of Aristophanes and Menander—is idealized. Whereas in Aristophanes and earlier Greek literature generally, the heroes insist on immediate and precise gratification of all their desires, in Plato displacement is already required—infinite sublimation of erotic energy until the realm of the Forms is reached. Plato, then, looks backward in that his erotic pattern is homoerotic (we can trace this to the pederasty of Aristophanes' old heroes and to that phenomenon in archaic and classical Greek culture generally) and forward in that it is based on sublimation and delayed gratification. In Menander, of course, for the first time in Greek literature, all of men's erotic attention is focused on young women, a fact probably associated with the absence of military, political, and cultural outlets available to young men in late fourth century Athens; they were all "dully sluggardis'd at home," like Proteus at the opening of *The Two Gentlemen of Verona* before he has followed his friend Valentine abroad.

In the *Symposium* and *Phaidros,* Plato develops his metaphysical system in a discussion of love. The kind of love he speaks of is that classic Greek pattern of pederasty in which the *erastēs* ("lover") is an older man and actively pursues the *erōmenos* ("beloved"), a younger man. These two figures represent originally distinct moments in the

Platonic dialectic, which finally resolves their difference: the *erastēs* sees beauty in the *erōmenos*, but comes to realize that the beauty he sees there is his own beauty reflected in the eyes of the *erōmenos*, as in a mirror, and then that this beauty is not really his own beauty but rather a reflection of absolute Beauty in him. The *erastēs* therefore needs the *erōmenos* as a kind of catalyst to define himself to himself, or rather to reflect the metaphysical constant of Beauty in himself. (This later becomes the Neoplatonic distinction between self and Self—"the mystic self"—as Zweig has shown.)[1] The *erōmenos* also benefits from this relationship, seeing the beauty of the *erastēs* (which is derived from absolute Beauty) re-reflected from himself in the other.

In the *Symposium*, Diotima explains to Socrates the difference between the physically expressed love of men for women, which results in babies, and the self-revelatory love of the *erastēs* for the *erōmenos*, which results in philosophy:

Those whose procreancy is of the body turn to women as the object of their love, and raise a family in the blessed hope that by doing so they will keep their memory green "through time and eternity." But those whose procreancy is of the spirit rather than of the flesh—and they are not unknown, Socrates—conceive and bear the things of the spirit. . . . his procreant nature is attracted by a comely body rather than by an ill-favored one, and if, besides, he happens upon a soul which is at once beautiful, distinguished, and agreeable, he is charmed to find so welcome an alliance. It will be easy for him to talk of virtue to such a listener, and to discuss what human goodness is and how the virtuous should live—in short, to undertake the other's education. And, as I believe, by constant association with so much beauty, and by thinking of his friend when he is present and when he is away, he will be delivered of the burden he has labored under all these years. And what is more, he and his friend will help each other rear the issue of their friendship—and so the bond between them will be more binding, and their communion even more complete, than that which comes of bringing children up, because they have created something lovelier and less mortal than human seed.[2]

We see here not only the pattern of the dialectic—subject and object gradually transcending themselves in contemplation of their shared essence—but also two important aspects of erotic relations. Plato shares with Aristophanes an insistence on the active quality of love, displaying a disdain for the passive posture of the *erōmenos* (who sees only the reflection of a reflection, like the imitation of an imitation);[3] we recall the disdain of Aristophanes' old heroes for catamites. There is also in

Plato, though, a distrust of sensual experience, a derogation of the physical: the *erastēs* never consummates his desire for the *erōmenos;* if he did, then the philosophical circuit would be broken.

The particular quality of this kind of relationship could not be made clear without reference to the mirror and to Ganymede, whom we recognize as Zeus' "cup-bearer," Rosalind's male persona, and the original Greek name which the Romans replaced with Catamitus:

So as he continues in this converse and society, and . . . [they meet] . . . in the gymnasium and elsewhere, that flowing stream which Zeus, as the lover of Ganymede, called the "flood of passion," pours in upon the lover. And part of it is absorbed within him, but when he can contain no more the rest flows away outside him, and as a breath of wind or an echo, rebounding from a smooth, hard surface, goes back to its place of origin, even so the stream of beauty turns back and re-enters the eyes of the fair beloved.[4]

In my reading of the individual comedies of Shakespeare I shall position him not only in the comic tradition beginning with Aristophanes, and in the philosophical tradition beginning with Plato, but also in that longer and more inclusive tradition of which Freud, too, is a part, that attempts to define the nature of love. I shall always insist that though we might occasionally use bipolar oppositions such as narcissistic-anaclitic, homosexual-heterosexual, and phenomenological-metaphysical, we must always try to think dialectically. One could claim, for instance, that love of the narcissistic type leads almost inevitably to philosophical speculation, that the motto Socrates took for himself from the temple of Apollo at Delphi—*gnōthi seauton* ("know thyself")—is the basic philosophical imperative, and that this should be contrasted with the Neoplatonic Christian effort to lose the self in the Mother, the anaclitic orientation. Shakespeare could then be seen as spontaneously restoring the original nature of Platonic love by showing young men first bonding with each other to know themselves before they approach the dangerous other of women.

Other critics share my contention that Shakespeare presents in his comedies marriage as a solution that is more socially than individually satisfying. Lyons, among others, has made this distinction.[5] A loss is felt—the same loss we feel in the transition from Aristophanes to Menander. Even though Menander seems to have discovered the capacity of women for attracting men's desire, a compensatory change

in the dynamics of comedy consequent upon this discovery is noticeable and significant: the focus of attention shifts from the character
who is successful in his quest—who is now the young man winning
the young girl—to the blocking character. This is a shift of attention
Frye and others have also noted in Shakespearean comedy. We must,
though, with Hunter,[6] credit Shakespeare, following Lyly, with having "discovered" women for Renaissance comedy. There are great differences, as we have seen, between Menander's women and Shakespeare's: Menander's marriageable young women scarcely speak—only
his courtesans have anything to say, any active role to play—whereas
Shakespeare's young women are eloquent and extremely active (though
it often takes transvestism to liberate their wit and energy), and they
become the focus of our attention.

Davies presents a typical appreciation of Shakespeare's transvestized heroines:

The convention of male disguise . . . allows the transcendence by the heroine
of normal social limitation, so that these characters are at liberty. In this state
of liberty, the feminine is seen as an active principle, with its own kind of
absolute intelligence and strength. Such individuals have a great wholeness of
being.[7]

Two main features are remarkable in this statement, beyond its clear
good sense: a tendency to ignore the erotic implication of transvestism, and a tendency to hypostatize constant qualities. These two
tendencies are closely related: if one can talk about the forms of things,
what actual experience only represents, then one flies from the particulars of that experience, which include erotic phenomena. L. Jardine
provides a salutary correction to all this by insisting that we always
appreciate the significance of the transvestism behind transvestism,[8]
i.e., that boy actors are playing girl characters who disguise themselves as boys. She cites many contemporary sources, especially from
the negative side of the war over the morality of stage production, to
show that the Elizabethans' response to this doubled transvestism in
the theatre would have been based on their pederastic interest; this
reminds us of the Greek interest in adolescent sexuality generally. Jardine argues that Shakespeare's contemporaries associated transvestism
with "hermaphroditism" and hermaphroditism with pederasty. She even
cites an authority who makes the classical connection:

There are affinities between hermaphroditism and pederasty. . . . In late antiquity, *androgyne*, with the derogatory overtone which *gynandre* had always had, is often used for either a eunuch, or an effeminate.[9]

She comes finally to the point: "Whenever Shakespeare's female characters in the comedies draw attention to their own androgyny, I suggest that the resulting eroticism is to be associated with their maleness rather than their femaleness."[10]

This is very difficult territory conceptually, especially when we are trying to consider two cultures simultaneously, and one of those cultures as it changed over time. Delcourt, Jardine's source on classical conceptions of the masculine and feminine, specifies "late antiquity" for the derogation of the androgyne. (We recall that Menander wrote a comedy called *Androgynos*.) If we look at characterizations in the visual arts, there is certainly nothing effeminate about Ganymede in the famous late sixth-century group at Olympia: Zeus strides off resolutely with a perfectly formed, completely masculine young boy of about twelve tucked under his arm, both of them smiling "archaic smiles." We need remind ourselves of Devereux's point about Greek "pseudohomosexuality." He suggests that the predominant pattern of Greek homosexuality, at least among Athenian aristocrats, was actually an extraordinarily extended period of adolescent sexual experimentation characterized by five major traits: fascination with penile erection; self-centered erotism (i.e., interest in the object in and of itself is not so important a determinant of sexual excitement as the effect of the object on the subject); lack of differentiation in object-choice (male or female will do); pseudodifferentiation under social pressure (young men fell into the pattern of homosexuality because it was fashionable), and sexual immaturity (lack of clear comprehension of sexual roles).[11] What seems to have been erotically appreciated then was the seeming potential in the young to become either male or female, rather than the actualization of male and female traits in maturity. This relates to the general tendency in erotic relations for men to choose objects young and unfulfilled, where there is a kind of negative capability to return the subject's idealized image of himself. We wonder, though, whether Greeks of the classical period, and Elizabethans, saw in young boys and girls the potential for becoming both male and female, or only the potential for becoming male.

Again, the evidence from the visual arts is instructive. From the early fifth-century "Kritios Boy" to the late fourth-century "Apoxyomenos" of Lysippos, or from the "Doryphoros" of Polykleitos (ca. 450) to the Hermes of Praxiteles (ca. 340), a clear evolution in the ideal of (masculine) beauty takes place. Characterized by a gradual effeminization and a less clearly defined musculature, the contraposto in the later examples suggests languor whereas formerly it showed readiness for action, and a certain fleshiness becomes apparent. (We might compare the Elizabethan "Portrait of a Youth with Roses," by Nicholas Hilliard.)[12] As the distinctions between the sexes begin to blur in sculpture, the decline of that militant homosexuality noticeable in Aristophanes is already under way. The two termini for this development are contained in the comedies of Aristophanes and Menander; predatory pederasty is a major theme of the former, but it is completely eclipsed by monogamous heterosexuality in the latter. We agree then finally with Jardine, against Davies: there is a traceable pattern among the Elizabethans, as among the fifth century Athenians, to seek "masculine potential" in all objects of desire. This is to be distinguished from a celebration of true androgyny. Philophically stated, in both cultures masculinity was the conceptual model and femininity only a distance from it. What men particularly liked in women was their ability to assume the positive qualities of masculinity—the wit, the charm, the elegance, the suppleness of limb and efficiency in action—and thus to become libidinally attractive while lacking the aggression of men.

If we think of a continuum in the history of Greek psychosexuality beginning with the Homeric poems and ending with tragedy (the eighth century through the fifth), we see a shift from a totally masculine world, where women are neither feared nor desired, to a world in which women begin to be seen as not only different from men in that they are not men—definition by negation—but different from men in that they are something else. At the same time, though, misogyny becomes evident where it had not existed before. Aristophanes' comedy might be the last statement of this totally masculine Greek world view; his contemporary tragedians (Sophocles and Euripides) present things differently, with threatening women at the center of life: men are locked up with them in their houses and become victims to their mysterious powers. What have we in Shakespeare? Again, the difference seems to be a function of genre: There is certainly misogyny in the tragedies, but in the comedies a seemingly unitary view of sexuality prevails in which there are men and non-men, or women capable of becoming men, but no women in and of themselves. The definition of comedy as wish-fulfillment illuminates this distinction: tragedy deals with the realities of sexual difference and antagonism; comedy fantasizes a world in which the sexes are assimilated to a masculine ideal. Menandrean comedy, as we have seen, takes the patterns of domestic strife which Greek mythology supplied to Greek tragedy and bowdlerizes them, so, to some extent, it should be read as melodrama rather than as pure comedy.

Is it useful to compare the patterns of psychosexuality to contemporary patterns of ontology? Parallel to the continuum of Greek psychosexuality stretching from the Homeric view of the world as entirely masculine to the Greek tragic view in which men and women are condemned to mutual destruction is a philosophical development beginning with the fragmentation of Homeric man's view of the world (and himself) and culminating with Platonic unity. For Plato, of course, unity is masculinity: in the *Republic* women are consigned to exercising naked in the gymnasium and to becoming guardians, thus assimilating to all the old masculine virtues; in the *Symposium* we see that philosophical growth takes place between—is the child born to—two male lovers. It is tempting to call Plato's search for unity a pattern of wish-fulfillment not unlike Aristophanes'. What, then, of Shakespeare? The same, I think. He saw the world fragmented by new modes of perception—the relativism of the astronomers, the philosophers, the lovers, and poets—and depicted this in his tragedies. In his comedies, however, he fulfills the masculine wish of a sexually undifferentiated world. That shaping erotic vision—looking at men and women and seeing only young boys—is comparable to his overall artistic vision, of seeing a bear in a bush or dignity in a rustic. I think the emotional affect at the ends of the comedies—so strong and completely unique— is the result of a crumbling nostalgia: like the pageants that are fading, the sexes are settling back into their old patterns of hostility. We awake from man's dream of returning to the garden where he was one with God and himself before women become known.

There is no study of homosexuality in Elizabethen England comparable to that by Dover of homosexuality in Greece from the archaic through the hellenistic periods.[13] Nevertheless, those familiar with the period cannot ignore the presence of this subject in both literary and social documents. For A. L. Rowse, the exceptional Dr. Forman proves the rule:

Forman is simply interested in the facts, every fact about himself and other people, especially women—who were an open book to him, and many laid themselves open to him, for he was abnormally heterosexual: there is not a trace of any other interest, in an age distinguished by the homosexuality (or ambivalence) of Bacon and Marlowe, Oxford and Southampton, and Lord Henry Howard, or with the Court of James I.[14]

Did the convention of boys playing girls' parts, and those girls then playing at being boys appeal to the homosexual interests of Shakespeare's audience, to those whose actual or fantasized pattern of sexual experience was with mature members of their own sex? I cannot believe that this was so, but if we specify pederasty I think we are closer to the mark. To appreciate the difference we need only compare the traditional Elizabethan practice of young boys, perhaps even prepubescent, playing the women's parts, and that recent experiment of the Royal Shakespeare Company with *As You Like It:* men with hairy chests were seen in ladies's silk bodices.

Devereux associates what he calls "pseudohomosexuality" with the "Greek miracle." It was essentially a worship of the promise of youth, its capacity to do anything, to become anything. He even invokes such modern prodigies as Mozart, appealing to the belief that creativity is often found in the childlike nature, the man who refuses to accept the limits which normally come with maturity. I have elsewhere written about the "childlike Achilles," claiming that that hero's experience of the undivided attention of his mother, his total innocence of oedipal conflict, created in him absolute demands for gratification of every desire—and his greatest desire was for his dear friend Patroklos, his childhood companion whom he used ontogenetically as a double. I have claimed that this is a pattern for all human experience, that we all suffer an "Achilles complex" to some extent, not only in our early attempts to define ourselves, to capture an image of ourselves from our mothers toward which we can assimilate, but also in adolescence, when we repeat the process and see that image of ourselves in our same-sex friends.[15] All this occurs in Shakespearean comedy, as we shall see, constantly varied but always recognizable.

Where then does desire for the woman come from? It is oedipal, of course, and pre-oedipal in the anaclitic type of object-choice, but what turns young men finally to young women and away from other young men, in the world of Shakespeare's comedies, which is to an important extent our world? Like all erotic questions, I think this one has basically an ontogenetic answer, and Shakespeare repeats it in many variations. The young men become fascinated with the young women when the young women become like the young men, but then the young men realize that, unlike their male companions, these young women need not always be their adversaries, their rivals in military, intellectual, and other endeavors. The swords the women have worn in their roles as swaggering pages, will be put aside; these weapons could never have symbolized anything, anyway. It is the young women's lack that the young men like, a kind of reverse penis envy.

The last time Achilles sees Patroklos alive, he chides him as a young girl:

> Why then
> are you crying like some poor little girl, Patroklos,
> who runs after her mother and begs to be picked up and carried,
> and clings to her dress, and holds her back when she tries to hurry,
> and gazes tearfully into her face, until she picks her up?
> You are like such a one, Patroklos, dropping those soft tears.
>
> (*Iliad* 16.6–11, R. Lattimore, tr.)

Patroklos then explains that the best of the Greek fighters have been killed or wounded and convinces Achilles to allow him to enter the battle wearing Achilles' armor, and perhaps thus to turn the tide, or at least give the harassed Greeks some respite. Hektor then kills Patroklos wearing Achilles' armor and dons that armor himself, so that when Achilles kills Hektor he is killing a mirror image of himself; this predicts his own actual death, which lies beyond the scope of the *Iliad*. We might call this the tragic outcome of narcissism—the ashes of Achilles and Patroklos will be mixed in an urn and set as a monument on the Hellespont—and compare it to the comic outcome wherein marriage rather than death unites the young man with his feminized image of himself.

Achilles sees something effeminate, something soft, in Patroklos, some break in the constant male-on-male aggression which makes up his experience, and our experience of the *Iliad*. Patroklos is like him, but he lacks that tremendous aggressive drive which characterizes Achilles. He lacks even the armor and weapons, the "phallic" equipment of the warrior, and this is why Patroklos dies trying to be Achilles. Achilles' aggression is narcissistic throughout the poem, and he always establishes his own identity by doing violence to a single opponent; this pattern finally concludes in his killing his mirror image in Hektor, a kind of suicide.

The pattern in Shakespearean comedy is similar. The young men see mirror images of themselves in their male companions and then in the transvestized young women. This image is armored, accoutered for battle, the violent, aggressive battle of self-assertion, the battle of establishing one's own identity at the expense of another who is similar to oneself. We actually see transvestism in the context of battle in Sidney's *Arcadia:* Pyrocles dresses as a warrior maiden to pursue his mistress, and attracts the admiration of his male companion Mucidorus. In The *Two Noble Kinsmen,* the friends Palamon and Arcite fight over a woman, but the result is a kind of *Liebestod* for the two of them. Rosalind knows about the violence of young men, their compulsion to compete, and therefore knows exactly how to appear in male persona. She says to Celia before they enter the forest:

> Were it not better,
> Because that I am more than common tall,
> That I did suit me all points like a man?
> A gallant curtle-axe upon my thigh,
> A boar-spear in my hand, and in my heart,
> Lie there what hidden woman's fear there will,
> We'll have a swashing and martial outside,
> As many other mannish cowards have
> That do outface it with their semblances.

> (*AYLI* I.iii.110–18)

Portia also knows what she is about; she answers Nerissa's objection that their husbands shall see them in Venice:

> They shall Nerissa: but in such a habit,
> That they shall think we are accomplished
> With what we lack;

(*MV* III.iv.60–62)

As I shall show in my discussions of individual plays, what finally persuades the young men that the young women they have learned to love as young men are even more to be desired than young men, is this lack, not only of a penis—that "addition" which the Poet observes in the Fair Youth (*Sonnet* 20)—but of all those accoutrements of conflict and aggression with which young men, seemingly of necessity, provide themselves. "Desire of a lack" is a difficult concept, and I do not mean that men do not come to recognize in young women some positive, peculiarly female virtues, but I do maintain that the major attraction these particular young women have for young men is that they promise relations in which the violence of self-definition through aggression with mirror images of the self can be avoided, that there can be some relaxation into a relationship with an other who is similar to the self, but lacks that insistent signifier of aggression, that sword which must be crossed with another sword, that "armor of an alienating identity."

In the early comedies this stage is barely reached. The young men struggle through their relations with other young men and with their attempts to impose upon young women their Neoplatonic expectations of perfection, but as far as establishing lasting relations between young men and young women, *The Comedy of Errors, The Two Gentlemen of Verona, Love's Labor's Lost* and *The Taming of the Shrew* are unambiguously aporetic. There is still a hint of this unsettledness in the mature comedies, but progress has been made, marriages are arranged, and young men are made to feel that their relations with young women are their only opportunities to find happiness.[16] Though we might feel uneasy about the future of these marriages—this is particularly true in *A Midsummer Night's Dream, Much Ado About Nothing*, and *The Merchant of Venice*—the negative paradigms of Antonio in *The Merchant of Venice* and Antonio in *Twelfth Night* (not to mention Malvolio, who continues to be "sick of self-love") warn us of the dead-end to which the persistence of narcissistic object-choice leads. To various extents, the struggle is over for the young men who have allowed themselves to be absorbed into these couples. It is in the late romances that we see the final chapter in this kind of arrangement. When the middle-aged fathers choose their daughters as objects, one feels the old fervor; the struggle begins again, and it is strangely narcissistic since the fathers see in their daughters younger, more beautiful, transexualized images of themselves.

One way of considering this sequence is to recognize that in the early comedies young men flee the threat of absorption and lack of identity posed by the women who appear awesome and overwhelming (the oedipal mother, or the pre-oedipal, anaclitic object) in pursuit of the self in the mirror image of the self which the friend provides. This tension persists into the mature comedies, but there the two figures are combined: friend and lover become one, and fear of the all-powerful, absorbing mother is allayed. (In the problem comedies, as Wheeler has shown, oedipal fears are so pervasive that all forms of sexuality are debased.) The late romances seem to transcend all these differences, but death makes its imminence so strongly felt that it almost seems we have come full circle. The lack of differentiation of self from other which was so much the concern of the early comedies—"I to the world am like a drop of water / That in the ocean seeks another drop"—is accepted and associated with the mature woman. In *Pericles* and *The Winter's Tale*, the father relinquishes his erotic claim upon his daughter and renews his bond with his aging wife, but life seems to be over for him. In *Cymbeline* and *The Tempest*, the father relinquishes his daughter and contemplates a renewal of life generally, under the auspices of this daughter and the young man to whom he gives her in marriage—but what awaits him is death.

We return to Hobbes' statement of the primacy and persistence of struggle in erotic and intellectual life, and proceed to his definition of power:

The felicity of life consisteth not in the repose of a mind satisfied. For there is no such *finis ultimus*, utmost aim, nor *summum bonum*, greatest good, as is spoken of in the books of the old moral philosophers. Nor can a man any more live, whose desires are at an end, than he whose sense and imaginations are at a stand. Felicity is a continual progress of the desire, from one object to another, the attaining of the former being still but the way to the latter. . . . So that in the first place, I put for a general inclination of all mankind, a perpetual and restless desire of power after power, that ceaseth only in death (*Leviathan*, chapter XI).

The release of tension, the end of the narcissistic struggle, the love of that lack which I claim the young men attain in the mature comedies with their marriage to young women, and the cessation of those hostilities against mirror images which is figured in the earlier comedies by tranvestism all become in the late romances the prelude to death itself.

It seems that Shakespeare began his career by debunking the Neoplatonic adoration of the idealized maternal object which characterizes the courtly love tradition and the late medieval church; this kind of orientation is traceable in Petrarch and the first English sonneteers, especially Sidney; and also in Italian romance and comedy and its English adpaters, especially Lyly. In his sonnets and early comedy Shakespeare makes a strong statement for the necessity of a narcissistic balance to, or at least preparation for, the young man's confrontation of and combination with a great lady. We have enough negative examples in the mature comedies of perversely maintained narcissism to begin to see that it is death-directed. Shakespeare's concerns here are remarkably close to those of Freud and Lacan, though he celebrates the possibilities rather than the limitations. To define the world in terms strictly and purely of the self is to reduce the great variety and surprise of life to death; allowing the other, as figured first in the mother, to redefine the self, to introduce fresh richness into life from an alien source, is the only proper response, and we see Orlando make it finally with Rosalind. The renunciation of narcissism, which gives life in the mature comedies, is, however, the prelude to death in the late romances. The only validation given there is of the creative effort which went into casting an illusion of love and of infinite possibility in youth; we look back upon it all as a faded pageant in which we played the part we now bequeath to the young. This closely resembles Freud, especially as he has been interpreted phenomenologically and dialectically by Lacan. Mutually constitutive relations between self and other are possible only through the creative efforts of the individual who simultaneously confirms and denies his derivation from his society and its traditions. Shakespeare's comedy is the fullest statement of this philosophical position. It is appropriate historically to that time between the breakup of the medieval world order and its replacement by the rationalism of the late seventeenth century; it is timeless in being one of those reactions which always set in when men have become too complacent, too reliant on the ageless, changeless forms of truth which they, like men in a cave, project to give meaning to the shadows.

III

THE EARLY COMEDIES

I am not concerned here with the various attempts to establish relative and absolute chronologies for the early comedies; I only assume that *The Comedy of Errors, The Two Gentlemen of Verona, Love's Labor's Lost* and *The Taming of the Shrew* are all early, probably written and originally produced before 1595. Since I do not trace patterns of development in them, a study of Shakespeare's influence on himself, it does not matter how we arrange them. The important thing is to recognize their central, shared concern, the danger to a young man of committing himself—his happiness, his whole identity—to a young woman in courtship and marriage. Barber concerns himself only with *Love's Labor's Lost* of this group, but holds generally that in the festive comedies it is the irony and stylization with which individual characters solve their erotic dilemmas that distinguish this kind of play and reveal their self-conscious derivation from games, fêtes, and other social rituals. He, too, however, is sensitive to the point of view, to the insistence in each play that one particular character is defining love in his own terms; in *Love's Labor's Lost* this central character is Berowne, and when Berowne defends himself against his friends' charge of perfidy—he has broken his oath to avoid women by writing to Rosaline—Barber observes:

The speech (IV.iii.333–49) is a perfectly fitting counterstatement to the ascetic resolutions with which the play began. The "doctrine" it derives from "women's eyes" is a version of the Renaissance cult of love as an educational force, especially for the courtier. But notice how little Berowne is concerned with love as an experience between two people. All his attention is focused on what happens within the lover, the heightening of his powers and perceptions.[1]

We are reminded of the way Devereux defines adolescent sexuality as "self-centered erotism" (see above, II.3, note 11).

Wheeler has made nice distinctions between the different affective states in which Shakespearean lovers find themselves. He begins by claiming that "Shakespearean comedy, like New Comedy, dramatizes the cultural crisis perpetually re-enacted when bonds of family and friendship must yield to sexual passion and the bond of marriage."[2] He then considers Frye's comic Oedipus situation objecting that "in Shakespearean comedy, however, the young man rarely seems to be driven by overpowering sexual longing."[3] Appealing to Freud's observation that originally oedipal desires are often displaced "toward sexual relations with women who are in some way degraded, and toward idealized and sexually inhibited relations with women chosen after the model of the mother,"[4] he finds, at least in *The Merchant of Venice* and *As You Like It*, that the idealization pattern is followed. There the young male lovers are not liberated from it, and they express "no compelling sexual ardor," indeed, "they are less driven by a desire to possess their women sexually than to be possessed by them, and the possession they long for seems to exclude or minimize sexual desire."[5] Indeed, "Bassanio and Orlando pursue an image of the beloved that builds on a child's need to inhabit a world presided over by a benevolent, powerful mother, a need strong enough that a boy sacrifices his sexual claim on a mother to it when desire and dependence come into conflict with each other."[6]

This seems the long way around, to return to a "corrected" comic oedipal pattern. It is interesting in that it almost duplicates some failed attempts to define "true love" in psychoanalytic terms, as a merging or blurring of distinctions between self and object. Kernberg, on the other hand, insists that mature love must be based on a balance of aggressive and libidinal investments of parental images consolidated in the same object, and this is only possible after the consolidation of a sense of self (through the normal progress of narcissistic investment of self-objects) which is capable of bearing the burden of such true object-choice.[7] We must account for Barber's observation that Berowne's experience of love is strangely self-referential. This suggests to me the effectiveness of considering the problem of narcissism in the genesis of desire, both originally and in maturity, i.e., if the child has originally two objects of desire, himself and the woman who tends him, and the woman is desired only because she tends him, so that his desire for her "leans up against" his desire for himself—and desire is by definition the need felt for something which is lacking: he has no "self" yet—then this very self-reflection is not an unlikely determinant in later object-choice.

On the question of idealization, we certainly have a wealth of Shakespearean material. It has generally been dealt with in terms of its evolution from and parody of Petrarchism. One of the questions Shakespeare seems often to be asking in his comedy is whether women can be loved without being idealized. Must Silvia be a moon goddess? Must Berowne and his friends write sonnets? We certainly know the operation of the mechanism of debasement in comedy; we might call it after its most obvious and effective example outside Shakespeare, *She Stoops to Conquer*. I am not sure that Shakespeare's greasy Joan and Nell fulfill this function. Rather, I think they are phantasms of misogyny thrown up to frighten the young lovers off their marital paths. Assimilation seems more the pattern of Shakespearean comedy, and this, like idealization, is accomplished in language—women learn to feint and parry the wit of their lovers—as well as in plot and staging: young women must transvestize to win the trust of their lovers.

Of the four comedies in this group, each presents a solution to the problem of male-female bonding, or the threat posed to the self by a liaison with the other. In *The Comedy of Errors* there is a remarkably strong statement of the danger confronting a man when a woman determines to integrate herself with him. The madness of Antipholus of Ephesus is circumstantial, of course, a function of the confusion between him and his twin brother, Antipholus of Syracuse, but the problem lies in identity, and it is the twins' mother who finally explains the situation when she accuses Adriana of nagging her husband into madness. The irony here is shocking: the mother, who must be seen as the source of the twin's misogyny, as figured in the overwhelming Adriana, is the one person, the only person, who can dispel the threat of engulfment which is the consistent theme-image of the play: "I to the world am like a drop of water." The end of the action of *The Comedy of Errors* is the reunion of the two twins: this signifies that an integrated sense of self is essential before investment in an object is possible. Marriage and remarriage are predicted at the conclusion, but all that has actually been accomplished is the reintegration of the nuclear family and thereby the integration of each twin's ego: the two Antipholi must be seen as one subject and that subject's projected, idealized image of himself.

If, then, *The Comedy of Errors* insists on the consolidation (through recapitulation) of the gains made in the phase of primary narcissism, with some suggestion of later true object choice, *The Two Gentlemen of Verona* deals with the threat of the overwhelming mother in a slightly different way: she is "Platonized." Julia is an inhibition to Proteus' free movement in the male world outside Verona; when Valentine leaves to create his identity abroad, Proteus will be "dully sluggardis'd at home." The dynamics of Proteus falling in love with Valentine's mistress Silvia are complex, but, as Vyvyan has shown, the essential dialectic of the play is Platonic, or Platonistic.[8] Silvia is the Form of Truth and Beauty, and the way to full appreciation of her is blocked by concern with the self. She is ageless and changeless and can teach those who worship her constancy. She is also a moon goddess, a mother-figure, and therefore calls up the myth of Endymion, which is to anaclisis what the myth of Narcissus is to narcissism: it represents the extreme of the satiated child lulled to sleep at the mother's breast, a nostalgic recapitulation of the symbiotic phase.

In *Love's Labor's Lost* we have a slightly different statement of the same dilemma, but it is still Platonized: does one complete oneself in company with those like the self (friends), or does one need the other (a female lover) to reflect one's image of oneself. It is commonly known that this play suggests an actual historical conflict between rival factions, Southampton's romantics against Raleigh's intellectuals.[9] Certainly the strongest themes in the play are those concerned with identity—whether the self is to be discovered in inner or outer reflection, found in the mirror of the soul or in the mirror of the mistress' eyes (the most persistent image is the mirror, along with visual stimulation of the erotic process—the phenomenology of desire). Implicit here is the difference between the self and the Self,[10] the individual who seeks a separate and unique image of himself in "autistic" contemplation, and the seeker after unity who finally appreciates that he participates in and is derived from a higher pattern. What is fascinating in all this, of course, is the twist of the Platonic logic. In Plato, truth is perceived as a result of the dialectical process which begins with the contemplation of the *erōmenos* by the *erastēs:* the erotic basis of Platonic love is then, in Plato, homoerotic. Renaissance Platonism, of course, heterosexualized the process, so that the adoration of the unapproachable mother is the way to truth. Basically this is the difference between philosophy—know thyself—and religion—lose thyself in the contemplation of a higher form different in degree and kind from the self: "I AM THAT I AM" (and you can never know me by your pattern).

None of these plays actually ends in marriage: marriage is proposed at the end of each, but postponed, most strikingly at the end of *Love's Labor's Lost.* It is in *The Taming of the Shrew* that marriage is the beginning and end of the pattern of action, and it is also in this play that we find the strongest statement of misogyny. As with the debate on Shakespeare's treatment of Jews in *The Merchant of Venice,* so with the debate on his treatment of women in *The Taming of the Shrew:* are these plays to be read straight or as irony? Or, more specifically, is he pushing conventional portraits of Jews and women to the point of caricature in order to reveal the absurdities of such traditional portrayals? This difference is clearest in the concluding remarks of Morris, the Arden editor,[11] and in Kahn. Focusing on Kate's obedience speech (V.ii.137ff.), but insisting on its context, Morris contends that Petruchio has given Kate an opportunity to make a willing display of her dependence on her husband an "unsolicited act of love and generosity." He thinks that the speech itself is "a solemn affirmation of the great commonplace that a wife was inferior in degree to her husband, and owed him submission and obedience."[12] Kahn thinks Kate's transformation is too quick and is therefore farcical, that the obedience speech, coming so soon after the sun/moon and maiden/father scene is a reductio ad absurdum of the male claim to supremacy, and therefore must be taken as ironic and satiric: "But on the deepest level, because the play depicts its heroine as outwardly compliant but inwardly independent, it represents possibly the most cherished male fantasy of all—that woman remain *un*tamed, even in her subjection."[13]

I must finally agree with Morris, for I feel that Shakespeare, in the relatively gentle mode of this play (though, of course, he can be vicious on the same theme elsewhere, as in *Henry VI, Richard III*, and *King John,* plays of roughly the same vintage as *The Taming of the Shrew*)[14] settles his male audience's misogynistic fantasies by creating a threatening female bogey, and then emasculating her.[15] I say "emasculate" because I think that is the point of much male maneuvering to avoid the threatening female: he both sees her as castrating because she is castrated and thinks he himself must castrate her before she castrates him. We are back with the phallic mother in either case, and there is a lot of typical but significant wordplay in *The Taming of the Shrew* which presents this spectre to our view, not the least of which is Kate's almost concluding line: "But now I see our lances are but straws" (V.ii.174.).

Many critical and theoretical issues must be settled before our discussion of these plays is complete. We must define point of view in each play, locate the prevalent fears and fantasies as stage- or phase-appropriate, and deal with the very difficult problem of the relations between identification with, and idealization of, the object of desire. Now, however, it is enough to state that there is in these early comedies a variety of reactions to the threat to the male of bonding with the female. (I use this awkward term because it suggests derivations from the fashionable phrase "male bonding." Of course, I think that is the essential problem in Shakespearean comedy, that men must first define themselves in terms of themselves before they can commit themselves to women, and this represents either narcissistic or homosexual choice of object depending on whether one thinks the plays represent pre-oedipal or adolescent and later patterns of desire.) We ask, then, without raising the question of the chronology of the plays since we are not indulging in psychobiography, is there emergent in this period of Shakespeare's exploration of the comic pattern a constellation or configuration, a continuum even (developmentally, or of relative pathology) of men's means of dealing with their compound, conflicted feelings of dread and desire, need and renunciation, of women?

Kernberg outlines "a continuum of configurations of pathological development regarding the capacity—or, rather, the incapacity—to fall and remain in love." The essential thing to appreciate here, as with so many critical models in psychoanalysis, is that there is a double axis. Included in the polarity of perverse and normal is the polarity of infantile and mature, the implication being that in a perverse adult the severity of the pathology is in direct proportion to the extreme of youth at which his emotional development was fixed, or to which he has regressed. The great paradox here, then, is that though we think of the relationship between mother and child as absolutely setting the pattern for all later object-choices, so that the child's relation with his mother is the early experience on which his later ability to love depends, nevertheless love is a learned ability, an aspect of the emotional life of the normal adult, and there are various prefigurations of this mature ability from infancy through adolescence. This all takes us back to two primary truths, both clear in Kernberg's work: there is a tension in early childhood between the child's choice of two objects, himself and the mother, and, in later life the ability to love another is a function of an integrated sense of self. Further, he stresses the same "primitive" types of sexual activity we noticed earlier in the comic tradition; indeed we see the difference between Aristophanes, with his celebration of polymorphous perversity, and Menander, with his introduction of romantic idealization, as the difference between Kernberg's third and fourth "constellations":

1) Narcissistic personalities who are socially isolated and who express their sexual urges only in polymorphous perverse masturbatory fantasies representing the most severe pathology of love relations. 2) Narcissistic personalities with sexual promiscuity are at the next fixation point along the continuum. 3) The chaotic, polymorphous perverse activity of the ordinary borderline patient is one step ahead of narcissistic pathology. Paradoxically, although ordinary borderline patients' feeling in love, their primitive idealization, and their sexual promiscuity may appear disturbed, inappropriate, and immature, they do have a much better prognosis for further development than the descriptive pathology of their love relations would initially suggest. In contrast to narcissistic patients, they have a better capacity for investment in others, or a less

active deterioration of their subject relations. These first three configurations represent the pathology of "stage one," that is, before the achievement of an integrated self and an integrated conceptualization of others,—in short, before the achievement of libidinal object constancy. 4) Next along the continuum is the presence of various sexual inhibitions, masochistic love relations, a greater capacity for romantic idealization and tenderness coupled with sexual inhibitions and other characteristics of patients with ordinary character pathology and symptomatic neuroses whose main etiological conflicts are in the triadic, oedipal realm. 5) The final configuration was the normal integration of genitality with the capacity for tenderness and a stable, deep object relation.[16]

For our purposes the distinction between pathological narcissism and borderline conditions is not crucial. Their relative seriousness as pathologies is dependent upon their relative primacy of origin: pathological narcissism is earlier in origin and more severe. They share certain symptoms—anxiety, phobias connected with the body, polymorphously perverse sexual patterns, tendencies toward the psychotic personality disorders of paranoia and schizophrenia—and they have a common diagnosis: ego weakness, characterized by the archaic feature of splitting, oral conflicts, and the maintenance of pregenital aggression.[17] As I emphasized above, one of Freud's great accomplishments was to show that human behavior cannot be categorized and pigeonholed. Pathological narcissists and anal retentive types do not appear in nature the way towns do on a map, isolated and unrelated to their surroundings. To the extent that followers of Freud categorize in this way, they distort their master's model. As the only valid model, the continuum shows that we have all at some stage in our development been what some few unfortunates continue to be, that we are all still, in a way, Malvolio and Shylock.[18]

A sense of self is a function of internalized object relations, beginning with parents, and if these relations are not adequately idealized, with their libidinal and aggressive components balanced under the predominance of the libidinal components, then all psychic energy remains fixed on a sense of self which is distorted. The paradoxes proliferate, but we might concentrate only on these: the self is a function of the perception of difference from others; an unintegrated sense of self focuses all attention on that "pathological self" so that "normal" object-relations are impossible; mature love is possible only for those who have consolidated a sense of self against love and hate feelings toward parents.

Kernberg helps us see all this in relation to Shakespeare by comparing object-relations symptomatic of pathological narcissism and normal adolescent sexuality:

> Here [in narcissistic pathology characterized by a more profound deterioration of object relations] the relation is no longer of self to object, nor of object to self, but of self to self. . . . This is a very different situation from what occurs under some normal circumstances, such as in adolescence, when mutual identifications occur with other objects as representations of the self simultaneously with the consideration of these objects as such, in their own right. Temporary or partial projections of an ideal self in normal friendships of early adolescence (which may include derivations of homosexual conflicts and infantile libidinal investment) onto an object perceived as similar to the self go hand in hand with object-libidinal ties to such an object.[19]

We should recognize in this distinction the pivotal role of Berowne, torn between friends and lover, self and other, intent on his experience of love rather than on the mutuality of love. Using Kernberg as a critical model for the early comedies, we see truth on many levels: the situations in the plays are realistic portrayals of adolescent or postadolescent sexuality, but I insist that adolescent sexuality is a recapitulation of primary narcissism. I do not claim that Shakespeare's friends and lovers are homosexuals or pathological narcissists, but I do insist that the primary goal of the comedies, their teleology, is a definition of love, and this involves a consideration not only of stages in the development of object-relations but also some attention to pathology. Obviously Shakespeare is concerned to show us that Adriana does not love as well as Luciana; neither Shylock nor Antonio loves as well as Bassanio; Orsino does not love well, but he is able to improve, whereas Malvolio is hopeless, incurably "sick of self-love."

The issues which keep emerging and always require different resolutions are the relations between identification and desire—do we love in others what we want to see in ourselves?—and the relations between idealization and desire—how do we abstract or objectify others in order to make them acceptable as the objects of our desires? This latter question is perhaps the most continuous throughout the Shakespearean corpus. The kind of idealization we see as a feature of the preliminary object-choices of characters in the early plays, such as Romeo and Proteus, persists, but is more completely and comprehensively presented in the object-choice of Orsino; and then, at the end of Shakespeare's career, in *The Winter's Tale*, we find that ultimate statement of the role of idealization in object-choice. There the living, aging, changing woman is replaced with a statue of herself, which one would expect to be an ageless, changeless Platonic form of the faithful and sexually attractive wife[20] (though Shakespeare constantly shows us that these two features are mutually contradictory in a bewildering variety of ways). But the husband must finally accept age and change in the object of his desire, that is, he must deidealize, deobjectify and love an actual woman.

The Comedy of
Errors

A common structural aspect of the early comedies is delayed marriage; this fact emphasizes the importance to these plays of the young male's trepidation at committing himself physically and emotionally to a woman. In three of these plays the alternative of identification with other males is first tried, and then, only with regret, dismissed as inadequate. In *The Two Gentlemen of Verona* and *Love's Labor's Lost* the other males are friends, but in *The Comedy of Errors* the protagonist seeks his twin brother, whom he speaks of as "myself." It is in this play that we are closest, then, to the narcissistic pattern of object-choice. We do not find in Antipholus of Syracuse the sensational aspects of the love life of pathological narcissists as defined by Kernberg—polymorphous perversity and sexual promiscuity; rather social isolation is his characterizing feature. We might rather choose to use the Elizabethan term melancholy for this, and associate him with Antonio, *The Merchant of Venice*, and Jaques in *As You Like It*, those outsiders who know not how to love.

Before defining this trait further with an examination of the "drop of water" speeches, and before pressing the contention that it is from Antipholus of Syracuse's point of view that we see the action of the play, I think it would be helpful to show that this kind of investigation does not raise new problems, but responds to those raised by other critics, namely, that the play is strangely without an end in marriage, and thus seems not to fit the romantic pattern of comedy. Legatt observes of the final scene and of the relation between Antipholus of Ephesus and his wife Andriana: "The director may contrive a forgiving embrace, but nothing in the text requires it. . . . For the critic, with only the text before him, the final state of the marriage must remain an open question."[1]

Palmer and Bradbury, in their preface to the collection of essays *Shakespearean Comedy*, explain why this play is not included in their discussion:

> Of the ten comedies which belong to the first half of Shakespeare's career, only *The Comedy of Errors*, *The Taming of the Shrew* and *The Merry Wives of Windsor* are not given detailed consideration here: an omission which reflects less on their merits than on the volume's prevailing interest in the more "romantic" plays.[2]

I have argued elsewhere that the comic tradition prejudices us against *The Comedy of Errors*, and this might account for its low estimation by critics in the Shakespearean corpus.[3] We have been accustomed by Menander, Plautus, and Terence, and their successors, to expect marriage to be not only the end of comedy, but its goal, i.e., that the genre's teleology is marriage and the immersion of the individual in society that marriage symbolizes. Frye, Barber, and Salangar, as we have seen, epitomize the criticism propounding this romantic tradition in comedy. There is, however, a different kind of comedy, represented for us by Aristophanes, some Plautus, some Shakespeare, Molière, and a few later comic poets, in which desires are fulfilled, but not for the male in the female. Rather, this tradition focuses on the male's search for and expression of himself, and this is figured with twins, doubles, friends, and other mirroring devices. I call this kind of comedy narcissistic, and in Aristophanes, at least, I find the polymorphous perversity and sexual promiscuity which Kernberg places at one extreme of his continuum of configurations.

J. R. Brown says that "the audience of Shakespearean comedy is not led towards an intimate knowledge of a single character,"[4] and that the doubling of pairs of lovers in Shakespearean comedy is a means of "dispersing our interest, and giving us range rather than concentration."[5] This seems to me again a function of the socialized view we have been encouraged, at least since Barber, to impose on the comedies. In *The Comedy of Errors* we are introduced to Antipholus of Syracuse by his father, and from this beginning we know that the driving force behind him is his search for his lost twin brother, which we soon come to realize, through language and incident, is a search for himself. Egeon tells us:

> My youngest boy, and yet my eldest care,
> At eighteen years became inquisitive
> After his brother, and importun'd me
> That his attendant, so his case was like,
> Reft of his brother, but retain'd his name,
> Might bear him company in the quest of him;
> Whom whilst I labour'd of a love to see,
> I hazarded the loss of whom I lov'd.
>
> (I.i.124–31)

Then, immediately, we meet Antipholus of Syracuse, and almost his first lines create an image of his self-concern; he meditates in an aside on a local merchant's valediction, "Sir, I commend you to your own content":

> He that commends me to mine own content
> Commends me to the thing I cannot get.
> I to the world am like a drop of water
> That in the ocean seeks another drop,
> Who, falling there to find his fellow forth,
> (Unseen, inquisitive) confounds himself.
> So I, to find a mother and a brother,
> In quest of them, unhappy, lose myself.
>
> (I.ii.33–40)

Rhetoric is overripe in parts of the play, but this is not one of them; here the paradox is a function of the psychological condition described, not of the language used to describe it. The whole content of the play is figured in "content": he cannot find "contentment" until he finds his "content," his brother, his external self. The drop of water image flows then naturally from this notion of the lost object as the whole of the subject. In order to assure himself of his own existence Antipholus of Syracuse sets out to find his brother (and mother), but in that search he loses the image of himself in the world which teems with others. The project in the stage of primary narcissism is for the subject to introject the image of himself which first his mother and then others project to him. Until that task is accomplished the choice of objects different from the self (both unlike and distinct from the self) is impossible. Indeed, first the mother and then the entire world are seen as a threatening, engulfing void.

Kernberg describes the overcoming of these feelings, and, with reference to an image first used by Freud himself, speaks directly to the dilemma of Antipholus of Syracuse:

> Sexual passion assumes the capacity for continued empathy with—but not merger into—a primitive state of symbiotic fusion (the "oceanic feeling" of earlier psychoanalytic literature), the excited reunion or closeness with mother at a stage of self-object differentiation, and the gratification of oedipal longings in the context of overcoming feelings of inferiority, fear and guilt regarding sexual longings.[6]

It is, of course, these oedipal feelings that Wheeler concentrates on; indeed he sees the great comic problem (especially in the "problem comedies") as overcoming the guilt oedipally associated with sexuality because of the incestuous pattern which is the origin of its longings. But I stress the anxiety which is a consequence of pre-oedipal fragmentation in the sense of self: the child is still shoring up fragments of his object-relations against the ruins of his symbiosis with his mother. Kernberg always insists that ego boundaries must be maintained in a happy love relationship, just as he insists that ego boundaries must be securely drawn before mature love is possible; hence his distinction between "empathy" and "merger." It is about merger that Antipholus of Syracuse fantasizes, and not as an experience of love, but rather as a consequence of having failed to integrate his ego through a normal sequence of object-relations beginning with his mother, but focused on his brother.

I am not constructing a psychobiography for Antipholus of Syracuse; I am not treating the separation from his mother, almost at birth, as the traumatic genesis of recurrent pathology. Rather I am suggesting that Antipholus of Syracuse is the focus of attention in *The Comedy of Errors* because we readily identify with him, and we readily identify with him because we have all passed through the phase of primary narcissism—more or less successfully. The less successful we have been, the more compulsive we become at recapitulating its pattern, and thus we understand what Antipholus of Syracuse tells us about his sense of deprivation. He raises to consciousness in us memory traces of our own psychic development—not because we have all had twins and lost them, but because we have all struggled to find in our early environment ("the precursor of the mirror is the mother's eyes") an image of ourselves we can assimilate towards, or, rather, introject as ourselves. In this way, by a very complicated (here completely abridged) argument, we can claim that Antipholus of Ephesus represents the ideal ego of Antipholus of Syracuse, and that, ontogenetically speaking, the ideal ego preexists the ego.

Just as Antipholus of Syracuse was introduced to us by his father, and we hear first from another that the young man seeks his twin and then hear from his own lips that this is his sole concern; so we first hear of Antipholus of Ephesus from his wife and his sister. Next we meet not him, but Antipholus of Syracuse again, confused by them for him. From all of them we learn of two different attitudes toward marriage: should the wife restrain, inhibit, and bind her husband to her, claiming he is a part of her, or should she allow him his free movement in the world, waiting patiently at home, never presuming to question or complain? The two Antipholi move in different directions: Antipholus of Syracuse seeks his mother and his brother, and in the process loses himself, while Antipholus of Ephesus flees his wife to find himself. Adriana and Luciana, the dark, binding wife and the bright, liberal wife-to-be, clearly polarize the sexual argument that runs through all the early comedies: the man's sphere is outside, the woman's inside; the man acts and the woman obeys. Though we might find the strongest statement of the first proposition in *The Two Gentlemen of Verona*, and of the second in *The Taming of the Shrew*, it is in *The Comedy of Errors* that the overriding theme of male and female identity is clearest: women define themselves by their relations to men, but men define themselves in their own terms. Adriana hauntingly recapitulates

the drop of water imagery of Antipholus of Syracuse's opening speech,
and, thinking she is speaking to her husband, speaks to a stranger and
so drives him mad, as later her husband will appear.

> How comes it now, my husband, O, how comes it,
> That thou art then estranged from thyself?—
> Thyself I call it, being strange to me,
> That undividable, incorporate,
> Am better than thy dear self's better part.
> Ah, do not tear away thyself from me;
> For know, my love, as easy mayst thou fall
> A drop of water in the breaking gulf,
> And take unmingled thence that drop again
> Without addition or diminishing,
> As take from me thyself, and not me too.
>
> (II.ii.119–29)

The dominant point of view in the play is that of Antipholus of Syracuse, and hence the male's. Here we have a strong statement by the
woman of what she requires from the man, but it is negated by another woman, that man's mother, at the conclusion of the play.

> And thereof came it that the man was mad.
> The venom clamours of a jealous woman
> Poisons more deadly than a mad dog's tooth.
>
> (V.i.68–70)

The extraordinary thing that Shakespeare accomplishes in all this is,
of course, first the expropriation of Antipholus of Syracuse's own image by Adriana, a threatening, demanding, inhibiting woman. I mean
to play on the two meanings of image: she speaks of him as a drop of
water just as he had spoken of himself as a drop of water earlier, and
in that drop of water we see, of course, his mirror image, his twin
brother, his ideal ego, his external soul—but certainly not his wife.
Then the reunion of the twins occurs under the mother's auspices: she
is the woman who matters most, and she effaces herself.

The situations and language of the play so specifically equate individual psychological needs with socially imposed sexual roles that we
are encouraged to add, from later comedies, the physical distinction of
the sexes as an explanation. Adriana and Luciana debate the nature
and convention of sexual difference:

Adr. Why should their liberty than ours be more?
Luc. Because their business still lies out o' door. (II.i.10–11)

Shakespeare follows the social convention of domesticating women: they stay at home. When they go out into the world, they are dressed as men, equipped with swords, and their tongues are sharpened to a rapier wit. Julia and Portia will debate their wearing of codpieces, the addition to their lack. Clearly Shakespeare encourages us to see for these women an identification between the house and the body: while they are women they stay inside, hidden, like their genitals; but when they become men, they go outside, and wear their genitals openly, even accentuated, in the male fashion of the day. Adriana is usurping male prerogatives, so that she frightens the man she thinks is her husband to madness, and locks him up inside; she is corrected in this behavior by her sister and by the mother of both that man and her husband. Portia and Rosalind are threatening to males in their transvestism; Julia, Viola, and Imogen are not. We shall consider their difference. Now we need only appreciate that Shakespeare, playing upon men's fears, figures women as expansive, absorbing, engulfing creatures whose roles and natures must be defined by walls and social conventions.

The second drop of water speech, in which Adriana pleads conjunction with her husband—the first half of which was quoted above— continues with a suggestion of venereal disease:

> How dearly would it touch thee to the quick,
> Shouldst thou but hear I were licentious?
> And that this body, consecrate to thee,
> By ruffian lust should be contaminate?
> Wouldst thou not spit at me, and spurn at me,
> And hurl the name of husband in my face,
> And tear the stain'd skin off my harlot brow,
> And from my false hand cut the wedding-ring,
> And break it with a deep-divorcing vow?
> I know thou canst; and therefore, see thou do it!
> I am possess'd with an adulterate blot,
> My blood is mingled with the crime of lust;
> For if we two be one, and thou play false,
> I do digest the poison of thy flesh,
> Being strumpeted by thy contagion.
>
> (II.ii. 130–44)

One need only compare Sonnet 129 to appreciate what Antipholus of Syracuse would hear in all this:

> The expense of Spirit in a waste of shame
> Is lust in action, and till action, lust
> Is perjured, murderous, bloody, full of blame,
> . . . .
> All this the world well knows, yet none knows well
> To shun the Heaven that leads men to this Hell.

From the male perspective the sin of fornication and the threat of disease are both in the woman, in that waist of shame, that Hell, to which is compared the Heaven of the Poet's union with the Fair Youth, and Antipholus of Syracuse's reunion with his lost brother.

The basis of Shakespeare's male characters' fear of the females who would marry them is derived from their fear of reincorporation by the pre-oedipal mother. Water we know to be the most frequent dream-symbol for the birth process.[7] In his drop of water speech Antipholus of Syracuse acknowledges his origin from the mother but, deprived of some image of himself in another drop of water (his twin brother, but also his ideal ego), he fears reversal of the birth process. Of course, this is the latent content of this dreamlike speech; the manifest content (though it, too, is unconscious, so only we, the audience, having just heard the family history, can appreciate it) is the separation of child from mother by shipwreck. The sea is actually prominent in several other plays where reintegration of the nuclear family is a goal: *Twelfth Night, The Tempest, Pericles.* This fear of the overwhelming mother is, then, articulated by Antipholus of Syracuse, and reenforced by Adriana, who would lock him up, and indeed does lock up her own husband, claiming he is mad, the state to which she has almost driven Antipholus of Syracuse. The whole situation can be corrected only by the real mother Emilia, who appears at the end and says, essentially, everything is going to be all right: "You two boys have found each other and me—your father is here, too, but he is not so important in this pre-oedipal struggle for identity which you are recapitulating—and now you can even think about marriage."[8] Shakespeare develops the theme of madness then in the framework of the nuclear family: madness is being two of the same or nothing at all. The twins are confused for each other, so they each think there is an other of them in the world, which is maddening, but they also fear the loss of self entirely, so that two became none, all being absorbed by the sea, the threatening mother and her representations.

Kernberg points out that male fears of close relations with women are derived originally from memories of the pre-oedipal mother, that because men know themselves to have been originally dependent on an all-powerful being different from themselves, they resist such attachments in maturity.[9] Women obviously have a different perspective. I think it is best argued that Shakespeare's perspective is always that of the male, though his so-called bisexuality is often hailed as the hallmark of his genius. Adriana is a male's nightmare image of the overwhelming mother; the chaste Emilia is its correction. Luciana also presents herself as a correction of Adriana's threatening persona. Psychoanalytic critics have pointed out that the names are significant: Adriana is the "dark lady" (*ater*) and Luciana the "bright lady" (*lux*). Antipholus of Syracuse spontaneously responds to this heavenly creature, and the play on love and reflected light, on self and other occurs, which also dominates *The Two Gentlemen of Verona* and *Love's Labor's Lost:*

> *Luc.* What, are you mad that you do reason so?
> *Syr. Ant.* Not mad, but mated, how I do not know.
> *Luc.* It is a fault that springeth from your eye.
> *Syr. Ant.* For gazing on your beams, fair sun, being by.
> *Luc.* Gaze where you should, and that will clear your sight.
> *Syr. Ant.* As good to wink, sweet love, as look on night.
> *Luc.* Why call you me love? Call my sister so.
> *Syr. Ant.* Thy sister's sister.
> *Luc.*   That's my sister.
> *Syr. Ant.*   No,
> It is thyself, mine own self's better part,
> Mine eye's clear eye, my dear heart's dearer heart,
> My food, my fortune, and my sweet hope's aim,
> My sole earth's heaven, and my heaven's claim. (III.ii. 53–64)

This is the Neoplatonic figure of the man defining himself by reference to the woman: he sees himself in her eyes, thinks indeed that he is but a reflection of her light. There is also play on the names: Luciana is light; Adriana is night. We shall see that in *The Two Gentlemen of Verona* Silvia will be a moon goddess, and first Valentine, then

Proteus will play Endymion to her. Here, in *The Comedy of Errors*, the figure is not developed, but implied in the extravagance of Antipholus of Syracuse's language is the distinction between self and Self which Zweig traces from the earliest Christian literature through Shakespeare and beyond. What Narcissus gazes *at* is only a deceptive image of himself (the imitation of an imitation), but the true Christian, or the true Neoplatonic lover, sees *in* himself a manifestation of God's grace, as the world of physical objects participates in *(methexis)* the Forms. This gives a metaphysical model for love which is generally contradicted in Shakespeare; indeed the extravagance of the language here suggests parody.

Having questioned whether Shakespeare ever centers desire or the universe in Truth or Being, having found instead that both erotically and philosophically he sees a tension of opposites mutually defining each other, we offer the following hypothesis: the Neoplatonic worship of the woman represents oedipal orientation of desire; the search for the self in a twin or friend represents primary narcissism; the fear of the overwhelming mother can be read as either oedipal or pre-oedipal, depending on the imagery of its expression. The "oceanic feeling" suggests those pre-oedipal anxieties which come with the recognition that the mother is separate and independent, i.e., anxieties occurring at the end of the symbiotic phase. The sexualized imagery of binding, of locking in or out of the house, suggests oedipal anxieties, i.e., fears of sexual incompetence. That there is no strong father figure, but only strong women in the play, tilts the argument to the pre-oedipal side. Emilia is awesome; Dromio's kitchen wench is disgusting; Adriana is threatening; Luciana is benevolent but colorless. We do not yet see that assimilation between self-images and images of the desired female which, beginning with *The Two Gentlemen of Verona*, becomes Shakespeare's major comic concern.

The Two Gentlemen
of Verona

R eaders of *The Two Gentlemen of Verona* might well feel dis-
comfort throughout the play, moving forward as they do
under a burden of ignorance about all the issues involved in
the developing situation, but this feeling becomes a certainty when, at
the climax, they reach the passage:

Proteus My shame and guilt confounds me.
  Forgive me, Valentine: if hearty sorrow
  Be a sufficient ransom for offence,
  I tender 't here; I do as truly suffer,
  As e'er I did commit.
Valentine   Then I am paid;
  And once again I do receive thee honest.
  Who by repentance is not satisfied,
  Is nor of heaven, nor earth; for these are pleas'd:
  By penitence th' Eternal's wrath's appeas'd.
  And that my love may appear plain and free,
  All that was mine in Silvia I give thee. (V.iv.73–83)

We have no problem with the suddenness of friend forgiving friend
for the perfidy of trying to win his mistress from him; the comic tradition has accustomed us to that requirement. We are impressed with

the quality of forgiveness: it is absolute, like God's grace, but also, being human, sensible of the community of human suffering, and we know that Shakespeare returned again and again to this feature, most notably in *The Tempest*. What bothers us is that the wronged friend bestows his own beloved upon this same perfidious friend. And then, to compound our dismay, this lady herself is given no opportunity to protest such misplaced liberality.

The critics are unanimous both in their rejection of this ending and in their realization that it is a stopgap, that Shakespeare had created problems in this play which he could not solve in this play.

Is the failure of the ending evidence that Shakespeare realized that the philosophy he was exploiting was inadequate in the face of the issues?[1]

If the ending is an example of ineptitude in early Shakespeare, then the very ineptitude suggests the troubled vision of a man who cares immensely about love and friendship, what they do to people and make people do to each other.[2]

The Two Gentlemen of Verona is not as easy to like as the other comedies, but it has a quality of its own—cool, reticent, and somewhat rueful, counseling us, if it counsels anything, not to expect too much.[3]

The philosophy is, of course, some version of Platonism,[4] and the issues are the seemingly contradictory drives toward sexual union and individual identity. Since one of the strongest statements Plato gives his metaphysical system is in the context of a discussion on the nature of love—the *Symposium*, which Shakespeare could only have known through such interpreters as Ficino—it is not unreasonable for us to seek a structural relation between these two models. Indeed we shall find that Shakespeare, in trying to balance the demands and attractions of friends and lovers, spontaneously restores the homoerotic origins of the Platonic model to the idealizing, heterosexual model adopted by his Neoplatonist contemporaries.

Not the least disturbing aspect of the play is Shakespeare's insistence that we see the action primarily through the eyes of its most reprehensible character, Proteus. His name indicates that a major concern will be his lack of constancy, and indeed, it is in his experience that we trace Shakespeare's deconstruction of Platonic love: Proteus himself must learn to contradict his nature, must learn to be constant in his love for Julia even though she is not constant in her physical appearance after she transvestizes to a young male page to follow Proteus in his pursuit of Valentine. What, then, is the quality of the love which Proteus bears Valentine, and what of his love for Julia? These two relations are starkly contrasted at the opening of the play where we find clearly stated the dichotomy so essential to all the early comedies, that men should move widely in the world to fulfill their potential in martial and intellectual endeavor, while women must stay inside, waiting at home for their men to return:

Val. Cease to persuade, my loving Proteus;
   Home-keeping youth have ever homely wits.
   Were 't not affection chains thy tender days
   To the sweet glances of thy honour'd love,
   I rather would entreat thy company
   To see the wonders of the world abroad
   Than (living dully sluggardis'd at home)
   Wear out thy youth with shapeless idleness.
   But since thou lov'st, love still, and thrive therein,
   Even as I would, when I to love begin. (I.i.1–10)

All of this is recapitulated in the scene where Julia determines to follow Proteus, who has followed Valentine. In answer to Lucetta's question, "But in what habit will you go along?" Julia replies:

   Not like a woman, for I would prevent
   The loose encounters of lascivious men:
   Gentle Lucetta, fit me with such weeds
   As may beseem some well-reputed page.

            (II.vii.40–43)

Lucetta then insists that Julia wear a codpiece, even so elaborate a one as to stick pins in. Though Julia first protests ("Out, out, Lucetta, that will be ill-favour'd"), she finally relents:

Jul. What thou think'st meet, and is most mannerly.
   But tell me, wench, how will the world repute me
   For undertaking so unstaid a journey?
   I fear me it will make me scandalis'd. (II.vii.58–61)

One way, then, of seeing the action of the play, is as a sequence beginning with the close identification of two young men, whose intimacy is broken when one seeks his adventure abroad and the other

stays home with his mistress. After an extraordinary scene in which
Proteus, the young man at home, lies about the contents of a letter
from his mistress Julia, and tells his father it is a letter from Valentine, his friend abroad urging him to join him, the situation changes,
and the two friends are reunited, but this time it is Valentine who has
the mistress—Silvia. Proteus attempts, through the worst kind of lying
and cheating, to displace Valentine in Silvia's affections, but she then
pursues Valentine, when, through Proteus' perfidy, he is exiled. Proteus pursues her and is in turn pursued by Julia, who is still disguised
as a page, and has been engaged to press her former lover's suit to his
friend's mistress. All four meet in the forest, and there the infamous
line is spoken by the true friend to the false friend: "All that was mine
in Silvia, I give thee."

The play, then, begins with the separation of the two friends and
ends with their reunion, but whereas at the beginning only one had a
mistress, at the end they both have mistresses. Marriages are arranged, but there can be no doubt that the play as a whole, and not
just that one line, values friendship between men over the love of men
for women that leads to marriage. What is the quality of this friendship? Proteus speaks of it first:

> Wilt thou be gone? Sweet Valentine, adieu;
> Think on thy Proteus, when thou (haply) seest
> Some rare noteworthy object in thy travel.
> Wish me partaker in thy happiness,
> When thou dost meet good hap; . . . .
>
> (I.i.11–15)

When Proteus lies to his father about the letter he has received from
Julia, it is as if he were fulfilling his own desire; by projecting his love
for Valentine upon Valentine, he can claim that Valentine loves him;
or, by projecting Julia's love for him upon Valentine, he can claim
that Valentine loves him. In either event, Valentine is on his mind:

> he writes
> How happily he lives, how well-belov'd,
> And daily graced by the Emperor;
> Wishing me with him, partner of his fortune.
>
> (I.iii.56–59)

In his commendation of Proteus to the Duke, Valentine admits to such love, and even reverses the accusation he had earlier made, so that now he claims it is he who is "dully sluggardis'd," whereas Proteus has been expanded and transformed by his love of his mistress, an abbreviated statement of the dispute in *Love's Labor's Lost:* do men learn to know themselves by study among themselves, or through their society with women?

> I knew him as myself; for from our infancy
> We have convers'd, and spent our hours together,
> And though myself have been an idle truant,
> Omitting the sweet benefit of time
> To clothe mine age with angel-like perfection,
> Yet hath Sir Proteus (for that's his name)
> Made use and fair advantage of his days:
>
> (II.iv.57–63)

These lines have marvelous resonance throughout the Shakespearean corpus. We recall both the lament of Antipholus of Syracuse at the opening of *The Comedy of Errors:*

> He that commends me to mine own content
> Commends me to the thing I cannot get.
> I to the world am like a drop of water
> That in the ocean seeks another drop,
> Who, falling there to find his fellow forth,
> (Unseen, inquisitive) confounds himself.
> So I, to find a mother and a brother,
> In quest of them, unhappy, lose myself.
>
> (I.ii.33–40)

and, at the end of Shakespeare's career, in *The Winter's Tale,* Polixenes' description of his friendship with Leontes:

> We were, fair queen,
> Two lads that thought there was no more behind,
> But such a day to-morrow as to-day,
> And to be boy eternal . . .
> . . . .
> We were as twinn'd lambs that did frisk i' th' sun,
> And bleat the one at th' other: what we chang'd
> Was innocence for innocence: we knew not

The doctrine of ill-doing, nor dream'd
That any did.

(I.ii.62–71)

When we come to discuss *The Winter's Tale* in some detail, we shall
face the issue of the exact nature of this relationship. It has, of course,
been argued that Leontes projects upon Hermione his own love of Polixenes, that this is the origin of his sudden jealousy. We cannot deny
the importance of a judicial consideration of homosexuality to some
plays: Antonio's relation to Bassanio and Iago's to Othello must be
considered in this manner. In these three plays, however—*The Comedy of Errors, The Two Gentlemen of Verona,* and *The Winter's Tale*—
the relations between two young men are central to the action, and yet
homsexuality would be a distorting term to apply. What is at issue
here is not one man's desire for another, either for physical intimacy
or for exclusive spiritual communion; rather for the men to establish
relations between themselves seems to be the prerequisite for their establishing relations between themselves and women. The young men
begin by defining themselves in terms of their male companions—"find
his fellow . . . lose myself," "I knew him as myself," "We were as
twinn'd lambs"—but they proceed tentatively toward relations with
women, and the previously sound relations with other men are helpful
in this process. Shakespeare accurately portrays adolescent sexuality,
which is characterized by self-centered erotism and a lack of sexual
differentiation in objects;[5] this phase is a recapitulation of primary
narcissism where the male child chooses first himself as object and only
then the woman who tends him.

In these three plays we have one pair of twins who seek each other
to find themselves, a pair of unrelated young men who are nevertheless so similar as to be called "twinned," and then Proteus and Valentine. It seems that we are about to be told, in the scene where Antonio and Pantherino decide on sending Proteus to join Valentine, that
they are first cousins, that their fathers are brothers. This is certainly
the pattern that Menander favored; when he wanted to double his love
plots and introduce complications, he contrasted the romantic pursuits
of two brothers, e.g., in the *Adelphoi.* Then confusion could arise, and
one brother could accuse the other of stealing his mistress, or the friends

and relatives could have that misapprehension: this is what Proteus actually attempts to do to Valentine. In the *Dis Exapaton,* however, Menander does not insist that the two young men be brothers when he creates the conflict over a mistress (actually two women with the same name), but he does bring in the young men's fathers at the end and suggest that each father and son pair will share the same woman. We could then claim that there is implicit in the brother-against-brother pattern a suggestion of sibling rivalry for the mother, and that this rivalry can even be given an oedipal variation, i.e., between father and son for the same woman. To proceed further here we must understand the way Shakespeare presents Silvia.

The story of the two friends can be traced through Sir Thomas Elyot's *Governour* (1531) to Boccaccio's *Decameron,* the eighth story of the tenth day, the story of Titus and Gisippus. In Boccaccio the friends are raised as brothers, since Titus is a Roman and has been sent to Athens to live and study under the protection of Chremes, Gisippus' father. Throughout the opening episode—in which Gisippus introduces Titus to his betrothed, Sophronia, Titus falls in love with her, and Gisippus arranges for Titus to take his place in Sophronia's bed and marry her in his stead—the emphasis is on idealism. Titus compares himself to the men of myth and history who have indulged their incestuous desires, but then insists to himself that he is not so reprehensible as they, since not only is neither Gisippus nor Sophronia related to him by blood, but it is not even jealousy or emulation of Gisippus that incites him to love Sophronia (whose name suggests her Platonic function): "It is not because she belongs to Gisippus that I love her, but purely for her own sake, and I should love her no matter to whom she belonged."[6]

In Shakespeare the situation is not so clear. Proteus questions his sudden passion for Silvia:

> Even as one heat another heat expels,
> Or as one nail by strength drives out another,
> So the remembrance of my former love
> Is by a newer object quite forgotten.
> Is it mine eye, or Valentinus' praise,
> Her true perfection, or my false transgression,
> That makes me reasonless, to reason thus?

> (II.iv.188–94)

This puts us in mind of Girard's principle of mimetic love, which he first determined for nineteenth-century French and Russian novels, but then extended to Shakespeare's *A Midsummer Night's Dream:* Demetrius only loves Hermia because Lysander does.[7] The Platonizing of *The Two Gentlemen of Verona* gives a new dimension to this pattern. The triangulation of desire for Girard is the creation of erotic interest in a woman as a result of competition between two men, but in *The Two Gentlemen of Verona* and its sources that erotic interest derives not so much from the men's competition as from their mutual appreciation in Silvia of the essence of Truth and Beauty: through her they are in touch with the ultimate Idea or Form. It is this idealization in the erotic process which reminds us of Wheeler's application to Shakespeare of Freud's observation that the oedipally inclined male will deny his sexual interest in the mother either by choosing sexual objects like her and then idealizing them, or by choosing debased objects which "could not possibly be like her." Is there then some kind of repressed oedipal pattern in *The Two Gentlemen of Verona?* Certainly idealization is the key in Boccaccio's story. When Titus confesses to Gisippus that he has fallen in love with Sophronia, Gisippus argues:

The fact that you have fallen in love with Sophronia, my promised bride, does not surprise me in the least; indeed I should be most surprised if you hadn't, considering her beauty and your own loftiness of spirit, which renders you all the more susceptible to passionate feelings, the greater the excellence of the object that arouses your liking . . . . But because your love for her is greater, and because you desire more fervently than I to possess so precious an object, you may rest assured that she shall enter the bridal chamber, not as my wife, but as yours.[8]

Now, clearly, Shakespeare was not interested in devising a dramatic proof of this kind of argument; he did not follow his sources' lead to a conclusion where the switch actually took place, but he did tease us with its possibility in the line "All that was mine in Silvia, I give thee." Rather he seems concerned to make Proteus, the Titus-derivative, as reprehensible as possible, since he is faithless not only to his friend but also to his former mistress. Just as the intimacy of Proteus and Valentine reminds us of the twin brothers in *The Comedy of Errors,* so the almost scholastic thoroughness of Shakespeare's treatment of the friends' and lovers' debate in *The Two Gentlemen of Verona* reminds us of the debate between romanticism and asceticism in *Love's Labor's Lost*. In both cases the romantic wins out over the ascetic or intellectual, which is also the narcissistic. The men must turn their attention from their images of themselves in each other to women. In *The Two Gentlemen of Verona* the idealized quality of Silvia can be traced back to Boccaccio—at least the lovers there *claim* that Sophronia is ideally beautiful. But Silvia is also the focus of another story pattern in *The Two Gentlemen of Verona*, and we need to examine its source briefly to understand how the idea of her beauty joins the two patterns together.

The other story line in *The Two Gentlemen of Verona*—a transvestized young lady pursues her former lover and becomes involved in his suit for another lady—seems to derive from a Spanish romance, Jorge de Montemayor's *Diana Enamorada*, through an English play, *The History of Felix and Felismena* (1585).[9] It is a long and involved story in which the betrayal of an old love for a new is only one episode. Felismena is beloved of Don Felix, but when he goes abroad he falls in love with Celia. Disguised as a boy, Felismena follows him, and when she finds out that his affections have been alienated from her, she joins his service as a page. The duty then falls to her of furthering his suit with Celia, but Celia falls in love with the page and kills herself when she receives no encouragement. There is nothing extraordinary in Montemayor's Celia, though her name suggests that she is a "heavenly" beauty. She is not the princess of the place, and Don Felix's man Fabius thinks her less beautiful than Felismena. One point is stressed: Don Felix has fallen in love with Celia in Felismena's absence, not in preference to Felismena. They are finally, after many subsequent adventures, reunited. The Diana of the title is Felismena herself, not Celia, since Felismena's mother is Delia and she has a twin brother whose adventures are also recounted. There is a superfluity, then, of moon-goddess types, and this is important for Shakespeare's adaptation, since it is precisely this kind of erotic attachment—the worship from afar of a divine lady by a mortal man—which he examines in his play. We know these women usually under one of those titles derived from the worship of Artemis.[10]

Silvia is secured by her father the Duke in a tower; she is thus physically as well as socially superior to Valentine and Proteus. The

Duke explains all this to Valentine when he comes with his ropeladder
to fetch her down:

> Why, Phaëton, for thou art Merops' son
> Wilt thou aspire to guide the heavenly car?
> And with thy daring folly burn the world?
> Wilt thou reach stars, because they shine on thee?
>
> (III.i.153–56)

Valentine continues the identification of Silvia with celestial lights when
he laments his failure to obtain her:

> What light is light, if Silvia be not seen?
> What joy is joy, if Silvia be not by?
> Unless it be to think that she is by
> And feed upon the shadow of perfection.
> Except I be by Silvia in the night,
> There is no music in the nightingale.
> Unless I look on Silvia in the day,
> There is no day for me to look upon.
> She is my essence, and I leave to be,
> If I be not by her fair influence
> Foster'd, illumin'd, cherish'd, kept alive.
>
> (III.i.174–84)

We identify, then, because Shakespeare does, the moon goddess with
the mistress of the Neoplatonic courtly love tradition, and in her we
see, because Shakespeare does, maternal qualities: she is distant, the
source and sustenance for the male lover, light, life, and the essential
self to which the physical is just a shadow.

If we note parody in this kind of praise of the mistress by the lover,
we identify Shakespeare's model as Lyly's *Endimion,* a play of 1591,
which also has a friendship theme. Whereas Shakespeare's characterization of Silvia is multidimensional, Lyly's associations are purely
Neoplatonic, being simply the distinction between the perfect universal and the flawed specific:

Endimion. The time was madame, and is, and ever shall be, that I honoured
your highnesse and above all the world; but to stretch it so farre as to call it
love, I never durst. There hath none pleased mine eye but Cynthia, none de-
lighted mine ears but Cynthia, none possessed my heart but Cynthia. I have
forsaken all fortunes to follow Cynthia, and here I stand readie to die if it

please Cynthia. Such a difference hath the gods set betweene our states, that all must be duties, loyaltie, and reverence, nothing (without it vouchsafe your highnesse) be termed Love. (V.iii.)

This certainly sounds oedipal: the moon goddess is then like the mistress in the courtly love tradition and the Virgin who becomes the object of cult-adoration in the medieval church, the desirable but forbidden maternal object. I claimed earlier that Neoplatonism takes the Platonic dialectic away from its model in the homosexual attraction of the *erastēs* for the *erōmenos*, where the search is for the self, and assimilates it to the search for the mother which comes to dominate Christian thinking and iconography as early as Augustine. In his weighing of the demands of friends and lovers, Shakespeare spontaneously restores to the tradition some of its original force; so I believe that he restores to the moon goddess some of her original pre-oedipal associations. All these celestial females trace their descent back to Diana and Artemis, more to Diana than to Artemis, and more to the many-breasted Diana of Ephesus than to the Amazonian ("breastless") Diana of Virgil and Ovid.[11]

The desire of the male lover, then, is to restore symbiosis with the mother, to reincorporate himself in her, so that he is physically and emotionally indistinguishable from her, rather than to possess her as a true object, won in competition with the father. Again we are reminded of Wheeler's point that the comedies generally present the woman not as sexually desirable but rather as a being who will absorb the lover and in this way put an end to his desires; the male lovers "are less driven by a desire to possess their women sexually than to be possessed by them, and the possession they long for seems to exclude or minimize sexual desire."[12] He, of course, is speaking of that fear of sexuality which he associates with the male's attempt to deny his oedipal attraction, a dynamic pattern he sees most fully developed in *Measure for Measure* and *All's Well*, where strong maternal women threaten to dominate men; the men flee them, seek sexual satisfaction with unthreatening socially debased women, or deny their sexuality altogether, only to be reunited with these women finally in changed but still mysterious forms.

I claim something altogether different for the early comedies—a pattern of action and a system of associations which will persist through the middle comedies and which will only finally be resolved in the romances. The complex figure of Emelia/Adriana/Luciana; Silvia; the wonderfully transformed Katherina, who finally surpasses and instructs her sister Bianca (this pair should recall Adriana/Luciana) in how to be *morigera* to her husband; the quadrupled persona of the originally denied but ultimately desired woman in *Love's Labor's Lost*—all of these female figures express the ambivalent feelings of the male child toward the mother in the very first months of life.

His defense against her is the friend, in whom we see the resurrection of his original mirror image of himself, his ideal ego. This image, paradoxically, is more real to him than those women he actually encounters, but whom he must idealize lest they seem, like the mother, too threatening. Shakespeare suggests in *The Two Gentlemen of Verona* an antidote to the kind of relationship Lyly depicts in his *Endimion* (who fell into an endless sleep in contemplation of his mistress the moon goddess), and we can take that figure from Greek mythology to counter our figure Narcissus, taken from the same source. We easily see the contrast in developmental and erotic terms: Narcissus chooses himself as object, while Endymion chooses the woman who tends him; Narcissus refuses all love relations to contemplate his own image, while Endymion loses all sense of the reality of himself in his contemplation of his beloved.[13] (In Endymion we see the satiated child asleep at the mother's breast; in the moon as goddess we see the faintly determined features of the mother's face.) More difficult is the conceptual or philosophical projection, but Shakespeare insists upon it: men have appreciable being in the world, but women are abstracted from it. In order to come into being women must move in the male world outside, as Julia does, in male clothing, or as Silvia does, coming down from her tower and exposing herself to the threats of the forest.

I think that there is a framing device in the play's opening and closing scenes, an insistence that men can share in life's important moments and accomplishments. We have already noted that Proteus wants to be "partaker" in Valentine's happiness while they are separated, and later tells his father that Valentine wants him to be "partner in his fortune." If we construe these lines literally, then the middle and end of the play are predicted; Proteus insists on "partaking" of Valentine's mistress, and Valentine finally offers Proteus all that was his in Silvia.

But contradicting this notion of perfect friendship, of two men literally twinned and sharing all or exchanging it—Gisippus gives Titus his
wife; Titus gives Gisippus *his* life—is Shakespeare's consideration of
that other idealism, the worship of perfection in the lady. In an elaborate system of references to the idealizing tendency of love, its confusion of illusion and reality, he constructs a phenomenology of love
which undercuts the conventional metaphysics of love so prevalent in
his sources. The erotic issue is finally whether a lover should have in
his mind's eye an image of perfection which then can be attached to
any mistress, or whether he can learn from a specific mistress how to
love. Does constancy in love consist of loving always a preconceived
image (presumably dialectically derived or divinely inspired, but perhaps a pure oedipal memory or an oedipally adjusted memory of the
pre-oedipal mother) or loving a particular woman no matter how she
changes. Shakespeare's answer is clearly the latter, and he uses the
transvestism of Julia—a change in her appearance to prove the constancy of her love for Proteus—as a contrast to the two gentlemen's
pursuit of their mutually constituted image of perfection in Silvia, even
though it means that Proteus must go through as many changes as the
mythological figure he was named for. This occasions the irony of the
use of the moon goddess as the Form of Truth and Beauty: she is change
itself, so to be constant to her proves that there is no metaphysics of
love, no ideal object, but only a perspective, a way of seeing.

There is also in Shakespeare's use of this conventional material serious consideration of the reflective quality of object-choice, and again
the moon is the appropriate reference. In the long scene that opens the
second act, we find Valentine's love defined by his remarks to Speed
and to Silvia herself. First there is the insistence on the visual element:

Val. But tell me: dost thou know my lady Silvia?
Spe. She that you gaze on so, as she sits at supper?
Val. Hast thou observed that? Even she I mean.
Spe. Why, sir. I know her not.
Val. Dost thou know her by my gazing on her, and yet know'st her not?
   (II.i.41–46)

Then the Neoplatonic point is made by Valentine, but contradicted by
Speed:

Spe. Is she not hard-favoured, sir?
Val. Not so fair, boy, as well-favoured.
Spe. Sir, I know that well enough.
Val. What dost thou know?
Spe. That she is not so fair as, of you, well-favoured.
Val. I mean that her beauty is exquisite, but her favour infinite. (II.i.46–52)

This, of course, leads to, and can be reduced to, the topos that Love is blind (1.76), but what makes the argument in this play more than a commonplace, indeed a profound revelation of erotic truth, is that the attempt to constitute an ideal object of desire is made by two friends who are too close: they feed each others' illusions. (Valentine will insist that Julia is worthy only to carry Silvia's train, "Lest the base earth/ Should from her vesture chance to steal a kiss" [II.iv.154–55].) The essential point of the Valentine-Speed-Silvia exchange (II.i) is that Silvia has had Valentine write love letters for her to an unknown beloved, who is, of course, Valentine: he therefore makes love to himself, which is a further intensification and convolution of Girard's mimetic desire.

The figure Shakespeare uses to accomplish this reduction is that of the puppet show. Speed hails the arrival of Silvia:

> O excellent motion! O exceeding puppet!
> Now will he interpret to her.
>
> (II.i.89–90)

Since Silvia has required Valentine to write letters to her lover, she is like a puppet who requires his interpretation, as a dumb show requires commentary. There is another allusion, though, since Valentine has just previously said, "In conclusion, I stand affected to her," to which Speed has replied, "I would you were set, so your affection would cease" (II.i.80–81). "O excellent motion," then, refers not only forward to the figure of the puppet show, but also backward to the movement of planets: Valentine is the sun to Silvia's moon, and only by setting can he escape her affect.[14] When Silvia agrees with Valentine that the lines he has written were "for" her, i.e., at her request, but are now "for" him, i.e., directed to him as her lover, and then complains, "I would have had them writ more movingly" (1.121), the reference to planetary movement is still felt. Valentine's love of Silvia has caused him to make love to himself, to become the center of his own universe, though Silvia is the motive force. Again, in *The Winter's Tale*, "affection" will be the term to define how a man sees himself in both friend and lover: of Leontes and Polixenes it is said, "There rooted between them such an affection" (I.i.23). It will draw Leontes to the conclusion that his friend has usurped his place: "Affection! thy intention stabs the centre" (I.ii.138). Proteus attempts what Leontes suspects, and in both situations a cosmological figure is chosen to define their relations. Shakespeare seems always concerned to show that love is self-referential, that lovers seek in their objects what they would find in themselves. Thus all the Neoplatonizing language of love is just a vast pathetic fallacy, the projection upon the universe of the lover's own requirement for certainty and constancy. One feels here the breakup of the "Elizabethan world picture," perhaps under the influence of those very intellectuals whom Shakespeare caricatures in *Love's Labor's Lost*. Shakespeare suggests that men should no longer be confident of their fixed place in a well-ordered system, and gives them a premonition of the full force of the Copernican revolution which would so radically change all areas of men's thinking in the second quarter of the next century. (Bruno had already, in 1583–84, lectured at Oxford and had published in England on Copernicus' theory.) There is a kind of relativism in Shakespeare's presentation of love just as there is a kind of nominalism in his philosophy of language. Indeed, in all areas he refuses to make connections. There is no absolute form of Truth and Beauty to which men may ascend in proper love relations; there are no universals outside of language to which the universals of language (like Love) have reference; there is no correspondence between heavenly and terrestial events. Already in these early comedies there is implicit in Shakespeare that belief so strongly and negatively stated in *Lear* and finally with acquiescence in *The Tempest* that any order in nature is the result of men's art, and when men lose the energy and inclination to continue distorting nature to fit their fancies, then all will collapse leaving not a rack behind. There is no stronger statement of the power of the individual as creator of his own reality than the character of Prospero in *The Tempest*, and these early comedies prefigure that.

If Shakespeare shows us in *The Two Gentlemen of Verona* that there

are no absolutes in erotic attraction, what then does he allow to exist
between two people? He tells us that erotic attraction is a kind of fetishism, that we are all concerned with *idols, pictures, shapes, shadows,
forms* and *images,* and that we prefer these illusions to the actuality of
people who move close to us and far from us. He sets Valentine and
Proteus up in this kind of dumb show:

Pro. Was this the idol that you worship so?
Val. Even she; and is she not a heavenly saint? (II.iv.139–40)

Silvia is repulsed by Proteus' insistence on possessing a likeness of her,
if she will not herself be his: "I am very loath to be your idol, sir"
(IV.ii.125). Julia protests to Silvia's picture:

Jul.   O thou senseless form,
   Thou shalt be worshipp'd, kiss'd, lov'd, and ador'd;
   And were there sense in his idolatry,
   My substance should be statue in thy stead. (IV.iv.196–99)

Indeed earlier, in a strange exchange of figure for later fact, Proteus
admits that he has fallen in love not with Silvia herself, but with some
image of her, presumably that projected by Valentine:

   'Tis but her picture I have yet beheld,
   And that hath dazzled my reason's light;
   But when I look on her perfections,
   There is no reason but I shall be blind.

                        (II.iv.205–8)

The constant figure for love in the play is likeness, whether "waxen
image" or "impression" (II.iv.197–8; cf. "This weak impress of love
. . . / Trenched in ice [III.ii.6–7]) or shadow (IV.ii.124,127). What
is strange is that the lover must admit that loving a picture turns him
to but a semblance of himself. Proteus protests to Silvia:

   For since the substance of your perfect self
   Is else devoted, I am but a shadow;
   And to your shadow will I make true love.

                        (IV.ii.120–22)

He had admitted earlier of his love for Julia:

   O, how this spring of love resembleth
   The uncertain glory of an April day,

> Which now shows all the beauty of the sun.
> And by and by a cloud takes all away.

(I.iii.84–87)

The ambiguity here is thoroughgoing: the sun reveals the beauty in nature, so when the sun itself is concealed by a cloud all of nature is obscured; so, too, with love, for if the mistress is the sun, then the lover himself disappears if she is eclipsed.

Shakespeare shows us, then, by conflating two tales that celebrate love as an absolute, that love is only a fantasy, a creative force which men project upon some object out of their own needs, and they then depend on that object to reconstitute themselves. It is dangerously close to what Voltaire said about religion—that God created man in his own image and man returned the favor. Love to Shakespeare is a mutually constitutive operation; the lover comes into being as a conscious subject by his pursuit of an object. Where then is "constancy" and "essence"? It lies only in change, the change that true love can accept in its object. Julia says of her transvestism:

> It is the lesser blot modesty finds,
> Women to change their shapes, than men their minds.

(V.iv.107–8)

And Proteus replies, finally de-Platonized:

> Than men their minds? 'Tis true: O heaven, were man
> But constant, he were prefect. That one error
> Fills him with faults; makes him run through all th' sins;
> Inconstancy falls off, ere it begins.
> What is in Silvia's face but I may spy
> More fresh in Julia's, with a constant eye.

(V.iv.109–14)

Constancy lies not in the object, but in the lover's view of that object, just as we have frequently before been told that love is a function of seeming or seeing, not of being.[15]

Shakespeare demands that his lovers relinquish those images of perfect love objects which are derived from idealizations of oedipal and pre-oedipal maternal figures: these are not only the Adrianas and Lucianas (the split-off good and bad mothers) but also the universal force, the all-encompassing Silvia. Julia is our first example of the complete

Shakespearean mistress; through transvestism she has acquired those traits which Proteus himself feels the need of in his own nature, and so, in loving her he remakes himself in his own image. She becomes both Silvia and Valentine to him, the idealized image of himself and the woman who first projected that image to him. We return to Kernberg and find there the reminder that "there can be no meaningful love relation without the persistence of the self, without firm boundaries of the self that generate a sense of identity." [16] This kind of love, based on self-consciousness, is compared with those kinds of "infantile dependent relations with women representing mother images" which he finds in pathological types. [17] The extremes are Endymion and Narcissus, or the Neoplatonic religious lover and the original Platonic philosophical lover, or the man who views the world as ordered by ageless, changeless absolutes, and the man who sees truth only as a function of difference between similars. Shakespeare demands the mediation and combination of these extremes, thus arriving at some kind of erotic maturity.

There are many ways in which *The Two Gentlemen of Verona* is a pivotal play. Besides the emergence of the transvestized heroine, the deflation of Neoplatonic idealizing in love relations, and the emphasis on mutually correcting changes in the images and objects of desire, we should remark that once again Shakespeare has placed women inside (until they transvestize) and men outside. He does provide Julia with a confidante in Lucetta inside, as he does Proteus with Valentine outside, and this is an important prefiguration of the importance Nerissa will have for Portia in *The Merchant of Venice* and Celia for Rosalind in *As You Like It*. Nevertheless, the men move first widely in the world in mostly masculine company to educate themselves, and this activity, this struggle, is framed by their first feeling "dully sluggardis'd at home" and then finally by their embracing their mistresses at the end. This is the clearest of many ways in which Shakespeare recapitulates in each comedy, and by degree over the whole course of his comic career, the full history of Greek comedy. I argued above that the erotic horizons of young men in Greek comedy narrow as their opportunity for political power diminishes in late fourth century Athens: their attention is focused on domestic issues because there is no scope for their activity outside. If we remind ourselves of Hobbes' definition of power—"In the first place, I put for a general inclination of all mankind, a perpetual and restless drive of power after power, that ceaseth only in death." (*Leviathan,* chapter XI)—then we must ask whether dynamically there is any difference between tragedy and comedy. Do they both end in a kind of death, ontogenetic and erotic, or actual? Is "acquiring" the woman an end of the struggle tantamount to death? Or will the struggle continue with her (in *A Midsummer Night's Dream* the arguments seem to be just beginning) or over her (Shylock would keep Jessica for himself, as would also the fathers of the late romances)? In *Love's Labor Lost,* the question is moot because the marriages do not take place. The courtship must continue although the men are finally convinced that they can only see themselves in their ladies' eyes.

Love's Labor's Lost

The principles of Shakespearean comedy which I have delineated theoretically and have traced in *The Comedy of Errors* and *The Two Gentlemen of Verona*—variety and progression in the orientation of desire and its relation to worldview generally—are readily discernible in *Love's Labor's Lost*. I have suggested that Shakespeare distinguishes four types of object-choice and presents these in a continuum suggesting development. A young man is first obsessed with a mirror image of himself; the melancholy of Antipholus of Syracuse as he seeks his lost twin represents this case in its extreme. He then enjoys the companionship of another young man, and thinks that only in such company can he come to know himself and make a place for himself in the world. A transitional stage from this dependence upon a male friend to a dependence upon a female lover occurs when he becomes attached to a young woman transvestized as a young man. When he first begins to love a woman, he might either idealize her or debase her, in both cases projecting upon her preconceived notions of the nature of women. Finally he recognizes in the young woman a being of great complexity and novelty, an independent and constantly changing creature who contradicts all his expectations and leads him to new discoveries about himself and the world.

This opening up of a young man's heart to variety in erotic experience is shown by Shakespeare to stimulate an awakening of his mind.

He stops thinking and speaking in clichés, learns to learn from experience, and casts aside all those stereotypical notions upon which he previously depended. He sees himself ironically, both as a lover loving and as a man thinking, and he comes to know that these processes are the only reality of his experience. It is as if he stepped out of the medieval world of hypostatized abstracts and into the renaissance of active immediacy and concrete objects, separating himself from those authorities who would tell him the nature of the world and determining for himself from his own experience how the world works.

In *Love's Labor's Lost* our focus of attention is Berowne: we see the action through his eyes, and see it differently as he learns to love. His character changes in such a way that we see him pass through stages of development in the orientation of desire outlined above as a "normalized" Shakespearean comedy. At the opening of the play, he prides himself on his wit, and though he is loath to renounce the company of ladies, this is more because he will have less opportunity to be witty than because he has any deep admiration for women or cherishes any woman in particular. If we see solipsism in his wit—note how he interrupts his fellows, overrides them, and generally speaks in the opening scene to express his own feelings and to turn a fine phrase rather than to reason with them and to elicit their response—then, at least in his signing of the pact there is a movement toward company, some kind of social commitment, even if he does believe it folly.[1]

Certainly we see in Berowne's first love for Rosaline idealization of that sort we traced in Proteus' "love" for Silvia: his sonnet to her (IV.ii.101–14) is not without charm, but it is characterized, rhetorically, by hyperbole, and conceptually, by the Neoplatonic distinction between gross distorted matter (earth and lover) and higher truth (heaven and lady). His renunciation of this rhetoric and this conception in the speech "Thus pour the stars down plagues for perjury" (V.ii.394–415) also marks his attribution of wit to women; indeed he tells Rosaline "confound me with a flout" and later she describes him as having been "Full of comparisons and wounding flouts" (V.ii.836). Whereas he first worships her as a moon goddess (or, in this play, the sun itself), a passive object of adoration, he finally recognizes her as an active agent, someone who can meet him on his own terms and even beat him at his own game.

What else does Berowne learn? Though he speaks of distinguishing a lady from her favor, he suggests an appreciation of the danger of reading actual experience by conventional expectations:

> The ladies did change favours, and then we,
> Following the signs, woo'd but the sign of she.

(V.ii.468–69)

It is not just our own contemporary concern with semiotics that causes us to read deep philosophical significance into this analysis of signs. Berowne is somewhere between Montaigne and Descartes: he knows with the former that trousers do not make a man, and approaches the latter's doubt whether what looks like a man is a man or a robot. Who is he courting, anyway, and what signifies her wearing his sign of her? We remember Silvia's disdain for Proteus when he begs her picture of her:

> I am very loath to be your idol, sir;
> But, since your falsehood shall become you well
> To worship shadows, and adore false shapes,
> Send to me in the morning, and I'll send it.

(*TGV* IV.ii.125–8)

In each case the man loves his projection of an idealized object of desire upon an actual woman, and Shakespeare insists that we see in this the idolatry of love. When Berowne overhears Longaville's sonnet, in which he adores his lady as a goddess, Berowne exclaims: "This is the liver vein, which makes flesh a deity; A green goose a goddess; pure, pure idolatry" (IV.iii.71–72). The idolatry of love then works in two directions: a man may see in a picture a woman, or in a woman a goddess. Both functions, I maintain, consist of hypostatization, rendering a living being into a static figure. We should be inclined to call it a fetish, if a man loved more the retouched photograph of a woman who represents an exaggerated amalgam of all those features most admired by his culture, than any actual, flawed, living, aging, changing woman. We need to consider very carefully Shakespeare's use of the concept of idolatry, comparing it with his contemporaries'. This will help us see how the way men see women as objects of desire in Shakespeare

is a model for their seeing the entire world, so that when Berowne
learns to see Rosaline as a particular woman and not as the sun, then
he has changed not only the orientation of his desire but also his epis-
temology and ontology.[2]

The right way to approach this play—even more than other
Shakespearean plays—is through the language, and this has been done
in a model study by W. C. Carroll.[3] Among his predecessors he acknowledges M. Mack, who has shown that "language creatively used
is freedom,"[4] and J. Calderwood, who has shown the importance of
women in the play as "linguistic reforming agents."[5] Carroll applies
the same terms and reaches the same conclusions from his inductive
reading that I have from my deductive reading:

The men—high and low alike—are primarily narcissistic, projecting their own
desires and images onto those about them. . . . It is with the greatest surprise
and consternation that the lords find in the ladies not the image of their own
minds, but the image of strong, independent, superior minds which have a
life and will of their own.[6]

His finding that the play strangely deconstructs its own concern with
language by determining that the eye is more trustworthy than the
tongue in reporting the heart, congrues with my application of Lacan's distinction between *demande* in the symbolic realm and *désir* in
the imagistic realm.[7] "Deconstruction" is the correct term here since
Carroll's larger argument, against previous critics, is that the play does
not finally validate nature against art, but shows these two modes of
being to be interdependent, if not mutually canceling:

There is indeed a dazzling reversal in the play's movement. It is not, however,
from "Art" to "Nature," but from a false, sterile art, in Navarre's original
formulation, to a genuine "living art," one that is not less artificial (in the best
sense) but more so.[8]

At the end of the play then, the artful use of language succeeds in
"making strange" the experience of love, rather than making each new
experience of love like every other, and therefore a cliché.

This reading opens up startlingly when we balance Carroll's close
reading of the uses of "affection"[9] with similar attention to the uses
of "grace." These important word-themes appear together early on:

the King praises his companions in a way which suggests both the conventional dualism of body and mind, and an appreciation that each man is "affected" differently:

> Therefore, brave conquerors—for so you are,
> That war against your own affections
> And the huge army of the world's desires—
> Our late edict shall strongly stand in force.
>
> (I.i.8–11)

The latter is then emphasized by Berowne:

> For every man with his affects is born,
> Not by might master'd, but by special grace.
>
> (I.i.150–51)

Berowne articulates what the audience already knows—that every man is, more often than not, ruled by his own "affects," his "affections" or passions, rather than by his reason. Whether "grace" is capitalized or not, these "affects" amount to a kind of original sin that man cannot overrule by his own will.[10]

There certainly is a double dimension to Berowne's warning, and "grace" does suggest divine intervention: "We know that the 'huge army' will inevitably triumph since, as Berowne puts it, only a special grace can conquer it, and no one in *Love's Labor's Lost* is so blessed."[11] The clear perspective of the play is that each individual sees things and feels things in his own peculiar way and there is no cosmic force to unify men's experience. Grace is, however, used repeatedly in the play in several particular senses which relate finally to create new meaning for the term. It is consistently associated with the noble characters, as a quality to be expected of their class. (This impression is strengthened by the form of address for the King and the Princess, "your Grace.")

Boyet. Be now as prodigal of all dear grace
  As Nature was in making graces dear
  When she did starve the general world beside,
  And prodigally gave them all to you. (II.i.9–12)

Kath. The young Dumain, a well accomplish'd youth,
  Of all that virtue love for virtue lov'd:
  Most power to do most harm, least knowing ill,

For he hath wit to make an ill shape good,
And shape to win grace though he had no wit. (II.i.56–60)

This class-specific use is related to the concept of divine grace, i.e., of God's favoring man in spite of man's sins, rather than because of man's virtues.

Long. My vow was earthly, thou a heavenly love;
   Thy grace being gain'd cures all disgrace in me. (IV.iii.63–64)

Ber. Good heart! what grace hast thou, thus to reprove
   These worms for loving, that art most in love? (IV.iii.150–51)

Though Holofernes uses three different epithets to express his disappointment in the nobles' behavior, they all add up to want of grace: "This is not generous, not gentle, not humble" (V.ii.623). What was required of them is Theseus' attitude toward the rude mechanicals. In response to Hippolyta's objection "to see wretchedness o'ercharged," he explains grace:

The. Why, gentle sweet, you shall see no such thing.
Hipp. He says they can do nothing in this kind.
The. The kinder we, to give them thanks for nothing.
   Our sport shall be to take what they mistake:
   And what poor duty cannot do, noble respect
   Takes it in might, not merit.(V.i.87–92)

He finally admits that he can "read" what he wants into any speech he hears, that his "capacity" makes up their deficiency. When he continues in this vein during the "Pyramus and Thisbe," Hippolyta objects: "It must be your imagination then and not theirs"(V.i.216).

At the end of *Love's Labor's Lost* there is a similar insistence on the phenomenology of art. Moth approves the plan of making the Hercules he will play an infant carrying snakes:

An excellent device! so if any of the audience hiss, you may cry 'Well done, Hercules! now thou crushest the snake!' That is the way to make an offence gracious, though few have the grace to do it.

(V.i.128–31)

And Rosaline explains the penance she would impose on Berowne, to tell jokes to the painfully ill:

> Why, that's the way to choke a gibing spirit,
> Whose influence is begot of that loose grace
> Which shallow laughing hearers give to fools.
> A jest's prosperity lies in the ear
> Of him that hears it, never in the tongue
> Of him that makes it.

(V.ii.850–55)

It is not, then, what a performance deserves that matters in the relation between performers and audience, but rather what the grace of the audience grants. This theologically derived philosophy is given a particular application to art, but its general truth is clear: there are no absolute values, only perspective.

With this we are back to Carroll's point on "affection": men cannot control their passions with reason; God could with his grace, but that does not seem to apply here. What does apply here is man's grace. Men graciously accept each other's weaknesses, the more so the high of the low; they read into situations what is there only intentionally and not efficiently. In love, with the lady still exalted, this means that the lover is no fool, nor even a liar for having broken his oath not to love:

> *Ber.* And what in us hath seem'd ridiculous,—
> As love is full of unbefitting strains;
> All wanton as a child, skipping and vain;
> Form'd by the eye, and therefore, like the eye,
> Full of strange shapes, of habits, and of forms,
> Varying in subjects, as the eye doth roll
> To every varied object in his glance:
> Which party-coated presence of loose love
> Put on by us, if, in your heavenly eyes,
> Have misbecom'd our oaths and gravities,
> Those heavenly eyes, that look into these faults,
> Suggested us to make. Therefore, ladies,
> Our love being yours, the error that love makes
> Is likewise yours: we to ourselves prove false,
> By being once false for ever to be true
> To those who make us both,—fair ladies, you:
> And even that falsehood, in itself a sin,
> Thus purifies itself and turns to grace.(V.ii.751–68)

There is an extraordinary irony in all this, which falls only a bit short of Descartes' *cogito:* Shakespeare shows his lovers thinking about themselves loving; they are distanced from the experience; they are gracious toward themselves. Barber sees this in *As You Like It,* when he speaks of "leaving judgment free to mock what the heart embraces."[12] We shall certainly see this in Theseus' great speech, "The lunatic, the lover and the poet," in *A Midsummers Night's Dream.*

If we pursue the notion of irony as self-consciousness, we come to a greater appreciation of the rarified atmosphere of the play. It is certainly a main feature of the pastoral tradition that lovers should achieve instrospection simultaneously with true affection for their ladies. This experience is vouchsafed only to aristocrats, whose leisure to love is compounded: they escape the workaday world by being born aristocrats and escape their obligations as aristocrats by making the pastoral pilgrimage. (They clearly see in the clowns and rustics their own primitive, preconscious selves, still mingled with the grossness of actual existence, the "greasy" world.) They escape the artifice of court to find themselves in nature, but they cannot take nature as they find it and instead shed their grace upon it, so that it will become for them an adequate reflection of the new personae they are creating for themselves. These people are, then, gods, and in the end a combination of incipient boredom with the feast of love and language and the rude intrusion of mortality forces them back to court. Who but these people in this setting have the leisure to devote themselves to purely erotic, purely ontogenetic pursuits? When do we have the leisure to see ourselves in them except when watching Shakespearean comedy? Just as irony is the hallmark of sophisticated literature, so the questioning of one's orientation of desire is the hallmark of the absurdly advantaged. Shakespeare does this for us, taking us back through his pastoral artifice to those earlier gardens of our own experience.

The play shows us that love is a way of seeing ourselves and the world. When Berowne calls it idolatry we think of Bacon, for whom love is but one of many idolatries:

It is a poor saying of Epicurus, *satis magnum alter alteri theatrum sumus:* as if man, made for the contemplation of heaven and all noble objects, should do nothing but kneel before a little idol, and make himself subject, though not of the mouth (as beasts are), yet of the eye, which was given him for higher purposes ("Of Love").

For the mind, darkened by its covering of the body, is far from being a flat, equal, and clear mirror that receives and reflects the rays without mixture, but rather a magical glass, full of superstitions and apparitions. Idols are imposed upon the understanding, either 1. by the general nature of mankind; 2. the nature of each particular man; or 3. by words, or communicative nature. The first kind we call idols of the tribe; the second kind, idols of the den; and the third kind, idols of the market. There is also a fourth kind, which we call idols of the theatre, being superinduced by false theories, or philosophies, and the perverted laws of demonstration (*Advancement of Learnning* 5.4).

We easily see that Shakespeare presents love as an idol of all kinds in this play. It is a human condition; each man experiences it in his own peculiar way; it is expressed and encouraged by rhetoric and particularly by poetry; it is philosophized. Indeed the sequence of thought in Bacon's essay "Of Love" is essentially negated by the play's argument:

I. The stage owes more to love than does real life, and it is more the stuff of comedies than tragedies. Great men have never been subject to its excesses. (Marc Antony and Appius Claudius are exceptions.) Have we not more to look at than a little idol?
II. Hyperbole is characteristic of love, not only in expression but also in thought. Not even the most arrogant man makes as much of himself as the lover makes of his beloved. To love and to be wise are incompatible.
III. Love is either reciprocated or spurned; in the latter case the lover loses not only the world but also the object of his love. Paris gave up the gifts of Athena and Juno for Helen.
IV. Love must be controlled. Military men are particularly prone to it. Love is best displaced from the one onto the many, as monks do. In married love is man created, in friendly love perfected, by sexual love destroyed.

The essay was not published until 1612; otherwise it could have been considered Shakespeare's inspiration for *Love's Labor's Lost*. The central and repeated equation between the greatness of men and their control of love could explain the pageant of the worthies, and several other references in the play, such as Armado's "What great men have been in love?" (I.ii.60). Armado is a military man and is the most absurd lover. The nobles are determined to be monks for three years. The hyperbolic nature of love and its rhetoric is the central theme and mode of the play; the relation between love and knowledge is constantly questioned. Bacon's own immediate inspiration was probably Augustine, *Confessions* III.2–4, which moves from an account of his seduction by the theatre, to his sexual seduction, to his seduction by rhetoric and finally by philosophy, which in turn led him on to religion and God.

What is clearly lacking in Shakespeare is any reference to God. In his attack upon love, Bacon reverses the development of Neoplatonism: he would return to the stage of Augustine's Platonism where God is the end of man's knowledge by canceling the intermediate stage where God's place is taken by the lady of the courtly love tradition. If Shakespeare brings the lady down to earth, refusing to worship her as an idol, what happens to that whole sphere of reference which first the Forms and then God and then the lady occupied? It is simply not there; there is nothing beyond human experience—of love or whatever—each human being's own experience; there is no *tertium comparationis*, no universals, no plan, nothing. What then does a man do? He dispenses his shaping grace on that experience, turning it into something wondrous fine, and then he allows it to evaporate with him into thin air. This conception will be clearer in *A Midsummer Night's Dream* and *The Tempest*, but it already exists in *Love's Labor's Lost*.

Carroll points out that "affection" and "infection" are conflated in Elizabethan English.[13] There are passages that play on this conception:

Boyet. If my observation, which very seldom lies,
  By the heart's still rhetoric disclosed with eyes
  Deceive me not now, Navarre is infected.
Prin. With what?
Boyet. With that which we lovers entitle affected. (II.i.227–31)

Ber. Write 'Lord have mercy on us' on those three;
  They are infected, in their hearts it lies;
  They have the plague, and caught it of your eyes.(V.ii.419–21)

De Rougement observes, "It is well known that the Greeks and the Romans looked on love as a sickness . . . whenever it went . . . beyond the sensual pleasure which was considered to be its natural expression."[14] It is disturbing to see two thousand years of *eros* turned into *nosos*, but the point is valid: from Homer to Virgil, from Hippocrates to Lucretius, the control and satisfaction of desire was considered an aspect of physical and mental hygiene. One must except, however, at least Plato and Ovid, the Greek and Roman whose influence is most strongly felt in *Love's Labor's Lost*. They also provided the stimulus for the great erotic revolution of the twelfth century, when for the first time in the West, women were idealized as objects of desire, and the courtly love tradition began.[15] Shakespeare in his way, as Bacon in his, is trying to end it. If we say Bacon depends on reason, Shakespeare on the senses, then we reduce the dispute to the two static polarities posed at the opening of the play: "The mind shall banquet, though the body pine" (I.i.25). The play is a mediation of many such polarities, and one might say that it transcends some of them, but this, too, suggests something beyond, where Shakespeare sees nothing, or even that these oppositions themselves exist outside language. Shakespeare celebrates love as a creative force, a phenomenology, a shoring up of the fragments of our experience aginst the ruins of Christian metaphysics.

The Taming of
the Shrew

The Taming of the Shrew, like A Midsummer Night's Dream, invites analysis as the fulfillment of an erotic fantasy because it is framed as a dream. Although the Induction, with the hoodwinking of Christopher Sly, is not closed wth a return to that situation at the conclusion of the play as we have it from Shakespeare, there has been speculation, on the basis of his anonymous "source," The Taming of a Shrew, that such scenes did originally exist.[1] (Note that the indefinite article suggests the different tenor of this piece, which is clear from the extant fragments: it is a generalized lesson in how to handle any difficult women, rather than the drama of the wooing of one particular woman.) Certainly, continued reference to Sly would have confirmed his identification with Petruchio, and this would have made it even more imperative for us to see the action from his point of view. If we find his treatment of Katherina offensive and see that here again, as in The Comedy of Errors, The Two Gentlemen of Verona and Love's Labor's Lost, Shakespeare is using dramatic action to explicate the erotic orientation of one particular character, and that here, as in The Two Gentlemen of Verona, the character is not attractive, then we might consider the action of the main plot as the fulfillment of a male fantasy.

Do we read the play as a misogynistic tract? As suggested in my opening remarks on the early comedies, I agree with Morris and others that this is inescapable. With the kind of analysis we have applied to the other early comedies, however, I think we can explain why this is the case. Whereas the other early comedies work through various stages of erotic orientation to the establishment of reasonably benign relations between the sexes, only here, and perhaps in *The Merry Wives of Windsor* and the problem comedies, do the initial fear and resentment remain. One reason for this, I shall maintain, is that Petruchio, unlike the focal males in the other early comedies, is alone, without a male companion to secure him in his own identity as he seeks out a female companion.

Williams, in an interesting approach to the play, considers that the way the action is presented encourages us to see it as forms of behavior imposed upon characters who might, and indeed in the future outside the play may behave differently. This is, of course, very risky criticism, to project fictional characters outside their fiction, but it might help us with the problem of point of view. Williams points particularly to the first meeting between Petruchio and Katherina (II.1), the testing scene at the crossroads (IV.v), and the final scene, where Katherina instructs the other brides. His basic point is that both Katherina and Petruchio are playing the roles assigned them by other characters, and that we are not annoyed by this because we can imagine them playing other roles, perhaps their own "true" roles:

Can we be allowed to think that she is again playing a part [Katherina in the final scene], acting a new identity, and that their marriage will in fact settle down to a Beatrice and Benedick kind of association?[2]

What of Petruchio? . . . He is not known in Padua, so may this swashbuckling roughness of his be an assumed identity too, an *ad hoc* device to deal with a wealthy, attractive young termagant?[3]

Several issues are thereby raised. This reading suggests that the play is a farce, and thus we are discouraged from expecting serious and consistent characterization; it also reminds us of the approach Abel takes to Shakespeare, seeing in Hamlet, for instance, a character writing his own play and manipulating the other characters; it suggests that Petruchio's swagger might be defensive.

Petruchio wants "to wive it wealthily in Padua," but he has other criteria for his choice as well, and these are listed in those crucial scenes that begin and end our view of his relations with Katherina. He first describes her to her face as he would have her be, not as he (and we) actually see her:

> I find you passing gentle.
> 'Twas told me you were rough, and coy, and sullen,
> And now I find report a very liar;
> For thou art pleasant, gamesome, passing courteous,
> But slow in speech, yet sweet as spring-time flowers.
> Thou canst not frown, thou canst not look askance,
> Nor bite the lip, as angry wenches will,
> Nor hast thou pleasure to be cross in talk.
> But thou with mildness entertain'st thy wooers,
> With gentle conference, soft and affable.
>
> (II.i.236–45)

This is certainly a strong statement of the phenomenology of love: Petruchio defines his ideal object of desire, an image which he then projects upon Katherina, whom we know to contradict all its features, and then she is forced to conform to its pattern. Traditionally, those critics who have been offended by the way in which the woman's role is defined in the play have either tried to read it ironically, or have simply relegated it to some nether region of Shakespeare's canon. I do not claim it as one of his greatest achievements, but it does fill a gap left by the other early comedies in his examination of men's choice of sexual partners. I think Petruchio is consistent in his attitude toward women, but I do not think that necessarily means this is Shakespeare's attitude; I think that Petruchio feels women must be controlled before they are loved, because, deprived of a male friend or twin, he depends entirely for his masculine identity upon women.

No greater contrast could exist than that between Lucentio and Petruchio. Lucentio is immediately recognizable as one of those young men who go abroad for education: we know variations on this type in *The Comedy of Errors, The Two Gentlemen of Verona, Love's Labor's Lost, The Merchant of Venice,* and *All's Well.* The pattern is basic to romances of all periods, and I have claimed in discussing the other early comedies that part of its significance lies in the insistence that

women should stay inside, refining their domestic arts, while men pursue
their education outside, in the wide world. (If women are to go outside in the male world, they must transvestize, wearing sword and
codpiece.) The fact that Petruchio, too, puts himself in this category,
although his specific intention is to find a wife, suggests that he is played
against the pattern, to produce a kind of parody of conventional romance.

> Such wind as scatters young men through the world
> To seek their fortunes farther than at home
> Where small experience grows.

(I.ii.49–51)

In the pattern generally, the dichotomy between philosophy and
sensual experience is immediately set up, as in *Love's Labor's Lost;* here
we find it in the opening exchange between Lucentio and his man
Tranio. Tranio warns against becoming stoics (I.i.31), Lucentio agrees,
and then, like Proteus and all the young men in *Love's Labor's Lost,*
falls in love at first sight with the first young woman he sees, Bianca.
Interestingly enough, not only in view of his later service to her as
tutor, but also in the context of his general contrast with Petruchio,
he is first struck not with her beauty, but with her demeanor:

> But in the other's silence do I see
> Maid's mild behaviour and sobriety.

(I.i.70–71)

> Hark, Tranio, thou may'st hear Minerva speak.

(84)

> . . . . . this young modest girl

(156)

Now clearly, the contrast between the dark Katherina and the blond
Bianca is similar to the contrast between Adriana and Luciana, the one
threatening and the other benign. Petruchio's mistreatment of Katherina can be compared to Emilia's blaming Adriana for driving Antipholus of Ephesus mad. We might even have been content with *The
Taming of the Shrew* if Katherina had simply been forced to conform
to Bianca's pattern, as we think Adriana will conform to Luciana's in
The Comedy of Errors, by relaxing her possessive control of Antipho-

lus, if, paradoxically, she is to keep him—and the play makes no certain conclusion of that. In *The Taming of the Shrew*, however, Katherina advances beyond Bianca in becoming *morigera* to her husband, and takes Bianca to school, so that even our original model of the demure young woman must reform. It is, as most critics have pronounced it, a cruel overstatement. Control is the role of the male, and he must exercise it even on the most unthreatening of females, lest, becoming vicious in her freedom, she rise up against him.

Both Lucentio and Petruchio have valets; indeed Tranio and Grumio are taken from Plautus' *Mostellaria* where one is a city slave who encourages his young master's libidinous excesses and the other is a country slave who is surly, rude, and opprobrious. Lucentio is friendly with Tranio, and, of course, they eventually exchange roles, Tranio becoming his rich young master so that Lucentio can masquerade as a poor academic in his own service. Petruchio beats Grumio and all his other men. To say simply that this contrast is part of the characterization of the protagonists in the plot and subplot is to ignore the relation between their attitudes toward other men and their attitudes toward women. We remember Antipholus of Syracuse's opening statement of his melancholy, where he was seeking his fellow forth; we then see the predicament of Antipholus of Ephesus, who, lacking a brother, is overwhelmed by his wife; we recall in *The Two Gentlemen of Verona* how Proteus feels deprived of himself in the absence of Valentine; and we remember in *Love's Labor's Lost* that the young men define themselves together by the exclusion of women. Only Petruchio, then, of all the young heroes of the early comedies faces marriage alone. I claim that this lack of male support creates the pattern in which his violence toward Katherina makes sense; paradoxically, since generally I argue that in Shakespearean comedy men need the help of other men to face the threat of women, Petruchio is the most unflinching in the face of the greatest threat:

> Signor Hortensio, 'twixt such friends, as we
> Few words suffice; and therefore, if thou know
> One rich enough to be Petruchio's wife—
> As wealth is burden of my wedding dance—
> Be she as foul as was Florentius' love,
> As old as Sibyl, and as curst and shrewd

As Socrates' Xanthippe, or a worse,
She moves me not, or not removes at least
Affection's edge in me, were she as rough
As are the swelling Adriatic seas.
I come to wive it wealthily in Padua;
If wealthily, then happily in Padua.

(I.ii.64–75)

Hortensio is not the kind of friend (of the same age, twinned since birth) that Proteus has in Valentine, that Berowne enjoys in his three companions, or that the two Antipholi find in each other. Petruchio's association of wealth and marriage (the gold and the girl) is also unparalleled, at least until Bassanio seeks Portia in *The Merchant of Venice*. We cannot consider here, even briefly, the sociological, political, and cosmological significance of such an association. However, Petruchio, in his singularity, calls up such heroes of myth as Perseus, Herakles, and Oedipus, whose greatest achievement is destroying a female monster. Indeed Gremio makes the comparison:

Hor. Did you ever see Baptista's daughter?
Tra. No, sir, but hear I do that he hath two:
  The one as famous for a scolding tongue
  As is the other for beauteous modesty.
Pet. Sir, sir, the first's for me, let her go by.
Gre. Yea, leave that labour to great Hercules,
  And let it be more than Alcides' twelve. (I.ii.250–56)

Slater has argued that the peculiar prominence of female monsters in Greek mythology is due to a social phenomenon which he calls the oral-narcissistic dilemma: mature Greek men hate and fear women because in Greek households the women took out their frustration and resentment against their absent husbands upon their young sons.[4] I think we sense something like this pattern of familial strife in *All's Well*. Bertram is overwhelmed first by his mother and then by his wife; his father is dead and the king is ill, so there is no other male to protect him. In *The Taming of the Shrew* we learn that Petruchio is abroad partly because his father, "old Antonio," is recently dead (I.ii.188–89). In *The Merchant of Venice* Antonio is Bassanio's friend and benefactor, whereas in Shakespeare's source he is Bassanio's godfather, to whom the young man is commended by his dying father. Erlich has studied the significance of the absent father in *Hamlet*—it could be called an anti-oedipal theme, since it accounts for the son's misogyny—and traces close parallels in *The Comedy of Errors*.[5] Generally, then, in the middle period of problem comedies and tragedies, the lack of a protective older man is felt by the young hero; in the early comedies the hero misses a contemporary, a friend, or a twin. In this respect *The Taming of the Shrew* seems transitional: Petruchio lacks both friend and father.

Having located the pattern, I insist on examining its significance. I have claimed that generally the twin or friend represents for the hero's depth psychology his libidinally invested self-object. We have seen that when this investment is satisfactory, when it is presented by Shakespeare as a phase which his young men grow into and out of, it yields finally to a different kind of object-choice, a woman seen as fully independent of the man, often with transvestism acting as a catalyst, a medial stage in which the woman is both male and female, friend and lover, self and other. In the middle comedies Shakespeare will present us with men who are "sick of self-love," like Antonio in *The Merchant of Venice* and Malvolio in *Twelfth Night,* and these we shall recognize as representing failure to fix an adequate and supporting self-image— hence the constant self-reference of their object-choices. We find no place for Petruchio in Kernberg's continuum of configurations, if we try to see him as representative of a fixation in a particular stage of development and as a particular pathology of mature object-choice. He does, however, present some of the features Kernberg cites in his "normalized" picture of the pathological narcissist:

These patients present an unusual degree of self-reference in their interactions with other people, a great need to be loved and admired by others, and a curious apparent contradiction between a very inflated concept of themselves and an inordinate need for tribute from others. Their emotional life is shallow. They experience little empathy for the feelings of others or from their own grandiose fantasies, and they feel restless and bored when external glitter wears off and no new sources feed their self-regard. . . . In general, their relationships with others are clearly exploitative and sometimes parasitic. It is as if they feel they have the right to control and possess others and to exploit them without guilt feelings—and behind a surface which very often is charming and engaging, one senses coldness and ruthlessness.[6]

Do we not see Petruchio in this characterization, especially in the crucial scenes of wooing, wedding, and testing? Certainly, when he forces

Katherina to call day night and an old man a young maid (is there
significance in Lucentio being provided with a father while Petruchio
is deprived of one?), we see an insistence that the world respond to
his willful image of it. As Williams first pointed out, Petruchio reads
his parts into other characters and forces them to act accordingly. The
result is simultaneously farce and a chillingly accurate image of narcissism, a man incapable of love making a charade of love, and de-
meaning a young girl who, though originally overly willful, is (almost
tragically) shown to be more sinned against than sinning. Her "emas-
culation" is precisely the reverse of the action we see other comic heroines undergo through transvestism. Only Hippolyta, perhaps, in
A Midsummer Night's Dream, whom Theseus claims to have wooed with
his sword and to have won by doing her injuries (I.i.16–17), suffers
so, and she can still talk back, as the final scene shows. It seems that
Shakespeare, just to complete his paradigm of all possible love relationships, felt required to study the anaesthetic, misogynistic, and
narcissistic; this is how we must describe Petruchio, much as we might
enjoy his antics.

IV

THE MATURE
COMEDIES

n these plays the correspondences and paradoxes that were presented almost schematically in the early comedies are pursued to bewildering conclusions, in both plot and language. Transvestism is used to determine identity for both the young woman and the young man who learns to love her; the phenomenology of desire is examined against the metaphysics of reason and idealized object-choice; objects of desire are constructed of words and myths, which must then be deconstructed by actual experience. Recent critics have deepened our appreciation of these plays to such an extent that we can hardly recognize the readings given them only thirty years ago, not to mention what was made of them by the critical tradition from Hazlitt and Johnson to Knight. My reading will show the conjunction of the erotic and ontogenetic concerns of the plays—as revealed by contemporary psychoanalysis to be repeated in human experience—with their philosophical concerns, which we think of as culture-specific. If in suggesting that Shakespeare showed the inadequacies of such medieval hypostatizations as Reason and Passion, I seem simply to replace that system with another, by projecting back upon Shakespeare such hypostatizations as the ideal ego, I can only explain my method by analogy. Just as art language deconstructs the hypostatizations of common language to redeem physical reality, so a critical model that insists on the primacy of sensual experience can deconstruct a tradition of criticism based on the very hypostatizations which Shakespeare rejected and so restore to our reading the actual experience of desire.

Redemption becomes a key concept here, because I see Shakespeare in these plays facing the abyss of random experience, unsupported by the forms of Neoplatonism, whether Christian, courtly, or humanist, and yet finding some new bridge to cross it, some new sense in man's relation to the world. The Forms, God, the idealized lady, and those universal patterns of human virtue no longer serve as sources of desire; instead of the triangulation of desire from these static referents, there is the mutually defining dynamic tension between self and other. In Shakespeare the comic hero introjects difference, setting it up as an intrapsychic function, whereby he can love himself loving and think of himself thinking. This kind of comedy I trace back to Aristophanes, the last Greek poet to capture concrete experience in language, to think in poetry, to see the world as a mirror rather than as a book. The comic tradition Shakespeare is working against is that of Menander, Plautus, and Terence, in which the hero's ability to define himself in his own terms is limited by social and political forces, but more basically, it is contradicted by philosophy: Menander is post-Platonic and figures in man's relations with women the anxiety of separation, the recognition of difference, the nostalgia for lost unity.

By placing in the lover himself the shaping fantasy that is set by Neoplatonic humanists in universal virtues, by the courtly love tradition in the lady, by Christian Neoplatonists in God, and by Plato himself in the Forms, Shakespeare comes full circle, as we have seen from the dynamics of desire in *The Two Gentlemen of Verona:* Plato's original pattern for philosophy was homoerotic, or rather autoerotic, and this is the pattern Shakespeare restores. I must explain then why grace is so crucial a concept in this period, receiving its final statement only in *The Winter's Tale*. It is not the grace of God or of the lady, but the lover's own gracing of his experience, a freedom he allows his world, so that he can enter into a mutually defining relation with it. It is a kind of irony based on unfilfilled expectations, an embrace of potential and change.

Change we know as "mutability" in Spenser and other English poets of the third quarter of the sixteenth century. They use it against the ageless, changeless forms of Neoplatonism which were still available for reference to their generation. Shakespeare sees change itself as the only referent.

One way to trace this development is as Aristotle's correction of Plato: the focus of Aristotle's universe is the Unmoved Mover, whereas the focus of Plato's is static—the Forms. Bacon sets up his idols on the pattern of Plato's lower forms of being, those imitations that confuse us: "The idols of the den" are the shadows seen by the men chained inside Plato's cave (*Republic*, VII).[1] The creation of these idols, though, can be used to deconstruct Bacon's and Plato's metaphysics. Bacon thought of the idols as images, products of the imagination, which falsely interprets actual experience; these interpretations should be corrected or canceled by reason. It is clear that for Bacon reason has content, "select and approved notions" (*Advancement of Learning*, V.1),[2] whereas certainly for Hobbes, and I think for Shakespeare, there is only "contentless reason": "REASON, in this sense, is nothing but *Reckoning* (that is, Adding and Subtracting) of the Consequences of generall names agreed upon, for the *marking* and *signifying* of our thoughts" (*Leviathan*, I.5). Shakespeare shows that the real danger comes not from false perception but from false projection, when we allow preconceived notions to distort our experience. Since men's experience is constantly changing, so should their minds: idols only erect themselves in idle minds. He shows no interest or belief in anything constant, thinking that constancy is not characteristic of nature, so it should not dominate our thinking about nature.

Another way of seeing Shakespeare's difference from this metaphysical tradition is as inductive reasoning against deductive reasoning. Plato, of course, claims that he uses only hypotheses, and treats them as hypotheses, until, through the operation of his dialectic, he approaches the Forms; this sounds like inductive reasoning, but the Forms are always already there, and the philosopher has some preunderstanding of them from his soul's experience in previous incarnations. That these Forms could exist separately and independently of things in the world seemed illogical to Aristotle, who maintained rather that universals exist only in particulars. From there to Hobbes' nominalism, where universals exist only in language, is not so long a step, and I think Shakespeare took it. Certainly the way was prepared for his thinking about what each individual sees and feels and thinks about himself by Montaigne: "I have had only myself as object of my thoughts" ("Of Practice" [1574]). Whereas the search for universals continued in Italy into the seventeenth century, probably because of the tremendous impact there of the Counter-Reformation, in northern Europe during the sixteenth century men became more and more concerned with themselves as independent of the vast structures erected by medieval theology. One need only compare the *Sonnets* of Shakespeare with those of Michelangelo: though a significant number in both collections is devoted to a fair youth, and the poet sees his younger, more beautiful self in the beloved (his ideal ego), Michelangelo seeks through that experience some revelation of absolute beauty, whereas Shakespeare is concerned only with his own sensual experience and his gracious transformation of it into art.[3]

Galileo was still reading the Book of Nature in 1615 ("Letter to the Grand Duchess Christina") and claiming his authority there, as opposed to the priests' appeal to the authority of the Bible, both texts being considered revelations of the Mind of God.[4] Paradoxically, it was Galileo, in his plotting of the seemingly independent movements of the individual planets, who inspired Hobbes to make his revolutionary statement of men's independence of each other and of any universal controlling forces. Here, too, Montaigne is an important precedent: "Our ordinary practice is to follow the inclinations of our appetite, to the left, to the right, uphill and down, as the wind of circumstance carries us" ("Of the Inconsistency of Our Actions" [1574]).

Aristotle's influence is also clear in the philosophy of art that began to emerge among Shakespeare's contemporaries. Sidney and Puttenham allow the poet direct access to the shared qualities of things; they do not think of the poet, as Plato does, as an imitator of imitations.[5] The poet orders experience and presents it in appreciable patterns. This is what Shakespeare means by "grace"; it is a way of looking at things, of seeing in them perhaps more than is actually there. Who has it, and how does it operate? Is it condescending, as God's grace is to the Christian, and the lady's love is to the courtly lover? In some ways it is a restoration of that reason of which Shakespeare chronicles the eclipse, a recentering of man in his universe after Copernican displacement. But the difference is radical: Shakespeare's world is mortal; he gives a lover no illusion that his lady will remain lovely after he ceases to love her, or that any of the patterns he sees in nature will survive his eyes. The immortality of art is another matter, and is likened to the fathering of children: Shakespeare sees a progression forward in time but it is characterized by change rather than by permanence. Children are like their fathers but are not the same as their fathers; he would not disapprove of the insistence of contemporary phenomenological criticism that art can be read in different ways because he certainly shows how variously nature can be read. A man's grip on nature is ephemeral and idiosyncratic: grace is to phenomenology what control is to metaphysics. One certain misreading of Shakespeare's comedies is to see in them new variations on old dichotomies. If man is not subjecting nature to his control, then neither is he subjecting women, peasants, and Jews. All these old hierarchies are collapsed, and random relations become the rule—like the relationship of Lear and Poor Tom.

It is indeed difficult to argue against the operation of misogyny in Shakespeare's plays. It becomes easier, though, in the mature comedies and in the late romances. The bald statements of women's subordination to men made by Luciana in *The Comedy of Errors* and by Katherina in *The Taming of the Shrew* are the cantus firmus against which totally contradictory harmonies are played in *A Midsummer Night's Dream* and *Much Ado About Nothing*. Men are shown to think of women as their grosser parts and to have wild fantasies of women's sexual appetites and infidelities, but the women are always proved true—to themselves and their husbands, if not to their fathers. Shakespeare returns in the late romances to this pattern of action where the chaste woman is tortured: Hermione is the apotheosis of the type, but Imogen and Marina suffer similar ordeals. Portia is a more difficult case, and Rosalind and Olivia also have a tendency to overwhelm, but in Viola, at least, we see a clear picture of a woman who has escaped the bondage of male expectations and prerogatives, precisely because she has been able to think of herself as a man.[6]

IV.1

A Midsummer Night's Dream

 hakespeare announces near the end of *A Midsummer Night's Dream* a paradoxical concern which is distinguishable in most of his major work: concord in discord. Hippolyta delights in the voice of Theseus' hounds:

> I never heard
> So musical a discord, such sweet thunder.
>
> (IV.1.116–17)

Theseus comments on the peaceful sleep of Lysander and Demetrius lying side by side:

> I know you two are rival enemies:
> How comes this gentle concord in the world,
> That hatred is so far from jealousy
> To sleep by hate, and fear no enmity?
>
> (IV.i.141–44)

Theseus, reading the abstract of the rustics' play, wonders, "How shall we find the concord of this discord?" (V.i.60). Almost immediately the resolution is sought in an audience's grace, both the royals' ability, in viewing the mechanicals, to "find sport in their intents" (V.i.79) and our ability, in viewing Shakespeare, to be gentle, not to reprehend, but to pardon, i.e., to behave differently from the nobles of *Love's Labor's Lost*.

We can trace discord itself back to the play's beginning and see it in all nature and attribute it to the dispute of Oberon and Titania over the Indian boy. After describing all the chaos in the seasons and in the elements, Titania concludes:

> And this same progeny of evils comes
> From our debate, from our dissension;
> We are their parents and original.
>
> (II.i.115–17)

I cannot agree with Olson that Oberon and Titania represent Reason and Passion, and that "here Oberon, king of fairies, has lost his sovereignty over Titania, and things are topsy-turvy."[1] He appropriately refers to "Ben Jonson's belief that the inventions of court drama 'should always lay hold on more remov'd mysteries.'"[2] It is clear that Jonson's aesthetic, his whole way of looking at the world, was typological, but it is just as clear that Shakespeare's was not. Olson's reading of *A Midsummer Night's Dream*, as we shall see, recalls the bold figures in the tradition of morality plays behind Shakespeare, but their conventional traits and conflicts are infinitely elaborated and finally contradicted by Shakespeare. What are the most jarring discords as the play proceeds, and how may we resolve them?

One contradiction occurs in the opening scene. Helena, considering that the general estimate of her beauty is as high as that of Hermia's, can only conclude that she has lost Demetrius' love for some other reason:

> Things base and vile, holding no quantity,
> Love can transpose to form and dignity:
> Love looks not with the eyes, but with the mind,
> And therefore is wing'd Cupid painted blind;
>
> (I.i.232–35)

It is on the eyes, however, that Oberon directs Puck to distill the wild pansy:

> The juice of it, on sleeping eyelids laid,
> Will make or man or woman madly dote
> Upon the next live creature that it sees.
>
> (II.i.170–72)

It is the visual element that Theseus stresses in the madness of the lover:

> the lover, all as frantic,
> Sees Helen's beauty in a brow of Egypt:
>
> (V.i.10–11)

One of the certainties in the play is that Helena is tall and fair, while Hermia is short and dark, so we know, at least, that at the beginning Demetrius and Lysander do not follow the Elizabethan taste in choosing Hermia. Unless, we think then, that Shakespeare, like Lévi-Strauss, plays on the flower's name *Pensée sauvage (Viola tricolor)*, and thus insists the mind is affected, the action of the play develops out of a literal interpretation of the figurative expression "Love is engendered in the eyes." We are asked then to consider the phenomenology of desire, against any claim that some metaphysical explanation might be found for it.

Theseus seems to contradict himself on a related theme at the end of the play. He dismisses the lovers' tale of their adventures as a trick of their imaginations:

> Such tricks hath strong imatination,
> That if it would but apprehend some joy,
> It comprehends some bringer of that joy:
>
> (V.i.18–20)

When Hippolyta complains, however, that the rustics are over-extending themselves, Theseus explains that all performances are but shadows, "and the worst are no worse, if imagination amend them." Hippolyta reasonably responds: "It must be your imagination then, and not theirs" (V.i.207–10).

Both these contradictions come in the consideration of interpretation. How do we love—according to sense experience (eyes) or preconceived notions (minds)? How do we see things generally (in both art and nature)—according to what actually happens or what we "image" or intend or will to happen? This play, then, deals most straight-forwardly, because most dramatically—it presents as physical act what elsewhere is only rhetorical figure—with the relation between erotic orientation and general worldview. It faces its own implied contradictions. Is there some concord in this discord?

It has been almost universally assumed that the play does not focus our attention on any one character, that, indeed, there is not much development or even delineation of character, that its appeal is rather that of farce, though certainly intellectual as well as erotic farce. It has also been assumed that what happens to the lovers is the play's closest approach to truth, so that Theseus is wrong in questioning their constancy; at the same time, of course, many insist that Theseus' speech on the lunatic, the lover, and the poet represents Shakespeare's attitude toward his own craft. More discord. I want to argue against those who discredit Theseus—both the conventional critics and the psychoanalytic critics—and to suggest that he plays a part much like that of Berowne in *Love's Labor's Lost* and the other young lovers of the early comedies, i.e., as a man both introspective and analytic in his experience of love. He asks not only "What is happening to me?" but also "How am I responding to it?" I do not think he learns as much about love as Berowne does, or that he passes so clearly through the stages of love that Antipholus of Syracuse and Proteus do. I think that he is originally misogynistic like Petruchio, but that this is one of those discords which his grace finally allows him to harmonize, in his own mind.

Theseus announces after hearing the lovers' reports:

> More strange than true. I never may believe
> These antique fables, nor these fairy toys.
> Lovers and madmen have such seething brains,
> Such shaping fantasies, that apprehend
> More than cool reason ever comprehends.
>
> (V.i.2–6)

Young[3] and Fender[4] note the difference in Elizabethan usage between "apprehend" and "comprehend." Apprehension is the mental seizing of an isolated, concrete event, while comprehension is the integration of a particular perception into a previously formed structure of knowledge, a generalization. We shall consider soon why these critics think the latter more characteristic of Theseus, but now let us only consider what it is that Theseus calls "fables" and "toys," the products of the lovers' "seething brains" and "shaping fantasies." We do not know precisely, because their reports take place offstage. We surmise that they tell him what we have seen: how they all four entered the wood (Lysander and Hermia followed by Helena and Demetrius); how Hermia had a dreadful dream and awoke to find herself deserted by Lysander; how Lysander suddenly fell in love with Helena, who did not believe him sincere; how Demetrius then fell in love with Helena, and she doubted him, too; how Helena and Hermia abused each other verbally and Demetrius and Lysander began to fight physically; how they all fell asleep and woke to find themselves paired off as they had once been—Demetrius and Helena, Lysander and Hermia. What is true in all this? It did, of course, happen, but why? and with what significance?

Oberon caused all the confusion—or, rather, he began it all, and Puck compounded it. The King of the Fairies scolds his servant:

> What hast thou done? Thou hast mistaken quite,
> And laid the love-juice on some true love's sight;
> Of thy misprision must perforce ensue
> Some true love turn'd, and not a false turn'd true.
>
> (III.ii.88–91)

But Puck responds:

> Then fate o'er-rules, that, one man holding troth,
> A million fail, confounding oath on oath.
>
> (III.ii.92–93)

We can accept Oberon's claim that Demetrius' love for Helena was true and his love for Hermia false, that Lysander's love for Hermia was true and his love for Helena is now false. Girard has explained this as the operation of mimetic love: Demetrius only began to love Hermia because Lysander loved her; he did not trust his actual love for Helena, but assimilated to Lysander's pattern.[5] Puck's rejoinder, though, is equally convincing: my mistake, he says, goes with the way of the world, since most men are not true in love; therefore Lysander is now false, with all men, rather than true alone.

Why has Oberson interfered? He just happened to have the eye-drops on hand because of his planned deception of Titania. He thinks that if he puts her under a particularly loathsome spell, she will acquiesce in his demand to possess the Indian boy, if only to be released from that spell:

> Having once this juice,
> I'll watch Titania when she is asleep,
> And drop the liquor of it in her eyes:
> The next thing then she waking looks upon
> (Be it on lion, bear, or wolf, or bull,
> On meddling monkey, or on busy ape)
> She shall pursue it with the soul of love.
> And ere I take this charm from off her sight
> (As I can take it with another herb)
> I'll make her render up her page to me.
>
> (II.i.176–85)

At this point the young lovers stumble in, and so are accidentally involved in his plan. That accident is then compounded by Puck's error, so that what Theseus hears from them is more strange than true. What they have seen has been a comedy of errors begun by a god who is jealous and vindictive. Can we even say that his deception reveals their true desires or the true nature of human love?

Kermode sees great significance in Bottom's dream, i.e., what Bottom takes to be a dream, but what we know to have been his actual experience: Titania's infatuation with him. Kermode thinks Shakespeare presents this to us as a mystery, that because Bottom reports his dream in a parody of St. Paul, we are to understand that he has been vouchsafed a true vision.

I have had a most rare vision. I have had a dream, past the wit of man to say what dream it was. Man is but an ass if he go about to expound this dream. . . . The eye of man hath not heard, the ear of man hath not seen, man's hand is not able to taste, his tongue to conceive, nor his heart to report, what my dream was. (IV.i.203–12)

Eye hath not seen, nor ear heard, neither have entered into the heart of man the things which God hath prepared for them that love him . . . Which things also we speak, not in the words which man's wisdom teacheth, but which the Holy Ghost teacheth. (I Cor. ii.9ff.)

Bottom is there to tell us that the blindness of love, the dominance of the mind over the eye, can be interpreted as a means to grace as well as to irrational animalism; that the two aspects are, perhaps, inseparable.[6]

Certainly the pattern is correct: in Christian experience one opens oneself to God's grace not by seeking to understand His nature, but by accepting all He gives: thus Bottom, in all his bestialism, is closer to God's grace than those who would attempt to understand, and thereby only project their feeble images upon His perfect being. I think, however, that this reading of the parody of St. Paul in Bottom's speech is out of context. What Bottom has seen in his dream is Titania loving him as an ass, and Titania only loves him as an ass because Oberon has altered her erotic vision. The most we can claim that Bottom has seen is Oberon's projection onto Titania of his own fantasy of her sexuality. If we examine that fantasy, and see it not only in the context of the forest scenes, but also as framed by the court scenes, I think we must decide that the function of the parody of St. Paul is not to restore the mystic experience of St. Paul but to put all mystic experience in question. The mystery is that there is no mystery: truth exists only in concrete, individual experience, and not as some divine plan or absolute form which determines experience.

It is generally recognized that Shakespeare was inspired by Apuleius to metamorphose Bottom into an ass and make him attractive in that form to a woman. The *Metamorphoses* of Apuleius were available to Shakespeare in Adlington's translation, *The XI Bookes of the Golden Asse containinge the Metamorphoses of Lucius Apuleius*. Bullough, in citing this source for *A Midsummer Night's Dream* omits the crucial passage.[7] Even Adlington expurgates *propter honestatem;* I offer a full translation of the passage where Lucius describes his intercourse with a woman while he is an ass:

But she, as often as I, to spare her, pulled back my hips, so often did she yield herself with wild exertion, and pressing my spine down upon her cling with closer embraces, so that by Hercules, I thought I might fail to satisfy her, nor did I think it was for nothing that the Minotaur's mother took pleasure with a bellowing bull.[8]

Perhaps we should recall that the Minotaur's mother was Pasiphaë, who mated with a bull to produce that monster, and that the Minotaur's half-sisters—their father was Minos, not the bull—were Adriadne and Phaedra, who both attracted Theseus, one before he married Hippolyta, the other after. (The liaison with Ariadne is mentioned at II.i.80.) Certainly these myths meditate on the sexual insatiability of women, as seen through the eyes of man; Apuleius took that as his theme, and I believe Shakespeare did, too. We must not think of the ass as just a foolish creature, but as the prototype for ungovernable libido. The size of the ass's genitals is proverbial;[9] there might be some suggestion of this, through displacement upwards, in Titania's attention to the ass's ears:

> Come sit thee down upon this flowery bed,
> While I thy amiable cheeks do coy,
> And stick musk-roses in thy sleek smooth head,
> And kiss thy fair large ears, my gentle joy.
>
> (IV.i.1–4)

Roses are essential in Apuleius: when Lucius eats them as an ass, he returns to his human form. In another version of the story, discussed below, a coronal of roses graces the lover.

It is generally acknowledged that Apuleius adapted his story from Lucian, or that they had a common source which Lucian followed more closely than Apuleius. Apuleius adapted the story of the man metamorphosed into an ass to his own satyric purpose, ending with an account of the hero's conversion to a celibate life in worship of Isis. Lucian's account ends not with such a conversion, but rather with a return of the hero, in human form, to the woman he had had intercourse with as an ass. The sequel suggests to me Shakespeare's basic concern:

I thought that I'd appear more handsome in my human form. Indeed she welcomed me, enraptured, it seemed, by my odd adventure. She even invited me to dine and pass the night with her. I accepted, considering it would be unseemly if, after having been loved in my ass's skin, I showed disdain on becoming once more a man and scorned my old mistress. So I dined with her salved in scents and crowned with those beloved roses to which I owed my return to the world of men. When the hour grew late, and the time came for bed, I rose, and thinking to do a pretty act, I threw off my clothes and making myself quite naked, imagining I would please the woman far more when she compared me with the ass. But she, seeing that I was really a man, threw a glance of scorn on me and cried out, "Go and kick up your heels far away

from me and my house. Go and make your bed where you will, but not here."
"What crime then have I committed?" I asked her. "By the Lord on high,"
she said, "It wasn't you, it was the ass, that I fell in love with. It was with
him, not with you, that I lay. I thought you'd still have, even in your present
form, that great appendage of the ass, but I see that instead of that charming
and useful animal, you've changed into an absurd monkey.[10]

I have argued above that Shakespeare restores to the Neoplatonic courtly
love tradition the original form of love in Plato, the *erastēs-erōmenos*
relationship, without necessarily having had access to the *Symposium*
and the *Phaidros*. I argue here that Shakespeare restores to the story
of the metamorphosis of a man into an ass, and his sexual adventures
in that form, the essential concern of the original story: the insatiable
sexual desire of women, their preference for beasts with huge phalluses to men. I insist, though, that we not take this view of women as
Shakespeare's own or even as the argument of the play; it is not the
truth revealed to Bottom, but only the projection onto Titania of
Oberson's own nightmare image of her, the kind of debasement we
have considered elsewhere. So framed is this view of women by irony
and parody that we must be careful to unravel its implications.

Titania's love for Bottom as an ass is the center-piece of the play.
We cannot deny that it happens; we only question its significance. It
must be seen in relation to the opening and closing scenes. Egeus and
Theseus carefully develop the argument that Lysander has usurped the
place of her father in Hermia's heart and mind:

Ege. Thou, thou, Lysander, thou hast given her rhymes,
  And interchang'd love tokens with my child:
  Thou hast by moonlight at her window sung
  With faining voice verses of feigning love,
  And stol'n the impression of her fantasy
  . . . .
  With cunning hast thou filch'd my daughter's heart,
  Turn'd her obedience (which is due me)
  To stubborn harshness. . . . (I.i.28–38)

The. What say you, Hermia? Be advis'd, fair maid.
  To you your father should be as a god:
  One that compos'd your beauties, yea, and one
  To whom you are but as a form in wax
  By him imprinted, and within his power
  To leave the figure, or disfigure it. (I. (I.i.46–51)

The phrase "And stol'n the impression of her fantasy" is ambiguous: does it mean that Lysander stole an impression that already was set in her mind, or that he stole in and made a false impression of his own? The latter is supported by the following "With cunning hast thou filch'd my daughter's heart," but the former by Theseus' metaphor of Hermia being but an impression of her father, as if he were a seal and stamped himself upon her. We shall find in the late romances development of the theme that the daughter is an image of the father, and that his love for her is then, in a way, narcissistic and nostalgic, related to a young lover's choice of a friend like himself as his object of desire, and then his choice of a young woman dressed as a young man like himself. In *Othello* we see another father's wrath when his daughter chooses a lover without his permission: only that play rivals this in equating the erotic with the bestial. Brabantio is susceptible to Iago's metaphor "An old black ram is tupping your white ewe." He warns Othello, "Look to her, Moor, if thou hast eyes to see;/ She has betrayed her father and may thee"; Othello sees the sexual world as so many "Goats and monkeys."

Animals appear elsewhere in the play besides in Oberon's fantasy projected upon Titania: Helena sees herself as a bear (II.ii.93); she would become a fawning dog (II.i.203–7); Lysander would cast Hermia from him like a snake (III.ii.260–61), after she has dreamed that a snake ate her heart and Lysander laughed (II.ii.144–49). I do not follow Girard's argument that "the animal images are part of the process which leads from mimetic desire to myth; . . . the animal images are the price the self has to pay for its idolatrous worship of otherness." I do, however, agree with him that the animal images "express the self-abasement of the lover in front of his idol."[11] There is in Shakespeare enough of the medieval division of the world into three parts—angelic, human, animal—to explain this polarization: by idealizing one's object of desire, one debases oneself. While appreciating these dynamics, I think the animal imagery is as much content as abstract form: it is not just an extreme, but a particular extreme. What is most amazing is that the animal images cluster around the women. If female sexuality is at issue in the beginning and middle of the play, as discord, is there anything at the end of the play to make of it a concord?

What does Hippolyta mean by "something of great constancy"? Why is it she who tries to correct Theseus' attribution of the lover's experience to their imaginations?

Hip. But all the story of the night told over,
    And all their minds transfigur'd so together,
    More witnesseth than fancy's images,
    And grows to something of great constancy;
    But howsoever, strange and admirable. (V.i.23–27)

We have seen that all the lovers could agree on is the change in their affections, and that this was caused by Oberon. He does not treat them so harshly as he treats Titania, since he causes them only to fall in love with the next person they see, not the next beast:

                    Having once this juice,
        I'll watch Titania when she is asleep,
        And drop the liquor of it in her eyes:
        The next thing then she waking looks upon
        (Be it on lion, bear, or wolf, or bull,
        On meddling monkey, or on busy ape)
        She shall pursue it with the soul of love.

                                (II.i.176–82)

        What thou seest when thou dost wake,
        Do it for thy true love take;
        Love and languish for his sake.
        Be it ounce, or cat, or bear,
        Pard, or boar with bristled hair,
        In thy eye that shall appear
        When thou wak'st, it is thy dear.
        Wake when some vile thing is near.

                                (II.ii.26–33)

Hermia first uses the term "vile" in her disquisition on love:

        Things base and vile, holding no quantity,
        Love can transpose to form and dignity:

                                (I.i.232–33)

She seems to base her contrast solely on value, so that her sense of "vile" is the same as the Latin *vilis;* this is not, however, the most frequent sense of the term in Elizabethan English (*OED*, A.5). It is more often used to denote moral depravity in people (*OED*, A.1–2), and occasionally this use is extended to animals, presumably through the attribution to animals, being deprived of reason, of only the appetitive functions (*OED*, A.2.b). Lysander says on waking to his new love, Helena:

> Where is Demetrius? O how fit a word
> Is that vile name to perish on my sword.
>
> (II.ii.105–6)

Lysander casts Hermia from him:

> Hang off, thou cat, thou burr! Vile thing, let loose,
> Or I will shake thee from me like a serpent.
>
> (III.ii.260–61)

(In "Pyramus and Thisby" the lion is thrice called "vile"—but the wall is also twice "vile".) Shakespeare makes a point with this word which was clearer to his original audience; they would have more readily associated erotic desire with animals. Kermode cites Bacon's "Of love":

Made for the contemplation of heaven and all noble objects, should [man] do nothing but kneel before a little idol, and make himself subject, though not of the mouth (as beasts are) yet of the eye which was given them for higher purposes?

"Animal imagery" then becomes a complex concept and phenomenon: animals can only feel physical desire, a purely appetitive instinct, because they cannot contemplate a higher form of love; they cannot make images. We saw in *Love's Labor's Lost* that the concept of idolatry is generally complex: men make of living women static objects of desire that reflect themselves. Obviously animals cannot do this. Is Shakespeare showing, then, that animals love in a purer, less idolatrous way than men do? This seems unlikely, but it might be one step in a more elaborate argument. Kermode thinks Bottom combines the animal and the spiritual in his vision of love, but I question whether Bottom or any other Shakespearean character has access to such a world of spirits, to truth beyond experience. What is man left with, then, if he is denied "spiritual love"? What happens when the systems of idolatry are short-circuited so that man cannot love either what he wants to see of himself in others, or what he wants to see of himself in his gods?

What if a man is left alone with a woman who refuses to be a mirror, but insists on being?

Hippolyta seems to be such a woman. We cannot but see in her an arresting variation on the transvestized heroine: as an Amazon that is her constant mode.[12] We are shocked when Theseus says to her:

> Hippolyta, I woo'd thee with my sword,
> And won thy love doing thee injuries;
>
> (I.i.16–17)

We are reminded of Othello's account of his wooing of Desdemona; we wonder whether the woman in each case agrees with the man's suggestion that she finds his violence attractive. This play does not, however, encourage us to question the woman. Rather, I am convinced, it forces us to see Theseus and Oberon as two aspects or stages in the development of one man's attitude toward female sexuality. Again, it should be noted how the marriage preparations frame the adventures of the lovers in the wood, and how these adventures frame the love of Titania for Bottom as an ass, which is Oberon's deception. The conflation of Theseus and Oberon, Hippolyta and Titania, is encouraged by the fairies' admission that they have had previous relations with the royals:

> *Tit.*   Why art thou here,
>   Come from the farthest step of India,
>   But that, forsooth, the bouncing Amazon,
>   Your buskin'd mistress and your warrior love,
>   To Theseus must be wedded, and you come
>   To give their bed joy and prosperity?
> *Obr.* How canst thou thus, for shame, Titania,
>   Glance at my credit with Hippolyta,
>   Knowing I know thy love to Theseus?
>   Didst not thou lead him through the glimmering night
>   From Perigouna, whom he ravished;
>   And make him with fair Aegles break his faith,
>   With Ariadne and Antiopa?
> *Tit.* These are the forgeries of jealousy:
>   And never, since the middle summer's spring,
>   Met we on hill, in dale, forest or mead. (II.i.68–83)

If Theseus is Oberon, then there is a recognizable sequence to the orientation of his desire. First there is aggression against a woman who fights like a man; when she is subdued, the man can imagine sexual union with her. He can also imagine, however, once he sees her as a woman, that she will be sexually insatiable, that he could never possibly be enough for her, that her appetites will be bestial. Finally, he tries to put down these fantasies, to convince himself that these are the mad imaginings of a seething brain, and that he can shape them to his needs gracefully.

If Oberon is Theseus then there is some sense to the discord over the Indian boy, which is the first condition for all the play's action. Olson suggests that he represents Ganymede, as Ganymede represents in the old emblematic tradition the soul: "Ganymede's tale was commonly thought to be a parable of the capture of man's rational soul by the love of God." Ganymede, throughout the Middle Ages and the Renaissance, is the type of the *erōmenos*, the younger male beloved of the older male *erastēs*, just as he was in antiquity.[13] We shall meet him in *As You Like It* as Rosalind's male persona. If we can see the Indian boy as Ganymede, then he represents for Oberon, and by identification, also for Theseus, some form of naricissistic object-choice, spontaneously arising as protection against the threat of mature female sexuality. This might seem improbable if the Indian boy is thought of as a child, even an infant, as Titania suggests when she describes the presumably recent death of his mother giving birth to him (II.i.122–35). We need only recall, however, the gradual rejuvenation of Eros from antiquity to the Renaissance: he begins as a pubescent boy and ends up as a baby. Does this mean that the psychosexual significance of the figure has changed, or just the aesthetic of the representation? That the Indian boy is an Eros figure cannot be doubted, and by my definition that means he represents an archaic self-image. Thus the male facing marriage nostalgically returns to an earlier, easier pattern of desire. Theseus, unlike Petruchio, finds some protection against the phantoms of his own misogyny. Union with the other need not mean loss of self.

Holland claims that "throughout the play, the ruler, the father, the lovers, the king of the fairies, the amateur actors, and even the audience at the play within the play—all proclaim love, but they also threaten violence or humiliation."[14] Faber finds an imposition of "masculine control over unruly impulses associated with the lack of proper boundaries between male and female."[15] Olson sees Theseus in *A Midsummer Night's Dream* as not unlike Theseus in *The Two Noble Kinsmen:* marriage is a "natural" imposition of the masculine over the feminine.[16] Young sees Theseus as the consummate politician, organizing and controlling.[17] If, however, we see the dream as Theseus' and its resolution as his attempt to deal with his own fears and desires,[18] if we admit that Shakespeare never posits anything constant in nature and certainly no absolute truth available to man's reason, if we recognize the elaborate identification between the animal world and women and man's unconscious, then perhaps we will be less inclined to see Theseus as a pompous ass, a royal Bottom. In this reading the problem of the play is Theseus' imagination and its control by reason, but it is not Imagination and Reason. It is a bridegroom's nightmare, shared by Othello and, retrospectively, by Leontes. The several ways of dealing with women are the several modes of seeing women—transvestized, idealized, debased. All fail, just as the several ways of philosophizing nature—Christian Neoplatonism, humanism, scientificism—all fail. Man is left with his actual experience of the world and women, which is chaotic. He requires then the organizing force of art and his own natural grace to orient himself to their constant change.

The concord of discords is first achieved in Theseus' own mind, and then projected upon his world, a version of pathetic fallacy, perhaps, but not totally reprehensible. What else is there after all, Shakespeare asks us? Without God or the Forms to order human experience, the individual must create his own reality. Theseus' grace, which transforms the rustics' play and his whole world, but particularly his way of thinking about women, is, then, at the end of the play, what Helena says love is at the beginning of the play:

> Things base and vile, holding no quantity,
> Love can transpose to form and dignity.

> (I.i.232–33)

He might still *fear* women, but he will *think* the best of them. "Pyramus and Thisby," a romance in which love kills, is another way of thinking about women. Thus Shakespeare gives us not one but two failed patterns of men's imagining of women, debasement in the dream and idealization in the play. He suggests that there are other alternatives, but does not present them here; they become the subplot of *Much Ado About Nothing* and the main plots of *As You Like It* and *Twelfth Night*.

IV.2

Much Ado About Nothing

uch Ado About Nothing is a fascinating play, and finally satisfying if we allow our attention to shift from the romantic
protagonists, Hero and Claudio, in the main plot to the narcissistic subordinates, Beatrice and Benedick. It is closer in tone and
moral cast to *Measure for Measure* and *All's Well* than to the other
comedies of this period. Like *Measure for Measure* it has a prince who
messes about in the love life of his courtiers, and like *All's Well* it has
an unregenerate hero. For our purposes, though—tracing the orientation of desire in the comedies, and noting how it reflects and informs
worldview generally—the major interest is the correction made by the
love match in the subplot of the love match in the main plot. Hero is
completely passive and unimpressive; Claudio is first ineffective in love,
then effusive, then offensive, and finally frivolous. There is a pattern
to his behavior, a discernible consistency in his character, and it is that
same self-imposed role of the warrior, ferocious in battle but clumsy
in love, that so deforms Bertram and is the type against which
Othello's unique tragedy is played. It is this same polarity between sex
and violence that forces our attention on Beatrice and Benedick, because they not only articulate it precisely in their commentary on the
romance of Hero and Claudio, but they mediate and transcend it
through their wit.

It is clear that Beatrice is cast against the type of Katherina; Leonato and Antonio call her "shrewd" and "curst" (II.i.16–19), and she says of herself:

> And, Benedick, love on, I will requite thee,
> Taming my wild heart to thy loving hand.
>
> (III.i.111–12)

Katherina is not clever, however, nor finally as self-willed. Beatrice has strong sexual appetites; indeed she develops the analogy between sex and food and expresses the violence in both loving and eating:

Beat. I pray you, how many hath he killed and eaten in these wars? But how many hath he killed? For indeed I promised to eat all of his killing. (I.i.38–40)

Beat. Is it possible disdain should die, while she hath such meet food to feed it as Signoir Benedick? (I.i.110–11)

Bene. By my sword, Beatrice, thou lovest me.
Beat. Do not swear and eat it.
Bene. I will swear by it that you love me, and I will make him eat it that says I love not you.
Beat. Will you eat your word?
Bene. With no sauce that can be devised to it. I protest I love thee.(IV.i.273–79)

This last leads, of course, to Beatrice's demand, "Kill Claudio!" To understand the full significance of that, we must follow its preparation in all the attention to seeming and being, to men of fashion and men of action, to men of words and men of deeds, to men and women generally. We can note now, however, that several traditional identifications, important to the earlier comedies, come together here to create a new dimension of identity.

Beatrice and Benedick are at war with each other, their tongues being their swords, whereas the other men and women divide their libidinal and aggressive pursuits. Claudio, the conventional lover, gives us a conventional statement of the convention:

Claud. When you went onward on this ended action,
I look'd upon her with a soldier's eye,
That lik'd, but had a rougher task in hand
Than to drive liking to the name of love:
But now I am return'd, and that war-thoughts

Have left their places vacant, in their rooms
Come thronging soft and delicate desires,
All prompting me how fair young Hero is,
Saying I lik'd her ere I went to wars.(I.i.277–85)

It is fortunate for Claudio, who can speak no better than this, that he
has Don Pedro to speak for him. Beatrice and Benedick can speak for
themselves, in way of war:

There is a kind of merry war betwixt Signior Benedick and her: they never
meet but there's a skirmish of wit between them.(I.i.55–58)

In the last act there are several derogatory remarks about the confusion of witty tongues with swords: Antonio to Claudio (V.i.124ff.) and
Benedick to Claudio(V.i.182ff.). Then in a brief exchange Benedick
and Margaret supply the missing signifier:

Bene. Pray thee, sweet Mistress Margaret, deserve well at my hands, by help-
ing me to the speech of Beatrice.
Marg. Will you then write me a sonnet in praise of my beauty?
Bene. In so high a style, Margaret, that no man living shall come over it, for
in most comely truth thou deservest it.
Marg. To have no man come over me? Why, shall I always keep below stairs?
Bene. Thy wit is as quick as the greyhound's mouth, it catches.
Marg. And yours as blunt as the fencer's foils, which hit, but hurt not.
Bene. A most manly wit, Margaret, it will not hurt a woman. And so I pray
thee call Beatrice; I give thee the bucklers.
Marg. Give us the swords, we have bucklers of our own.
Bene. If you use them, Margaret, you must put in the pikes with a vice, and
they are dangerous weapons for maids.
Marg. Well, I will call Beatrice to you, who I think hath legs.
Bene. And therefore will come.(V.ii.1–24)

We know tongues as swords in the battle of wits, but now the identification between swords and penises is made explicit.[1] With the talk
of blunt swords that will not hurt, and pikes (spikes) vised into bucklers (shields), we are forced to think of sexual intercourse as a violent
encounter which men and women nevertheless take pleasure in. (If we
think of this complex of associations in tragic rather than comic contexts, we see that Desdemona is both witty and courtly, as well as ad-
miring, if not envious, of her husband's martial prowess; in Emilia we
see wit as the means of expressing women's sexual desires, just as it is

here with Margaret. Shakespeare then condemns women to death for their wit and desires in tragedy while he makes them triumphant in comedy. Portia, I think, is somewhere in between.) Kernberg notes the importance of ambivalence in erotic relations; libidinal and aggressive impulses combine only if good and bad object-images are combined.[2] He even insists that satisfying heterosexual relationships involve some projection of homosexual desires:

> It seems to me the normal love relationships include the following pre-conditions: first—at the level of actual sexual behavior—having the capacity for broadening and deepening the experience of sexual intercourse and orgasm with the expanded sexual eroticism derived from the integration of aggression and bisexuality (sublimatory homosexual identification) into the heterosexual erotic relationship; second, having developed an object relation in depth . . . third, having developed depersonification, abstraction, and individualization in the super-ego.[3]

Certainly Margaret and Benedick summarize here the whole play's consideration of sexual roles. This is particularly important after Beatrice's outburst:

Beat. O that I were a man! (IV.i.302)

Beat. O God that I were a man! I would eat his heart in the market-place.(IV.i.305–6)

Beat. O that I were a man for his sake, or that I had any friend would be a man for my sake! But manhood is melted into curtsies, valour into compliment, and men are only turned into tongue, and trim ones too: he is now as valiant as Hercules that only tells a lie and swears it. I cannot be a man with wishing, therefore I will die a woman with grieving.(IV.i.316–23)

Now this clearly fits the context of those other considerations of the seeming and being of men—Borachio's diatribe on fashion (III.iii.127–34) and the attacks on Claudio by Antonio and Leonato (V.i.45–109) and by Benedick (V.i.110–90).[4] Indeed yet another masculine accoutrement enters into the discussion: we have heard of penises, swords, and tongues, but we also hear of beards. Beatrice thinks a man without a beard is not a man, but a woman or a boy (II.i.30–37); Benedick calls Claudio "lackbeard" (V.i.190); Antonio speaks of "fashion-mongering boys" (V.i.94). Shakespeare's sexual perspective then seems to be that boys are like women, but with the potential to become men, whereas women can wish to become men, as Beatrice does to avenge Hero, but must die—perhaps there is even a sexual suggestion here—as women.[5]

As Hunter has shown,[6] it was first Lyly who introduced wit into dramatic love relationships and thereby freed women from the passivity imposed upon them by the medieval romance tradition. Shakespeare goes much further: by first identifying wit and warfare, and then giving women wit, he makes it possible for them to beat men at their own game. That, however, is a social issue; my concern is the erotic. What Shakespearean comedy shows again and again is that men want women to be like men, and *Much Ado About Nothing* makes the strongest statement of this so far in the corpus. Claudio and Hero follow the conventional pattern of love-relationships, and their union is diastrous; Beatrice and Benedick break all the rules and their union is perfect. It seems not to frighten Benedick that Beatrice wants to be a man; he has not Petruchio's fear of women. It seems that Theseus dominates Hippolyta; it seems that Rosalind dominates Orlando; Beatrice and Benedick are in perfect equilibrium. In *Much Ado About Nothing* the violence is sublimated. It is not with swords and genitals but with tongues that they fight. We see the preparation for the belligerent equality of Beatrice in the transvestism of Julia, and, of course, we see in Beatrice preparation for Portia, Rosalind, and Viola, those young women who will completely dominate the other comedies of this middle period.[7] Why is that figure satisfying? How does she represent the fulfillment of men's desires? Again, Kernberg is suggestive:

In men, the predominant pathology of love relations derived from oedipal conflicts takes the form of fear of and insecurity vis-a-vis women and reaction formations against such insecurity in the form of reactive and/or projected hostility and guilt toward the maternal figure. Pre-genital conflicts, particularly conflicts around pre-genital aggression, are intimately condensed with genital conflicts. . . . In men, pre-genital aggression, envy and fear of women reinforce oedipal fears and feelings of inferiority toward them: the pre-genital envy of mother reinforces the oedipally determined insecurity of men regarding idealized women.[8]

There can be no question that Claudio represents this pathology: he idealizes Hero, then loves her correspondance to an idealized image and not her actual being; because he still feels antagonistic toward both the pre-oedipal image of the mother as all-powerful, and the oedipal image as all-sexual, he readily mis-sees Hero as whore, and denounces her in the most scathing misogynistic terms.

Benedick, on the other hand, is reassured by Beatrice's assimilation to his type. She is aggressive, surely, but in such a way that he can fight back. Her threat is, as it were, up front: genital, lingual, martial. She is not the void of nonbeing that the pre-oedipal mother can seem, or the sexually insatiable oedipal mother. She is a clear and present danger, not a veiled threat. She is, indeed, his mirror image. Benedick finds in Beatrice the combination of friend and lover which previous Shakespearean comic heroes had pursued in separate objects. His union with her is then a restoration of the total self-referentiality of primary narcissism: he desires what he is and is what he desires. There is no other. His identity is in his tension with this mirror image of himself. Therein lies his being, not by some reference to an hypostasis of desire, an idealized object, a metaphysical constant. In this we see again the conjunction between Shakespeare's analysis of love and his whole worldview. Our overwhelming impression at the end of *Much Ado About Nothing* is of Benedick's superiority to the other male characters: he has achieved the most satisfying sexual union and with it complete self-knowledge. He is the secure center in a chaotic universe. The strongest statement of this occurs directly before the innocence of Hero is proved and therefore his duel with Claudio canceled. Benedick moves through three stages of identifying himself—first, as antagonist to Claudio:

But I must tell thee plainly, Claudio undergoes my challenge, and either I must shortly hear from him, or I will subscribe him a coward.(V.ii.53–56)

Then, as Beatrice's lover:

And I pray thee now tell me, for which of my bad parts didst thou first fall in love with me? . . . I do suffer love indeed, for I love thee against my will. . . . Thou and I are too wise to woo peaceably. (V.ii.56–66)

And finally as a man who knows himself:

If a man do not erect in this age his own tomb ere he dies, he shall live no longer in monument than the bell rings, and the widow weeps. . . . Therefore, it is most expedient for the wise, if Don Worm, his conscience, find no impediment to the contrary, to be the trumpet of his own virtues, as I am to myself. So much for praising myself, who I myself will bear witness is praise-worthy.(V.ii.71–81)

Benedick has introjected Beatrice's image of a perfect man, loved her for making him see himself in that image—a kind of mutually narcissistic relationship, since she describes the man she would be, which becomes the man she loves—and now he sees himself clearly.

When Claudio and Don Pedro try to nag Benedick about his capitulation to love, he disdains even to answer, knowing they are incapable of understanding what he has discovered:

A college of wit-crackers cannot flout me out of my humour. . . . Since I do purpose to marry, I will think nothing to any purpose that the world can say against it; and therefore never flout at me for what I have said against it; for man is a giddy thing, and this is my conclusion.(V.iv.99–107)

How do Beatrice and Benedick love each other? As reason itself (V.iv.74–77), and there is no higher authority. Note that here reason is not some sort of external force operating upon men's minds to shape their experience (as Descartes' passive acceptance of that force is the only way to self-knowledge), but rather reason is self-knowledge, which comes through a disparagement of the world and its expectations, and a fulfillment of one's own individual desire to recapture in one's own beloved the perfect, original image of oneself.

We must note also that the resurrection of Hero prefigures the resurrection of Hermione in *The Winter's Tale*. Both women have been wrongly accused of sexual crimes and their lovers made to lament their false judgement; thus, when they give themselves a second time to their husbands, this is the greatest grace and favor. Claudio accused Hero of seeming rather than being good, and she disputed him:

Claud. She's but the sign and semblance of her honour.(IV.i.32)

Claud. I never tempted her with word too large,
 But, as a brother to his sister, show'd
 Bashful sincerity and comely love.
Hero. And seem'd I ever otherwise to you?
Claud. Out on thee, seeming! I will write against it.
 You seem to me as Dian in her orb,
 As chaste as is the bud ere it be blown;
 But you are more intemperate in your blood
 Than Venus, or those pamper'd animals
 That rage in savage sensuality.(IV.i.52–61)

Claudio makes here the same kind of mistake that Berowne and his
friends make:

> The ladies did change favours, and then we,
> Following the signs, woo'd but the sign of she.

(LLL V.ii.468–69)

But, whereas Berowne only confuses one lady for another behind the
sign, Claudio actually confuses the sign for the lady, and then accuses
her of making that confusion herself. He has an image of the perfect
woman, the moon goodess, to which he will force Hero's assimilation.
Needless to say, it is an idealized, desexualized maternal image, a denial of all those fears and loathings that we know prey upon him and
keep him "infantile." Claudio rejoices in the restitution of this image
after the revelation of Don John's deception:

> Sweet Hero! Now thy image doth appear
> In the rare semblance that I lov'd it first.

(V.i.245–46)

It is much easier for Claudio to love a dead woman than a living, aging, changing woman, who in her cycles will fulfill and contradict all
his fears and desires of the female.

There is a significant echo of Claudio's comparing Hero, in her sup-
posed intemperance, to "pamper'd animals," in Hermione's description of herself and other women:

> I prithee tell me: cram 's with praise and make 's
> As fat as tame things: one good deed, dying tongueless,
> Slaughters a thousand, waiting upon that.
> Our praises are our wages. You may ride 's
> With one soft kiss a thousand furlongs ere
> With spur we heat an acre.

(WT I.ii.91–96)

This adds fuel to the fire of Leontes' madness. The image is first of
some guinea hen or rabbit being fattened for the table, but then these
creatures breed in captivity, having nothing else to do. That is what
Claudio and Leontes think of women, that they live "dully sluggardis'd at home" with nothing to do but think about sex. They are
Othello's "goats and monkeys," Oberon's "love-in-idleness."

Kirsch has shown how Claudio's misperception of Hero is based on his idealization of her.[9] He cannot see her properly, because he sees with other men's eyes, the mind of the past, the myth of women's infidelity and sexual insatiability. Girard compares Cervantes, Molière, and Dostoevsky on the hell of choosing love by another's eyes.[10] We have already noted the resemblance to *Don Quixote*, where Cardenio misreads an actual scene and sees his fiancée marry another man.[11] What these lovers lose is the actuality of their own experience: by insisting on reference to what they think are constant patterns in human experience, they are blinded to the present. Again, we might attempt to understand this both as a particular moment in the evolution of men's ways of looking at the world—Foucault's classical episteme: the representation of representation—and as a recurrent problem in psychosexuality. Claudio and Leontes, like Cardenio, have a preunderstanding of women, based on myth and romance; they impose it upon actual women, especially those they love. Shakespeare and Cervantes take an ironic view of this, showing us that men compulsively misread things, especially women. (Cervantes also, of course, shows us that Don Quixote's misreadings are sometimes right, and almost always more gentle and gracious (i.e., elevated and humane) than what actually occurs in the scene.) It seems to me that for Hobbes, and Lacan, and any serious thinker, the problem is language: it is our attempt to express in this alien structure imposed upon us, both to ourselves and to others—the distinction Hobbes makes between "marking" and "signifying"—what we see and what we feel. Desire is a function of the difference between what we actually need and the need we can express in language. Myths live in language, though they are thought to be preverbal: like words themselves they are arbitrary categories into which we organize our experience. This process of necessity short-circuits the connections between things (the real), our impressions of them (the imaginary), and our thinking and speaking about them (the symbolic): connections (necessarily false) are immediately made between things and words. By representing representation, Shakespeare restores the indirection of the original circuit, calling our attention to the genesis of false impressions. One consequence is that he is not so interested in presenting things as they are, but rather things as they appear to individual characters and the difficulty they have communicating these images to other characters. They all speak the same language, but they do not all have the same impressions.

When these phenomena are erotic, I argue, the images are largely self-images: love in Shakespeare, as in life, is not an idle entertainment, but a compulsive attempt to establish identity. The images, then, that we are projecting are of object-relations from our earliest childhood. If these have been consolidated into a substantial sense of self, then we can allow correction in them by the others they are projected upon. There are, however, two types of pathological projections which we know from life and from Shakespeare. There is the projection onto others of a grandiose self-image; this is pathological narcissism, which we see in Malvolio and Petruchio. Then there is the kind of splitting of the object we see in all those male characters who are obsessed with female sexuality: they deny it in their "ladies" and seek it in inferiors. This is Freud's distinction between idealization and debasement in object-choice, which Wheeler has applied so thoroughly and convincingly to the problem comedies that we need only refer to his work and pass directly on from the mature comedies to the late romances.

In this sense, too, Shakespeare produces a representation of representation: he forces us to see how characters without a consolidated sense of self force all their objects to fit archaic images of narcissistic and anaclitic object-choices. He shows us how characters learn to love and progress through the stages of such a consolidation, thereby creating a sense of self derived from early object-relations. Again we see, in a different way, the disastrous results of the "triangulation of desire": an immediate and complete correspondence is demanded between actual, experienced objects and those images of one's original objects, derived from one's own childhood or from the "childhood of man," which have solidified as symbols without any allowance for the mutual corrections which should take place in the relations between the real and the imaginary, on the one hand, and the imaginary and the symbolic, on the other.

IV.3

The Merchant
of Venice

he Merchant of Venice is an incalculably rich play. In addition to the conjunction of sexual and ontological issues which it shares with the other comedies, it raises issues of character, religion, and class which, if not unique in the Shakespearean corpus, are certainly nowhere else so deeply explored. To get a grip on this complex material it is tempting to set up a system of bipolar oppositions, such as Venice/Belmont, getting/giving, and male/female. I think this would be a mistake, though, because it seems to me that Shakespeare never mediates these polarities, never answers the questions they raise, never, indeed, even validates one side against the other. Rather he shows us infinite complications and contradictions in what we might originally think are simple, even simplistic, problems: is love more important than money? are friends more important than lovers? is one gracious to one's enemies as well as to one's friends? how is justice tempered with mercy?

Central to any interpretation of the play is "the Jewish question." Many critics have too readily accepted the historical solution to this,— that Elizabethans had a genuine prejudice against Jews and persecuted them without compunction. I do not want to raise large critical and

moral issues in my very brief discussion of this play, but I do not favor this kind of historical reading of a literary text: it tells us only how
it was written, not how it must be read. I think in this particular case
we must follow the lead of Jan Kott and read the horrors of our own
times back into Shakespeare, appreciating all the while that these horrors are somehow predicted in Shakespeare's text. An issue in the play
is certainly the use of the scapegoat, and one of the finest examples of
Shakespeare's manipulation of plot and character is the exchange of
places between Antonio and Shylock. It is historically the Jews' role
to be whipped, excluded, and sacrificed, but Shakespeare—playing with
the historical Jewishness of Jesus—makes Antonio, a rich, gentle
Christian, assume that role. It is Jews who are traditionally circumcised, but Shakespeare threatens the Christian's flesh. It is Jews who
were early forced into commerce because they could not own land, and
their commercial practices gave rise to their general characterization as
parsimonious and greedy, but Shakespeare shows us Christians finally
learning to "fast bind, fast find."

The radical nature of Shakespeare's consideration of these ironies is
suggested in his punning on "gentle" and "gentile." Lorenzo confides
in Gratiano his plan to steal Jessica:

> I must needs tell thee all,—she hath directed
> How I shall take her from her father's house,
> What gold and jewels she is furnish'd with,
> What page's suit she hath in readiness,—
> If e'er the Jew her father come to heaven,
> It will be for his gentle daughter's sake,

(II.iv.29–34)

As Gratiano and Lorenzo wait beneath Shylock's penthouse for Jessica
to descend, it is Gratiano who puns:

Jes. I will make fast the doors and gild myself
  With some moe ducats, and be with you straight.
Gra. Now (by my hood) a gentle, and no Jew. (II.vi.49–51)

At the trial, the Duke addresses Shylock; having argued that even Turks
and Tartars would feel pity for Antonio and forgive him his debts, he
concludes: "We all expect a gentle answer, Jew!" (IV.i.34). Superficially, then, an identification is made between race and religion (gen-

tile, non-Jew) and class-specific behavior (noble, gracious). In each use
of the pun, its significance is pointed up by the close proximity of the
term "Jew." One can argue then that this is simply heavy irony: how
foolish to expect gentle (i.e., gentile) behavior from a Jew, a contradiction in terms. Money, however, also appears in each context: Jessica will not simply elope with Lorenzo, but come gilded with her father's wealth; the Duke asks for financial sacrifice from Shylock. It
does no good to argue that the Elizabethan audience would have considered stealing from a Jew no more than he deserved, to make him
suffer the loss of that he overvalues being some kind of punishment
appropriate to his criminal nature. Shakespeare does not allow us to
hypostatize the Jewish nature; he presents us only with the remarkable character Shylock, and what we see is that he becomes what his
Christian antagonists think him to be. We must appreciate then that
Shakespeare presents us not with the metaphysics of racial difference,
but with the phenomenology of racism. The Venetian Christians create in Shylock the monster they hate and fear, and he is a vicious caricature of themselves.

There is no denying that Shylock suggests absolute evil. Like Iago
and Don John he is the outsider who hates irrationally, and his hatred
is overdetermined. He says (aside) of Antonio:

> How like a fawning publican he looks!
> I hate him for he is a Christian:
> But more, for that in low simplicity
> He lends out money gratis, and brings down
> The rate of usance here with us in Venice.
>
> (I.iii.36–40)

Iago similarly says he hates Othello because Othello preferred Cassio
as his lieutenant and because he seduced his wife; he portrays two di-
mensions of jealousy. I would argue (against Brown in the Arden edition) that Shylock's hatred of Antonio is not original and does not determine the peculiar quality of the vengeance he would take on him.
Iago is a *bricoleur;* like the slaves of Roman comedy he weaves anything that falls in his way into his plot. There is not, however, in
Othello the incredible mirroring that occurs in *The Merchant of Venice.*
Everything that happens in the subplot between Jews and Christians
happens in the main plot between Christians and Christians. Fiedler

has shown that not only is Jessica an ogre's daughter, but Portia is as well.[1] The myth behind all this, of course, is that of Persephone, as we have seen in an earlier chapter; the father of comedy and romance is the husband of cult and ritual: Hades, sterility, money rather than love, excrement rather than aliment, death itself. I shall come finally to consider Shylock's anal retentiveness as one of the configuration of attitudes toward sex and money which the play presents, but now it is important to see how Shylock's villainy develops under the influence of Christian example, and here I come straight upon the oral-aggressive aspects of the play.

Bassanio approaches Shylock with his proposition to borrow money and immediately attempts to transfer his business to hospitable circumstances, but Shylock insists on a distinction:

Bass. If it please you to dine with us.
Shy. Yes, to smell pork, to eat of the habitation which your prophet the Nazarite conjured the devil into: I will buy with you, sell with you, talk with you, walk with you, and so following: but I will not eat with you, drink with you, nor pray with you. (I.iii.28–33)

Shylock goes on to avow—and the determination of what is said aloud and what is said aside is disputed (see Arden and Cambridge editions *ad loc.*)—that he hates Antonio for two reasons. Then he considers:

> If I can catch him once upon the hip,
> I will feed fat the ancient grudge I bear him.
> He hates our sacred nation, and he rails
> (Even there where merchants most do congregate)
> On me, my bargains, and my well-won thrift,
> Which he calls interest: cursed be my tribe
> If I forgive him!
>
> (I.iii.41–47)

After some computation of his available resources, he finally acknowledges Antonio:

> Rest you fair good signior,
> Your worship was the last man in our mouths.
>
> (I.iii.54–55)

We have moved, then, from an invitation to dinner, to a figurative expression of revenge ("I will feed fat the ancient grudge I bear him"), to a literal, physical statement of a circumstance ("Your worship was the last man in our mouths," meaning only that he and Bassanio were just speaking of Antonio). Shylock has a compulsion to use bodily language:

> But stop my house's ears, I mean my casements,
> Let not the sound of shallow fopp'ry enter
> My sober house.
>
> (II.v.34–36)

> Some men there are love not a gaping pig!
> Some that are mad if they behold a cat!
> And others when the bag pipe sings i' th' nose,
> Cannot contain their urine.
>
> (IV.i.47–50)

There is a common theme here: control. But to understand Shylock's vengeance we must understand how his mind works, and it seems always to move from the figurative to the literal, from the word to the thing, from the abstract to the concrete, from the general concerns of life to the features and processes of his own body.

He says he will not eat with the Christians, but will eat the very flesh of the Christians. It is like that oldest of monster jokes, the one Polyphemos makes to Odysseus: "No, I won't ask you and your friends to dinner; rather you will be my dinner. No, I do not worship Zeus and do not keep the custom of hospitality he demands; the only grace and favor I shall show you is to eat you last." The rest of this scene of meeting and agreeing between Shylock and Antonio is taken up with an argument over usury, which leads to a straightforward exchange of abuse between them:

Ant.   Mark you this Bassanio,
  The devil can cite Scripture for his purpose,—
  An evil soul producing holy witness
  Is like a villain with a smiling cheek,
  A goodly apple rotten at the heart.
  O what a goodly outside falsehood hath! (I.iii.92–97)

Again, the prophetic quality of the imagery is staggering. I have spoken of both Shylock and Antonio as scapegoats: Antonio describes himself in the trial scene not as a goat but as a castrated ram and then proceeds to use exactly this image of fruit, previously applied to Shylock, of himself:

I am a tainted wether of the flock,
Meetest for death,—the weakest kind of fruit
Drops earliest to the ground, and so let me;

(IV.i.114–16)

It is precisely castration—a wether is a castrated ram—that Shylock, in his compulsive body reference, feels he has suffered from Lorenzo, whom he associated with Bassanio and Antonio:

A sealed bag, two sealed bags of ducats,
Of double ducats, stol'n from me by my daughter!
And jewels, two stones, two rich and precious stones,
Stol'n by my daughter!

(II.viii.18–21)

Fiedler claims that in Elizabethan minds circumcision was confused with both castration and cannibalism.[2] They were not alone in this conception; the Jews themselves in Genesis seem to meditate on these relations all as a function of their debt to God the father. God favors the blood sacrifice of Abel to Cain's offering of grain; Isaac favors the meat stew of Esau to the porridge of Jacob; Abraham would sacrifice his son Isaac at God's command, but a lamb is substituted at the last minute; God allows the Israelites in Egypt to save their firstborn sons from the Angel of death by smearing the blood of a lamb over their doorposts. Circumcision makes the Jews known to God as his chosen people and thus is the symbolic act for keeping the covenant, but a sacrifice as well. All of this is reversed in Christian myth when Jesus becomes the lamb of God, and Paul insists that circumcision be not of the penis but of the heart and spirit.[3] What we come down to is that Shylock is the God of the Old Testament insisting on the letter of the law, whereas these Christians are Paulists and want symbolic acts, the spirit of the law dependent upon the grace of God, not their own works, to save them.[4] It is no wonder Shylock and Antonio hate each other: one is a jealous God and the other is a passive victim; one moves in the clear world of absolute correspondence and the other in a vague world of representation; one thinks that men are what they do—flesh, feces, babies, money—and the other thinks there is some divine force operating upon men which transforms them into something rich and fine. Does Shakespeare ratify one or the other vision? Is this a Christian play? What about its erotic argument? What does it say about love's usury?

Carrying her father's wealth, Jessica flees with Lorenzo shortly after Shylock's reference to Jacob's trick for taking more sheep from Laban. All the striped and spotted sheep would be Jacob's in payment for his long labor for Laban, his dwelling with Laban for fourteen years to obtain the hand of Rachel. (Laban had cheated Jacob after seven years and had sent in his older daughter Leah to sleep with Jacob, so that Jacob had to marry her first, and then labor another seven years for Rachel. This is recalled by the bed trick in *All's Well* and *Measure for Measure;* this is the basis of Baptista's insistence in *The Taming of the Shrew* that his older daughter Katherina marry before his younger daughter Bianca.)

> And when the work of generation was
> Between these woolly breeders in the act,
> The skillful shepherd pill'd me certain wands,
> And in the doing of the deed of kind
> He stuck them up before the fulsome ewes,
> Who then conceiving, did in eaning time
> Fall parti-colour'd lambs, and those were Jacob's.
> This was a way to thrive, and he was blest:
> And thrift is blessing if men steal it not.

(I.iii.77–85)

When Jacob finally left Laban, taking his two wives and his sheep with him, "Rachel had stolen the images which were her father's" (Gen. 31:19) and had hidden them in the saddling of the camel. Laban pursued and searched Jacob's campsite for the images, but Jacob did not know Rachel had stolen them, and Rachel sat upon them and asked her father not to make her rise for his searching, "for the custom of women is upon me" (Gen. 31:35). Shylock's usury is answered then by the very kind of theft which he separated himself from, and the Christians approve Jessica's theft.

It is this crime that fuels Shylock's hatred of the Christians, and he directs it toward their scapegoat, Antonio. He demands of Antonio talion punishment: since he feels himself castrated by Jessica's flight and theft, he will castrate Antonio, but the penalty will be displaced upward, a pound of flesh taken nearest the heart. The division of the world into

Venice and Belmont, Jews and Christians—Shylock against the world—allows the collapse of all Christians into the one scapegoat figure. Antonio is closely associated with Bassanio, and Bassanio has won Portia in all her riches from her father; Lorenzo has stolen Jessica and her father's riches. Lorenzo's offending parts are his genitals; so too are Bassanio's; Antonio is old and impotent, but he loves Bassanio. It is here that Shakespeare's concern for the attitudes of love reveals itself as consistent with and yet somehow contradictory to what we have seen in earlier comedies. Paul's Christian must be circumcised of the heart; Antonio is threatened with castration of the heart.[5] What are the relations between Antonio and Bassanio? We know that in Shakespeare's source for the main plot of the play (Ser Giovanni Fiorentino's *Il Pecorone*, IV.1) the older man who finances the younger man's pursuit of the wealthy wife is his godfather.[6] Antonio's love for Bassanio is compulsively physical, however, like Shylock's whole world-view, though unlike Shylock, Antonio is pathic:

> I pray you good Bassanio let me know it,
> And if it stand as you yourself still do,
> Within the eye of honour, be assur'd
> My purse, my person, my extremest means
> Lie all unlock'd to your occasions.

> (I.i.135–39)

Antonio has already introduced himself to us at the opening of the play as a melancholic; he sounds very much like Antipholus of Syracuse at the opening of *The Comedy of Errors:*

> In sooth I know not why I am so sad,
> It wearies me, you say it wearies you;
> But how I caught it, found it, or came by it,
> What sutff 'tis made of, whereof it is born,
> I am to learn:
> And such a want-wit sadness makes of me,
> That I have much ado to know myself.

> (I.i.1–7)

As in the earlier comedy, we find the conjunction of erotic and ontic yearnings because we soon appreciate that only Bassanio can make Antonio happy, and, of course, the play's developments emphasize the impossibility of any real intimacy between them. Bassanio takes advantage of Antonio's generosity to pursue Portia, and Portia scolds Bassanio with renouncing her claim upon him in order to save Antonio. Antonio is not Bassanio's twin or contemporary, but is an older, weaker, sentimental male protector, a father without a father's authority or a father's demand for love and obedience. He is certainly not the possessive father, like God the Father, the jealous God, whom we see in Shylock.[7]

Again Shakespeare seems to be insisting on the stage-appropriate aspects of certain erotic attachments. We shall see the same in *Twelfth Night* with another Antonio and in *The Winter's Tale*, where Leontes' nostalgia for the lost bliss of his childhood when he felt twinned with Polixenes creates the tragic madness that "kills" his wife Hermione. In *The Merchant of Venice* Shakespeare is presenting a recognizable pattern of homosexual attachment—the older man who "idolizes" the beautiful youth, seeing in him his own younger, more beautiful self. This is the attachment so clearly described in the *Sonnets*, the love of the Poet for the Fair Youth. Erotic relations between men, then—and I do not consider whether these feelings are latent or manifest, but only that they are essential to men's identity—are presented by Shakespeare in two entirely different lights depending upon the age of the lover. Young men are shown to require such attachments for gaining some sense of themselves; this I claim to be adolescent recapitulation of primary narcissism. We see it in the relations of Valentine and Proteus, of the twin Antipholi, and of the gentlemen of the King of Navarre's court. Here, however, with Antonio, we see an older man who has been arrested in that phase-appropriate kind of object-choice. His melancholy signifies that he still has not consolidated an identity through mirroring, and that he has never been able to invest libidinally a true object, a woman, or, through that kind of relationship, other objects—his ships, his wealth, the world itself. He is still looking for that archaic image of himself, and thus his attachment to Bassanio, which Shakespeare shows us to be pathetic.[8]

Shylock fulfills, then, Antonio's paranoid fears, but also his desires. Antonio is the most complete of Shakespeare's portraits of failed lovers. In his melancholy and fixation on an unobtainable object, a self-object, we see the failure to integrate an image of the self from object-relations, to complete the work of primary narcissism. In his fixation on a threatening father figure we see the oedipal recapitulation of that failure. Freud traces the sequence of ideal ego, ego ideal, and superego in childhood development. The father should step into that place prepared by the completed work of primary narcissism: he is first the replacement for the child's narcissistic fantasy of his own perfection and then the figure who condemns the child for not being perfect. In the normal resolution of the Oedipus complex he is introjected as the superego, but if the Oedipus complex is not experienced in the normal way, because primary narcissism was not experienced in the normal way, then the father condemns his son for making the wrong sexual choice—the father (as oedipal replacement or extension of the narcissistic image of the self) and not the mother.[9] In Antonio we see the complex working both ways: he chooses the younger, more beautiful, narcissistic image of himself in Bassanio, and is punished for this by the oedipal father personified in Shylock.

We need not go into the trial scene and the reunion in Belmont in detail. It is clear that the profligate ways of the Christians (Antonio is the extreme example; he gives his love and his money with no strings attached, and he ends up alone) with regard to money (they freely spend other peoples' money) is not acceptable behavior with regard to love. Portia shows that she intends to "fast bind, fast find." There is some threat, then, left in the prospect of marriage. Portia is a numinous figure, and we feel in the end that she has overwhelmed all the men. They are not unlike Odysseus' men in Circe's sty: they have been touched by her wand, metamorphosed into married men, and they suddenly feel the constriction of those rings. Marriage is never unalloyed bliss in Shakespearen comedy, and in this one the figures of Shylock and Antonio, excluded from the pairings, loom large. In Greek and Roman comedy there is often the contrast between a *pater lenis* and a *pater iratus*, and the extremes of educational philosophy they represent are somehow mediated. For instance, in Terence's *Adelphoe*, based on Menander's *Adelphoi*, Demeas, the harsh father, is forced to admit that he has ruined his son and deprived himself of the pleasure of being loved. But he forces his profligate brother Micio to such outrageous expense that we realize moderation is the only answer. Shylock is to Antonio as Demeas is to Micio. In Aristophanic comedy, however, we often find the hero fleeing a world of graft and corruption to establish a new world of his own design elsewhere; for instance, in the *Birds,* this is Euelpides' intention. Then at the end, though, we realize that all he has succeeded in doing is building another Athens in the clouds.

The Merchant of Venice is more Aristophanic in its resolution than Menandrean or Terentian. We appreciate finally that there are no great differences between Belmont and Venice, between Christians and Jews. Shakespeare forces us to see the power of perspective: in this case, of prejudice and hypocrisy. Love is not an experience separate and different from other experiences: In love, as in commerce, we find chaos and have to apply our own pressure, so that its raw material becomes recognizable as a product. Then, stepping back, we sometimes wonder what we have wrought, or what we have been wrought into. *The Merchant of Venice* is unique among Shakespeare's plays for giving that strange feeling that the lovers we thought were so active, freely giving and receiving, have finally ended up in passive postures, bound by love, fast. They are better off than Antonio, whose kind of love has failed completely to give him any satisfaction; Shakespeare has shown here, however, and throughout the corpus of his comedies, that no kind of love gives complete satisfaction, because no kind of love fulfills the narcissistic demands Antonio makes of it. The merchant of Venice, is, then, both a positive and a negative pattern for love in his own play, and in every other play Shakespeare wrote about love.

IV.4

As You Like It

ur focus in this play must be on the character of Rosalind, since she surprises us by completely controlling the action: I have claimed that Petruchio in *The Taming of the Shrew* is harsh and vindictive towards Katherina because he is insecure in his suit, unaccompanied as he is, in a strange city, by male friends and relations to support and comfort him in his dangerous undertaking. Likewise this play becomes Rosalind's because she is given a strong female companion in Celia, who as "Aliena" becomes her alter ego (compare the childhood intimacy of Helena and Hermia) and then, after her transvestism, a doting male companion in Orlando. The play opens conventionally with Orlando expressing his impatience at being kept "dully sluggardis'd at home," but Orlando never develops into the strong male character that the other comedies depend upon for their erotic and philosophic centers. There seems indeed to be a kind of physical law operative in these plays, whereby the nature of love and an entire worldview are adumbrated from the central position of a male lover. Because of the weakness of Orlando and by means of the transvestism of Roslind, she takes up that position, thus filling what would otherwise be a vacuum in the play. It is her definition of love and her view of reality we finally accept.

We must reconcile these observations with those made by Barber and others on the peculiar version of pastoral Shakespeare here offers

us. Barber nicely contrasts the idealism or romanticism of Orlando's
love lyrics with the realism or even materialism of Touchstone's wooing
of Audrey:[1]

As the ox hath his bow sir, the horse his curb, and the falcon her bells, so
man hath his desires, and as pigeons bill, so wedlock would be nibbling.

(III.iii.71–73)

For Touchstone, then, love is instinctual: one experiences it because
one is part of nature, not because one just happens to meet the one
woman in the world whom one is meant to love. Rosalind's neat mediation of these two extremes is extremely sophisticated, and not unlike what Theseus says about art in *A Midsummer Night's Dream* and
what Prospero says about all man's undertakings in *The Tempest*. It is
a peculiarly human quality to animate nature with one's own creative
vision, to see things in a certain significant order, even if that order
be of one's own imposition. As in *A Midsummer Night's Dream*, then,
love here is "natural" and art is self-conscious.

Barber explains this view of love and implies its relation with worldview generally:

The reality we feel about the experience of love in the play, reality which is
not in the pleasant little prose romance, comes from presenting what was sentimental extremity as impulsive extravagance and so leaving judgement free to
mock what the heart embraces.[2]

This observation comes directly from the conjunction of such speeches
of Rosalind's as that ending "men have died from time to time and
worms have eaten them, but not for love" (IV.i. 89–103) and

That same wicked bastard of Venus, that was begot of thought, conceived of
spleen and born of madness, that blind rascally boy that abuses everyone's
eyes because his own are out, let him be judge how deep I am in love. I'll tell
thee Aliena, I cannot be out of the sight of Orlando. I'll go find a shadow and
sigh till he come. (IV.i.201–7)

If we ask, then, how it is that a young woman so completely takes
over the action of the play and yet there seems to be no masculine
protest, the answer must lie in Rosalind's complex attitude toward love:
she knows all the conventions are silly, but she feels finally their appropriateness. Latham has put this in context:

Rosalind, like her father, is deprived of her rightful inheritance and the life to which she is accustomed. In Arden she finds her freedom. She is no longer living on suffrance at the usurper's court, and in doublet and hose she is no longer confined to a woman's limited role. Her own temperament frees her from the restrictions of romantic love-cults. "Men have died from time to time and worms have eaten them, but not for love." This does not mean that she is in the least destructive of love itself or resentful of its compulsive tides, in which she is happily drowning. "Rosalind," says Mark Van Doren, "has found that there is only one thing sillier than being in love, and that is thinking it silly to be in love." What she will not countenance is an affected and humor-less intensity, the besetting fault of Elizabethan love-cults. Once in the forest, it is she who takes control—even of her father, to whom she makes herself known in her own good time—and Shakespeare puts the denouement into her capable hands. Without her earlier misfortunes she might seem almost too managing, but when we first meet her she is sad, so that it is a pleasure to watch her spirits bubble up. She comes into her own and into a better heritage than she has lost.[3]

Does Latham mean that Rosalind comes into the forest looking for her father and finds a lover instead? Certainly Shakespeare makes much of the intimacy between Rosalind and Celia, so we cannot take it simply as a necessity of the plot that Rosalind had originally chosen to stay at court with Celia rather than accompany her father into exile. The erotic and self-reflective dynamics of this arrangement are compelling, es-pecially when thought of in relation to the later romances. Comparing Rosalind, who has been separated from her father but continues in her intimacy with a relation of the same sex and age—"thou and I are one," Celia says to Rosalind(I.iii.93), as Helena calls herself and Hermia a "double cherry" (*MD* III.ii.209).—and Miranda, who has had only her father in all those years of his exile, one remarks the independence and self-assurance of the one and the childish simplicity of the other. Finally, one realizes that Shakespeare does not simply transvestize Rosalind to facilitate conventional pairings in the forest; rather he transvestizes comedy, and gives us a view of the erotic moment in all its complexity through the young woman's eyes.

It is not Rosalind's original sadness in contrast with her later ebul-lience that makes her authority acceptable to us, but rather her com-plete assimilation of all those masculine virtues which the comic tra-dition and Shakespeare's own earlier comedies have made conventional. In the play itself, isolated from its predecessors, we feel simply that she takes up the self-assertive space which Orlando is too simple to claim.[4] In the comic context, though, we see Rosalind as Berowne and Benedick, the male who scoffs at his fellows for falling in love, and then falls more deeply in love himself, but somehow more self-consciously than they, because with an object more like himself. For Rosalind, though, there is no sparring partner as Benedick is for Beatrice and Berowne for Rosaline since Orlando is no equal to her wit: he is a purely physical man, unable to do anything well but wrestle. Is she to any extent Portia, a mysterious, slightly threatening, woman, who, after transvestism, seems almost too much a match for her lover? It is significant that Shakespeare does have Rosalind claim for herself, in her persona as Ganymede, the power of a magician, who can manipulate people in love (V.ii.59–62), which is comparable to the mythic force behind Portia as an "ogre's daughter." Transvestism, then, as well as being a plot device is proof of the mysterious power of these women. There is, however, at the end of *As You Like It,* none of that binding which makes the end of *The Merchant of Venice* such a harrowing account of the demands of love. Rather, as the title suggests, everyone's desires are fulfilled, even Phebe's, though she has taken only the first step in love, from derision to doting, and still must learn to respond to Silvius' love for her, to see herself in his eyes.

When Rosalind scolds Silvius for doting on Phebe, she defines precisely that phenomenology of desire which I think Shakespeare is concerned with in all his comedy:

> 'Tis not her glass but you that flatters her,
> And out of you she sees herself more proper
> Than any of her lineaments can show her.

> (III.v.54–56)

The lover is then a flattering mirror for the beloved, so that not only does the lover change his own reality but also that of his beloved: he sees her differently, and she sees herself differently. At the same time that Rosalind exposes the transforming nature of Silvius' love for Phebe, she makes herself, as Ganymede, attractive to Phebe, and this phenomenon is similar to that of Orlando, who while learning from Rosalind as Ganymede how perverse a lady can be when she is loved, nevertheless falls in love with that lady even more deeply. In both cases the lesson in the deceptive nature of love increases love rather than releases from love. The nature of the love of Orlando for Rosalind is not, however, even that simple. Indeed one of the central problems of the play is the complexity of that relationship between a seemingly simple man and a very sophisticated lady. Clearly Orlando falls in love with Rosalind as Ganymede; indeed I think his original love for Rosalind as Rosalind is no more profound than Romeo's original love for his Rosaline or Berowne's for his Rosaline—and they all write bad poetry.[5] What then happens, though, is that Rosalind, appearing to Orlando simultaneously as a boy and as his lady—and undercutting love in both personae—nevertheless makes herself even more attractive to Orlando. Simultaneously, of course, she falls more deeply in love with him, but that is clearly because of his simplicity. As she weaves elaborate patterns of criticism and apology for love, he answers in simple sentences, like Socrates' straight man in a Platonic dialogue, and because of this her love deepens until it "hath an unknown bottom, like the Bay of Portugal" (IV.i.197). In contrast, Orlando loves Rosalind-Ganymede for her complexity. In the report of Oliver we have some indication of this:

> The lioness had torn some flesh away,
> Which all this while had bled; and now he fainted,
> And cried in fainting upon Rosalind.
> Brief, I recover'd him, bound up his wound,
> And after some small space, being strong at heart,
> He sent me hither, stranger as I am,
> To tell this story, that you might excuse
> His broken promise, and to give this napkin,
> Dy'd in his blood, unto the shepherd youth
> That he in sport doth call his Rosalind.
>
> (IV.iii.147–56)

In Oliver's report Orlando cried out upon Rosalind and sent the bloody bandage to the shepherd he calls Rosalind, i.e., Ganymede. Are these two figures any more separable in Orlando's love than they are in the play's reality? Surely, we must see in the bloody bandage a strange love token, a talisman, like the bloody scarf the lion left and Pyramus mistook for evidence of Thisbe's death. Rosalind faints in parody of Pyramus' suicide. It is Rosalind-Ganymede that Orlando now loves, not simply Rosalind, and that love is deeper because it involves an image of himself: he sees in Ganymede the clever fellow he is not, and while he makes love to Ganymede as Rosalind, he also identifies with Ganymede as the commentator on his love. His self-irony is then once removed, unlike Benedick's and Berowne's. The identity of the object of desire with the object of identification is a phenomenon which we have previously remarked in *The Two Gentlemen of Verona* and *A Midsummer Night's Dream*. That it somehow takes two men to love one woman is what Shakespeare manipulates the conventions of romance to reveal: the lover loves himself loving, it seems, for one male always introjects another in the very moment of loving a woman. Again, the crucial feature is self-consciousness, like the Cartesian *cogito:* "I think, therefore I am" means "I am because I can think of myself thinking."[6]

If we accept this as the basic pattern of Orlando's changing love of Rosalind—which is also of her changing, an indication that his love deepens from the idealizing type to the phenomenal type, loving objects as they appear rather than as they fit some preconceived notion of an appropriate object—then we must see that she and he learn to love the same way, self-consciously. They come to know what love is in others, to question and distrust it, but then when they feel it in themselves, they triangulate their desire internally, love themselves loving, or, at least, simultaneously feel love and think "I feel love."

IV.5

Twelfth Night

I agree with those who find in *Twelfth Night* a summary of and culmination to Shakespeare's early comic development.[1] I am particularly sensitive to the recapitulation here of the patterns of action of *The Two Gentlemen of Verona* and *The Comedy of Errors*.[2] I agree with Kermode that the largest theme of the play is identity.[3] I only insist that here, as always in Shakespearean comedy, identity is a function of erotic orientation, and that Shakespeare in *Twelfth Night* takes us over all the ground he has previously covered, showing us all the stage-appropriate kinds of object-choice and then their transcendence in a kind of love which is spontaneous and can accept change in its object.

As in other comedies of the middle period, Shakespeare is here concerned to show that erotic relations are stimulated by different types of experience. By stressing the ontogenetic (sexual ambivalence and ambiguity in adolescence is a recapitulation of primary narcissism) and epistemological (love is a way of seeing which can be a model for our appreciation of the world generally), we cannot afford to ignore the social. For some reason Malvolio is condemned to ridicule for making precisely that pretension to greatness which Olivia encourages in Viola-Cesario-Sebastian. Is this all set right by the revelation that Sebastian is not socially subordinate, but, perhaps, Olivia's equal? This would only ratify Elizabethan standards of marriage within one's class. Surely

Shakespeare pursues here those correlations of birth and worth which are strongly stated in *A Midsummer Night's Dream*, but seriously questioned in *The Merchant of Venice:* what is "grace," to be "gentle," and "generous"?

For my purposes the best texts to measure Shakespeare's text against are Freud's "On Narcissism" and "Mourning and Melancholy," two closely related papers of the middle period, written after he began to consider the dynamics of the ego libidinally investing itself, but before he postulated the death drive. We have seen several striking examples in the earlier comedies of the relation between melancholy and narcissistic choice of object, most notably Antonio in *The Merchant of Venice* and Antipholus of Syracuse in *The Comedy of Errors*. In *Twelfth Night* this association is compounded with mourning: Olivia will not respond to the love of Orsino, but does respond to Viola in her disguise as Cesario, because her brother has recently died; Viola, however, does respond to Orsino because she believes that her brother might recently have died.

We are presented then with two interwoven plots which move from deprivation of cross-sex self-object, to choice of same-sex self-object, to choice of cross-sex "true" object. We see peripherally two other kinds of erotic experience, which might be considered arrested or regressive: Malvolio is "sick of self-love," and Antonio's love of Sebastian is idolatrous.

It is Orsino, however, who delivers the main statements on the nature of love, and their internal contradictions give us not only an indication of the original weakness of his own philosophy of love, but also a negative standard against which to measure the loves of the other characters. To begin with, Orsino is in love with love, and Olivia is just an accidental object.[4] In Elizabethan terms he is melancholy; the congruence in his own statements about love, of imagery drawn from music, food, and the sea, however, encourages us to attempt more sutle distinctions. What is his great appetite for, that appetite which, like the sea, absorbs objects but is never filled, and what does music have to do with all this?

Duke. If music be the food of love, play on,
  Give me excess of it, that, surfeiting,
  The appetite may sicken, and so die.

That strain again, it had a dying fall:
O, it came o'er my ear like the sweet sound
That breathes upon a bank of violets,
Stealing and giving odour. Enough, no more;
'Tis not so sweet now as it was before.
O spirit of love, how quick and fresh art thou,
That notwithstanding thy capacity
Receiveth as the sea, nought enters there,
Of what validity and pitch soe'er,
But falls into abatement and low price,
Even in a minute! So full of shapes is fancy,
That it alone is high fantastical.(I.i.1–15)

Melancholy is associated with the sea in opening passages of *The Comedy of Errors,* where Antipholus of Syracuse compares himself to a drop of water, and in *The Merchant of Venice,* where Antonio's friends suggest that his feeling of loss (which we later learn is determined by the hopelessness of his love for Bassanio) is due to his merchandise being "squander'd abroad" in ships upon the sea. In both cases, then, an inadequate sense of self finds expression in comparison with the limitless void of the ocean. However, Orsino does not express the same kind of anxiety. If there were any indication that, in his love for Olivia, he felt somehow diminished, inadequate, and impotent, we might impose upon all three characters the Freudian explanation for melancholy:

The distinguishing mental features of melancholia are a profoundly painful dejection, cessation of interest in the outside world, loss of the capacity to love, inhibition of all activity, and a lowering of the self-regarding feelings to a degree that finds utterance in self-reproaches and self-revilings, and culminate in a delusional expectation of punishment.[5]

This suits Antonio of *The Merchant of Venice* perfectly, Antipholus of Syracuse less well, and Orsino, seemingly, not at all. When we appreciate that what Freud calls melancholia is what we now call pathological depression, and that he associates it with mania, which we still call mania, then we see the whole pattern, the manic-depressive, and wonder whether what Orsino describes in not the upward swing of that cycle. Freud himself cites Hamlet.[6] He explains that melancholy is like mourning in that some emotional adjustment to the loss of a loved one is worked out in a series of steps. But whereas mourning is "normal,"—the loved one is dead, and the empty feeling is gradually filled by new objects—melancholy develops when the object of desire refuses to be loved, the subject then disparages the object, and the disparaged object is introjected so that "a shadow falls across the ego" of the subject. This pattern of identification with the love-object is not, of course, unique to melancholia; it is the basis of that dynamic process by which we become those very objects we have desired, beginning with our parents, after we have idealized them.[7]

It is true, of course, that Orsino, being finally confronted by Olivia and forced to accept her rejection of him, does disparage her, and both music and food are imaged in the conception:

Olivia. If it be aught to the old tune, my lord,
   It is as fat and fulsome to mine ear
   As howling after music.
Duke. Still so cruel?
Olivia.   Still so constant, lord.
Duke. What, to perverseness? You uncivil lady,
   To whose ingrate and unauspicious altars
   My soul the faithfull'st off'rings hath breath'd out
   That o'er devotion tender'd—What shall I do?(V.i.106–13)

He does, then, turn violent, but not against himself—rather against Viola-Cesario, who is by then some part of himself. That his love for Olivia is idolatrous[8] makes it comparable to Antonio's for Sebastian, which is also hopeless:

Ant. Let me speak a little. This youth that you see here
   I snatch'd one half out of the jaws of death,
   Reliev'd him with such sanctity of love;
   And to his image, which methought did promise
   Most venerable worth, did I devotion.
   . . . .
   But O how vile an idol proves this god! (III.iv.368–74)

We know the association between "vile," suggesting the object of animal appetites, and "idol," a fetish-like replacement for a worthy object of affection—human reason should reject both—from *Love's Labor's Lost* and *A Midsummer Night's Dream*. Olivia's reference to music—Orsino's declaration of love is to her howling after the music of Viola-Cesario-Sebastian—recalls not only Orsino's opening remarks on the ability of music to calm the passion of love, but also an intermediate remark:

Duke. Give me some music. Now good morrow, friends.
  Now, good Cesario, but that piece of song,
  That old and antic song we heard last night;
  Methought it did relieve my passion much,
  More than light airs and recollected terms
  Of these most brisk and giddy-paced times.(II.iv.1–6)

Love as appetite persists as an image in the play, and brings us back to Freud and his description of the manic lover: "Moreover, the manic subject plainly demonstrates his liberation from the object which was the cause of his suffering, by seeking like a ravenous hungry man for new object-cathexes."[9] Before we claim that Orsino fits Freud's sketch of the manic-depressive type, and that the play only slightly distorts the sequence of libidinal investment, object loss, melancholy, recovery, new object-choice, we must consider the whole problem of object-constancy, a subject on which Orsino also has a great deal to say.

Orsino's constancy in love is a constant theme, but one whole scene is shaped around it—II.iv., from which I have already quoted the opening lines on the ability of music to relieve passion. He banters with Viola-Cesario on the nature of love and presents himself as its paragon:

        Come hither, boy. If ever thou shalt love,
        In the sweet pangs of it remember me:
        For such as I am, all true lovers are,
        Unstaid and skittish in all motions else,
        Save in the constant image of the creature
        That is belov'd. How dost thou like this tune?

                              (II.iv.15–20)

The use of "image" here, of course, puts the quality of Orsino's love in way of comparison with Antonio's for Sebastian—"And to his image . . . / . . . did I devotion" (III.iv.371–72)—which we have already noted, because finally Orsino tells us that his soul has breathed out offerings at Olivia's altar (V.i.110–13). This suggests the kind of problem raised in *The Two Gentlemen of Verona*, where constancy is also an issue: a metaphysics of love, after the Platonic fashion, would insist on the constancy of the ideal image of love, to which then an actual object is assimilated, rather than the discovery in an actual object of qualities previously unvalued. Moreover, the quibble is there made on whether one is constant to one's own ideal image of the perfect mistress or to a mistress one has chosen. Shakespeare shows us Orsino inconstant even in his definition of love, for just a few lines after he says that in all else he is unstaid and skittish except in the constancy of his love, he admits of his own sex:

> For boy, however we do praise ourselves,
> Our fancies are more giddy and unfirm,
> More longing, wavering, sooner lost and worn
> Than women's are.
>
> (II.iv.32–35)

At the end of the scene he contradicts this, claiming that men are stronger and more constant in their love than women are; indeed at that point he contradicts all he has previously said about love. But first we hear from the Clown, who again unites Antonio in *The Merchant of Venice* and Orsino, under the headings of melancholy and the sea:

Now the melancholy god protect thee, and the tailor make thy doublet of changeable taffeta, for thy mind is a very opal. I would have men of such constancy put to sea, that their business might be everything, and their intent everywhere, for that's it that makes a good voyage of nothing. (II.iv.72–78)

This is a very dense and multivalent speech. I agree with the Arden editors that the final phrase is ambiguous meaning either it turns nothing to good account, or it turns everything to bad account. I think, though, that the whole speech is metaphorical: lovers like Orsino resemble merchants like Antonio, who send their merchandise off in all directions and end up with nothing of themselves at home. To be plain, I think the Clown sees that Orsino's violent passion for Olivia is ungrounded in a secure self-image. He might have a constant object-image, but does not know himself. This is part of a larger argument, which, simplistic as it seems, is that Shakespeare constantly shows us that lovers must love themselves before they can love others. (The simplicity is deceptive, however, since he shows that lovers only know themselves through their love of others, first mothers, then friends, etc.)[10] Orsino comes to this self-knowledge through his attraction to Viola-Cesario, just as Orlando does through his love of Rosalind-Ganymede. This is a feature of adolescent object-choice: the sexual ambiguity of this stage reflects itself in sexual ambivalence, all of which Shakespeare figures in his use of transvestism. More difficult is my argument that adolescent sexuality recapitulates primary narcissism, in that originally the subject must constitute an image of himself from his relations with parental objects (the mirror stage) and only then can he invest an object with regard for its actual alterity (the oedipal stage). Shakespeare figures all this in his opposition of anaclitic choice of object—the moon goddess as an idealized, pre-oedipal image of the mother—with narcissistic choice—investment of similars in friends and transvestized lovers. Shakespeare shows all this moving toward a consolidation of narcissistic and anaclitic object-choice—or, as Kernberg puts it,[11] the consolidation of homosexual desires in a heterosexual union wherein the beloved is both self and other, not just self (the two Antonios' homosexuality) or just other (the originally idealized love of Orlando, Orsino, Proteus, etc.).

Orsino finally admits his lack of a secure self-image in describing what he thinks is the weakness of women's love; in fact he is describing himself as he has previously presented himself:

> There is no woman's sides
> Can bide the beating of so strong a passion
> As love doth give my heart; no woman's heart
> So big, to hold so much: they lack retention.[12]
> Alas, their love may be call'd appetite,
> No motion of the liver, but the palate,
> That suffers surfeit, cloyment, and revolt;
> But mine is all as hungry as the sea,
> And can digest as much. Make no compare
> Between that love a woman can bear me
> And that I owe Olivia.
>
> (II.iv.94–104)

This specifically refers back to his opening remarks about the effect love for him would have upon Olivia:

> O, she that hath a heart of that fine frame
> To pay this debt of love but to a brother,
> How will she love, when the rich golden shaft
> Hath kill'd the flock of all affections else

> That live in her; when liver, brain, and heart,
> These sovereign thrones, are all supplied, and fill'd
> Her sweet perfections with one self king!
>
> (I.i.33–39)

Olivia will shortly admit of Viola-Cesario:

> Methinks I feel this youth's perfections
> With an invisible and subtle stealth
> To creep in at mine eyes.
>
> (I.v.300–2)

More than just the anatomy of love and the idealization of the lover bind these passages together: the last two are concerned with "brotherly love." Olivia has lost her brother and will not keep company with men, until she meets Viola transvestized as Cesario, with whom she falls immediately in love. This is, then, the perfect pattern of mourning: when the object of one's love dies, the ego feels diminished, but the energy with which it formerly invested the object gradually returns to restore itself, and then it is capable of investing a different object. In Olivia's case, we must conclude, this working through of the mourning process is much abridged because Viola as Cesario is for her precisely the brother she has lost. Furthermore, since she has fallen in love with a youth like her brother, who is really a young woman like herself, we have an extraordinarily clear statement in the plot of narcissistic object-choice. As Freud says in defining melancholy, "The object-choice has been effected on a narcissistic basis, so that the object-cathexis, when obstacles come in its way, can regress to narcissism."[13]

Olivia loved her brother, and he died; Viola loved her brother, and she thinks he might have died. What is such "brotherly love" but the libidinal investment of the self in the sibling of the opposite sex, and when this narcissistic choice of object is lost, there is a mourning of the most profound kind, because the self itself is called into question. Here I thoroughly agree with Kermode that identity—in the double sense of "sameness" and "self-consciousness"—is the primary concern of the play. Viola and Olivia both use phrases that suggest masquerade, and Viola, of course, does masquerade:

Viola. Good gentle one, give me modest assurance if you be the lady of the house, that I may proceed in my speech.
Olivia. Are you a comedian?
Viola. No, my profound heart: and yet, by the very fangs of malice I swear, I am not that I play. Are you the lady of the house?
Olivia. If I do not usurp myself, I am.
Viola. Most certain, if you are she, you do usurp yourself: for what is yours to bestow is not yours to reserve. (I.v.180–90)

Both Viola and Olivia are described as melancholy (II.iv.114–15), II.v.203). Why has Viola "usurped" her masculine attire (V.i.248)? For purposes of the plot, to secure herself in a strange land, but for thematic development, to take her brother's place, whom she thinks she might have lost. Only here, in this play, does Shakespeare combine transvestism and twins; only here, then, can he tease us with all those erotic variations and confusions which are made possible by the one erotic circumstance that he is most deeply concerned with: all object-choice is narcissistic, so the closest thing to complete satisfaction must be the love of twin brother for twin sister. Shakespeare brings us to that same point with Viola and Sebastian that Wagner does with Siegmund and Sieglinde. But whereas Wagner condemns the male twin to death, and only allows the male offspring of the union to survive, Shakespeare celebrates the union itself, displaced only slightly with the addition of Orsino and Olivia.

Nowhere else in Shakespeare's comedy is the vocabulary of love so consistent, and the relations of characters so doubled, as in a mirror. Viola is saved and protected by the Captain, as Sebastian is saved and befriended by Antonio.

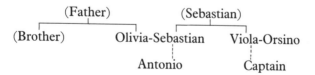

Only Orsino is completely without family, and in this perhaps, as with Petruchio, we find some reason for his disorientation. What strikes us more forcefully, though, is the oedipal pattern of all these attractions. No matter how young the actress playing Olivia, her social position must make her dignified, even exalted, so that when she falls in love with a page, she is stooping, and we feel the transgression of social barriers in erotic object-choice to be similar to the transgression of incest barriers. The same is true of Orsino's love for Viola-Cesario. Again, though, the complication that transvestism introduces makes of this pattern of oedipal object-choice, which seems to be anaclitic—mother-son, father-daughter—something transparently narcissistic. Olivia loves her brother in Viola-Cesario, but really loves herself. Orsino comes to do the same: he is prepared to love Viola when she reveals herself because he has fallen in love with Cesario. Of course, the pattern of the lover falling in love with the "page" who presses his suit for another mistress is known from *The Two Gentlemen of Verona* and *As You Like It*. It might be significant that the name of Julia's persona, the young man she pretends to be, is Sebastian; Rosalind's persona is Ganymede. These names certainly carry associations with pederasty.[14] I claim, though, that Shakespeare's use reveals patterns of narcissism, and that he validates it as a phase-appropriate kind of object-choice, and incorporates it in these sexually ambivalent young pages. Viola-Cesario moves from master to mistress like an Eros figure, hermaphroditic, fascinatingly beautiful because he can present to either sex what it wants to see in itself, and therefore in the object of its desire. Viola-Cesario is the perfect culmination of Shakespeare's development of this convention because she has a twin brother, but she is prefigured in Julia-Sebastian and in Rosalind-Ganymede.[15]

Finally we come to Malvolio, and appreciate that he is not at all a peripheral figure, but instead the negative paradigm of all that goes on erotically in the play. Olivia characterizes him precisely, and in terms that fit with Orsino's various attempts to define love:

O, you are sick of self-love,[16] Malvolio, and taste with a distempered appetite. To be generous, guiltless, and of free disposition, is to take those things for bird-bolts that you deem canon bullets.

(I.v.89–92)

Malvolio's disdain for the Clown is also an ethical issue, and Olivia reminds us of Theseus: grace transfigures the base, or at least renders it less obnoxious. The speech is also, of course, prophetic of Malvolio's disappointment in love, for his own suit of Olivia, encouraged by the fools he despises, results from his overestimation of himself.

The plot and subplot of the play are as tightly knit as is thematically and dramatically possible. Olivia's resistance to Orsino's suit is based not only on her grief for her dead brother, but also on her determination not to marry above herself (I.iii.106–9), and later, when she demands that Viola-Cesario reveal the secret of their love and marriage (which she arranged with Sebastian), she encourages her:

> Alas, it is the baseness of thy fear
> That makes thee strangle thy propriety.
> Fear not, Cesario, take thy fortunes up,
> Be that thou know'st thou art, and then thou art
> As great as that thou fear'st.
>
> (V.i.144–48)

Here, of course, is the phenomenology of love and identity. It recalls the earlier exchange between Viola-Cesario and Olivia:

Olivia. I prithee tell me what thou think'st of me.
Viola. That you do think you are not what you are.
Olivia. If I think so, I think the same of you.
Viola. Then think you right; I am not what I am.
Olivia. I would you were as I would have you be. (III.i.140–44)

This last line is very close to the subtitle of the play, "What You Will," and I suggest that its significance lies precisely in the kind of erotic object-choice here presented. Olivia wants Viola to fit her idealized image of her lost brother, but this makes of Viola a double mirror, for Olivia saw herself in her brother, and Viola is, of course, truly more like Olivia than she is like her dead brother. The persistent insistence on the social (and familial) determination of object-choice also receives emphasis here. The Arden editors rightly construe Viola's description of Olivia—"That you do think you are not what you are" as meaning both "that you think you are not in love with a woman, but you are," and "that you are behaving (in loving a page) as though you thought you were less nobly born than you are." Clearly, then, social and sexual identity is determined by object-choice, and everyone can be what he wills, by loving in another what he would see in himself.

Why, though, should Malvolio suffer for doing exactly what Olivia has encouraged Cesario to do? The false letter reads:

In my stars I am above thee, but be not afraid of greatness. Some are born great, some achieve greatness, and some have greatness thrust upon 'em.

(II.v.143–46)

This injunction is twice repeated, once by Malvolio himself (III.iv.38–44), and once by the Clown (V.i.369–70), so that it becomes an important reference point in the play. The Duke finally assures Olivia that Sebastian is socially acceptable—"Be not amaz'd, right noble is his blood" (V.i.262)—and Viola has previously ranked herself as "gentleman" (I.v.281–83). Olivia's triple definition of what Malvolio is not ("generous, guiltless, and of free disposition") recalls what Holofernes says the King of Navarre and his court are not: "generous . . . gentle . . . humble" (*LLL* V.ii.623). Class is seemingly one area in which Shakespeare allows no relativism: one either is, or is not, gentle, and birth will out—an argument which it is generally conceded he makes in *The Tempest*, in correction of Montaigne's "Of Cannibals." When Olivia says of Malvolio, "He hath been most notoriously abus'd" (V.i.378), the Arden editors rightly point out that her echo of Malvolio's own complaint, "Madam, you have done me wrong,/ Notorious wrong" (V.i.327–28), suggests that she "may express amusement, or amusement mingled with concern . . . but . . . hardly . . . complete seriousness, still less positive anger [against the Clown and others in on the plot]." She then shows the same condescension of all the courtiers in *Love's Labor's Lost* and all but Theseus in *A Midsummer Night's Dream*—and even he abuses the rustics, in spite of his protestations of amending imagination.

One of the invariables of Greek New Comedy is the social compatibility of young lovers who are to be married; many of the plots turn on the recognition of the young girl's parentage. Menander harks back to an earlier Greek equation between birth and worth and ignores the quibble that Euripides made in so many of his plays, that virute is a mode of behavior, not an inheritance, so slaves can behave more like free men than their masters. In most theories of comedy its primary function is to restore order out of chaos. I have argued that Shakespeare allows this order to be imposed by his heroes in their perception, rather than to be recognized as inherently there in nature. I have also suggested that he makes gods of his heroes by giving them the leisure to see themselves and others in this creative fashion. But he does not seem to distribute this gift universally, nor does he make those who receive it universally charitable in their use of it. Like most gods his young lovers are arbitrary and unaccountable, and we occasionally identify with the butts of their abuse.[17]

Twelfth Night closes with three marriages—Sir Toby stoops to take Maria—but Malvolio is left alone. His perversion is that he does not love at all. He despises Olivia along with all her retinue, and only pays suit to her to advance himself to the position of authority her husband would hold. He cannot see beyond himself to others, even to see himself in others. His appetite is distempered, so that he has a taste for nothing, nobody. In contrast, Orsino's appetite is ravenous but never satisfied and easily surfeited with any object because his desires are various, although the perfect image of his love is constant. He must learn to accept change in the object of his desire, to allow that object to remake his image. Antonio here, as also in *The Merchant of Venice*, is left alone. His love is idolatrous, the way Orsino's was before Viola taught him to love better.

There is a certain zaniness to all this, as there must be when there is so much erotic action and when it ends with each person having what he will. The great truth Shakespeare exposes here, at the end of this first period of his comic development, is that desire is not a static, absolute pattern, but rather a dynamic, changeable system of forces. In the late romances we shall see a mutual correction of idealizing and adjusting love, love that imposes its patterns upon its objects, just as in these middle comedies we have seen a mutual correction of the narcissistic and anaclitic orientation of desire. Orsino must be a bit bewildered by all this; Viola is still transvestized when he accepts her as his own, and he must fantasize her as a woman.[18] There could be no finer figure for Shakespeare's conception of "mature love" than this scene which concludes his "mature comedies":[19] it is love which moves beyond mirroring and idolatry to a point where it can accept change in its object because its subject is not only secure in himself but is himself capable of change, of assimilating to fresh, rich patterns.

It is Orsino who remarks, on seeing Viola and Sebastian together for the first time: "A natural perspective, that is, and is not!" (V.i.215). Sebastian then interprets to Olivia Viola's account of her transvestism:

> So comes it, lady, you have been mistook.
> But nature to her bias drew in that.
>
> (V.i.257–58)

What is natural about all this is that lovers have followed all the necessary steps in orienting their desire. We all have narcissistic longings, though few have twins. To see the embrace of these actual twins on stage, one male and one female, should be a *coup de théâtre* unsurpassed in romantic comedy. Unfortunately it seldom plays well, because the actor and actress do not look enough alike. The only scene which could surpass this in fulfilling the deepest narcissistic desires is if a mature lover could embrace his own younger, more beautiful self, since narcissism is essentially nostalgic.[20]

It could be argued that Shakespeare makes the high point of each of his comedies the recognition scene, which inevitably involves some kind of narcissistic pattern in desire and that then the marriages which follow—or do not follow—are anticlimatic, sometimes even unconvincing. This is not my reading. I think Shakespeare's exhaustive seriousness about depicting the operation of desire caused him to formulate the philosophy which we find so evident in the late romances, that of celebrating the capacity gracious men have to move beyond their search for themselves in others to the point of seeing others as independent, spontaneously developing subjects in their own right. I will admit, however, that this philosophy to some extent dissipates the erotic tension, so that the late romances do not share that fervor and obsession so characteristic of the mature comedies like *Twelfth Night*. Again, then, I agree with Kermode, who finds Shakespeare at the height of his powers in the mature comedies, whereas in the late romances he sees a tendency toward prolixity.[21] I see, however, psychosexual and philosophical patterns in Shakespeare to explain this aesthetic judgement. The early comedies do not end in marriage because Shakespeare cannot reconcile his young male lovers' narcissistic demands with the compromises inherent in that institution. In the mature comedies such reconciliation is almost complete, but the outsiders—especially the two Antonios, but also Malvolio, and, much less ~cifically, Jaques—are always there to remind us of those old, inescapable desires. These desires will come back at the end of the late romances—where there is marriage for the young lovers and reunion, sometimes, for the aged—as a clearly expressed wish for death. In all the ways Shakespeare states the case for the renunciation of narcissistic demands in oedipal compromise and the yielding of adolescent to mature object-choice, he never claims that such demands are ever met, that there is any end to the desire they express, except death. In Hobbes' terms, "Felicity is a continual progress of the desire, from one object to another . . . A special inclination of all mankind [is] a perpetual and restless desire of power after power, that ceaseth only in death" (*Leviathan*, XI).

V

THE LATE ROMANCES

There are many ways in which to determine the differences between the comedies of the 1590s and the romances written after 1610. Our interest, however, is the orientation of desire. Though nothing really happens in the later plays that does not happen in the earlier ones—fathers claim a sexual prerogative over their daughters, women are falsely accused of unchastity, families are divided and reunited by the sea, men dispute the possession of women but even in doing so show their great dependence upon each other— nothing seems the same. The perspective is entirely different, and this is a function, generally, of time. We are concerned with the desires of two generations, older married people and younger people just falling in love, whereas formerly all our attention was focused on the young people as they first learn to love. Whereas in the earlier comedies all energy was spent in the young man's attaining the object of his desire, relinquishing finally friend for lover—and we have noted that in several of the plays the young woman takes the role of the pursuer, having transvestized for the task—there is a release in the later plays, a relinquishing of control, almost a sigh of relief after the expense of energy.

This affect is not confined to the erotic concerns of the plays, but is pervasive of all their concerns. In *The Tempest* Prospero gives up not only his daughter, but his staff, his books, his control of the island, and, prospectively, life itself: "Every third thought shall be my grave." We relate this to the bond we found in the earlier plays between erotic orientation and general worldview. Love, like life generally, is a fanciful adventure, a projection of images upon malleable, changeable nature, a shaping of things to our own needs. To the Lunatic, the Lover, and the Poet, Shakespeare adds Everyman or at least every gracious man, every Gentleman. They show us that to live is to create, to impose our own principles of order upon the chaos of our world, and like love, this effort is exhausting, so that finally we tire and die. In all of this there is the phenomenology of the self, the mirroring of the self in nature, a narcissism which begins in the desire for another like the self, but reaches into every aspect of life, requiring all of nature to reflect the self, so that life itself is over when this tension subsides.[1]

We must discuss the shift of erotic focus from the sexually ambiguous friend-lover of the early and middle comedies, where the point of view is the young man's, to the faithful and innocent daughter who is the center of her father's world in the late romances.[2] We must discuss the simultaneous shift of attention from a worldview which defies ideals and absolutes and seeks truth in particular phenomena as shaped by the creative human spirit (the Lunatic, the Lover, and the Poet, but also the Constant Lover and the Gracious King) to a consideration of the misuse of authority. In exploring this theme Shakespeare shows the need for loosening control and for allowing natural patterns to assert themselves, or rather, for allowing other, younger, more erotically active people to assume control of those patterns, through whom they exist.

The Winter's Tale

The proposition that in Shakespeare's comedy the way young men look at women somehow determines the way they look at the world—that their psychosexuality is their philosophy—has been difficult to argue over the whole stretch of his career, and throughout each individual play. In *The Winter's Tale*, however, there is one, short crucial passage, where all the concerns of all the previous plays come together, and though the difficulty of this passage has inclined previous critics to declare its content almost ineffable, it might yield more readily to explication under the pressure of that proposition. It is, of course, when Leontes announces the onset of his jealousy:

> Affection! thy intention stabs the centre:
> Thou dost make possible things not so held,
> Communicat'st with dreams;—how can this be?—
> With what's unreal thou coactive art,
> And fellow'st nothing: then 'tis very credent
> Thou may'st co-join with something; and thou dost,
> (And that beyond commission) and I find it,
> (And that to the infection of my brains
> And hard'ning of my brows).

(I.ii.138–46)

My reading of the play is centered in this passage, and within this passage on the conception behind "affection."

Suddenly, Leontes becomes convinced that Polixenes, his dear friend from childhood, and Hermione, his wife, have become lovers. We never think of these characters as young, because they are always played by middle-aged actors, whose beards can be powdered white for the second half of the play, after the sixteen-year gap. Yet we should, in fact, compare them to the young lovers of the early and middle comedies. Leontes was only twenty-three years old when Mamilius was born, and Mamilius is still "unbreech'd" (I.ii.154–55). Leontes has replaced Polixenes with Hermione, just as Proteus must replace Valentine with Julia, and Orlando must replace Ganymede with Rosalind. Friends must yield to lovers, but what happens when friends and lovers are confused, when the likeness between friends creates the fantasy that one friend can take the other friend's wife, that the wife herself cannot tell the two friends apart? This is exactly what happens in the Titus and Gisippus story behind *The Two Gentlemen of Verona*: a bed trick is played on one friend's wife so the other friend can actually take sexual possession of her. Shakespeare did not allow this to happen in *The Two Gentlemen of Verona*—though Valentine does say to Proteus, "All that was mine in Silvia, I give thee"—but it is the fantasy behind *The Winter's Tale*.

The most obvious sense of "affection" is "sexual passion." The Arden editor, in addition to citations from Jonson and the Authorized Version of the bible, 1611 (where at Col. iii.5, "inordinate affection" replaces "unnaturall luste" in the Great Bible, 1539; and at Romans i.26, "vile affections" replace "shamefull lustes"), cites two representative passages from Shakespeare. Tarquin explains his intention to rape Lucrece: "Affection is my captain and he leadeth" (*Rape of Lucrece*, 271). Shylock explains his desire for Antonio's flesh:

> for affection,
> Mistress of passion, sways it to the mood
> Of what it likes or loathes.
>
> (*MV* IV.i.50–52)[1]

This comes at the center of Shylock's long speech on the idiosyncracy of men's fears and desires. His examples are the man who hates rats, the man who hates pigs, and the man who hates cats. Clearly, then, there is a twofold distinction: affection is not only distinguished from reason, but also from those universal fears and desires, which he calls "passions."

We might compare the King's opening remarks in *Love's Labor's Lost*—

> Therefore, brave conquerors—for so you are,
> That war against your own affections
> And the huge army of the world's desires—
> Our late edict shall strongly stand in force.

$$(I.i.8-11)^2$$

—and note the same distinction: "affections" are peculiar to each man, but "desires," like "passions," are universal forces. If affection in Leontes' speech is used in this special sense, with reference to those fears and desires peculiar to individual men, then whose affections are being considered: Leontes' own, Hermione's, or Polixenes'? The immediate context is Leontes' consideration of Mamilius' likeness to himself, and the possibility that Mamilius is not his son but Polixenes':

Leon. Art thou my calf?
Mam.   Yes, if you will, my lord.
Leon. Thou want'st a rough pash and shoots I have
   To be full like me: yet they say we are
   Almost as like as eggs; women say so,
   (That will say anything): but were they false
   As o'er-dy'd blacks, as wind, as waters; false
   As dice are to be wish'd by one that fixes
   No bourn 'twixt his and mine, yet were it true
   To say this boy were like me. Come, sir page,
   Look on me with your welkin eye: sweet villain!
   Most dear'st, my collop! Can thy dam?—may't be?—
   Affection! thy intention stabs the centre. (I.ii.127–38)

How is it that he associates the likeness of his son to himself with the difference of one man's property from another's? The connection is the falseness of women: they are as false, in the sense of weak and undependable, as are clothes which have been dyed so often with vitriolic black dye that they fall apart; as wind; as water; as dice which are rolled by a man who covets another man's property, who sets no limit ("bourn") between his property and the other man's, between

himself and the other man. In the consideration of likeness between
himself and his son, Leontes freely associates his wife with the unpre-
dictability of dice rolled by this indiscriminate man; the middle element is that she, and other women, say Mamilius is like him, but women
say anything, and therefore may do anything: "Can thy dam?—may't
be?" Later Leontes will accuse Hermione of not being able to tell the
difference between himself and Polixenes, of confusing them, of lik-
ening the one to the other:

> You have mistook, my lady,
> Polixenes for Leontes.
>
> (II.i.81–82)

Is it, then, Hermione's affection which is at issue? We might think
so, especially if we recall Emilia's conversation with Desdemona, her
admission of sexual passions for herself and all women, and her impatience with the artificial distinction society maintains between the
sexes on the very nature of such passions:

> Let husbands know
> Their wives have sense like them. They see and smell
> And have their palates both for sweet and sour,
> As husbands have. What is it that they do
> When they change us for others? Is it sport?
> I think it is. And doth affection breed it?
> I think it doth. Is 't frailty that thus errs?
> It is so too. And have not we affections,
> Desires for sport, and frailty, as men have?
>
> (*Othello* IV.iii.94–100)

"Affection" is here associated in an elaborate figure with appetite and
"change," "sport" and "frailty," to suggest "whim" or "passing fancy."
This is different, then, from Shylock's usage: there, though peculiar
to each man, "affection" is constant, like a character trait; here, however, not only are affections different from one man or woman to another, but they are also different for each man or woman from time to
time.[3] We note also that the basic figure finally is of affection as a creative force, a fertility: affection breeds sport. Leontes uses the same
figure later in his madness speech, as we shall see.[4]

Carroll points out in his remarks on the opening of *Love's Labor's Lost*[5] that "affection" is used by Shakespeare if not synonomously with, at least to suggest, both "affectation" (*OED*, V.13) and "infection" (*OED*, III.10). A particularly clear example of this is found in *Troilus and Cressida*, where Hector tries to diminish Cressida in Troilus' eyes:

> *Hect.* Brother,
>   She is not worth what she doth cost the keeping.
> *Tro.* What's aught but as 'tis valued?
> Hect. But value dwells not in particular will:
>   It holds his estimate and dignity
>   As well wherein 'tis precious of itself
>   As in the prizer. 'Tis mad idolatry
>   To make the service greater than the god;
>   And the will dotes that is attributive
>   To what infectiously itself affects,
>   Without some image of th' affected merit. (*TC* II.ii.51–60)

We have seen that Shakespeare consistently defines the idolatry of love as a kind of fetishism, where the representation of an ideal object of desire is projected upon an actual object and then that object is venerated not for what it is but for this representation. Here in *Troilus and Cressida* we hear that Troilus' love for Cressida is a closed circle of representation: the lover sets up an idol in his mind which then, like a disease, reduces to a likeness some lady who had no original likeness to that idol at all.[6]

All of these uses of "affection" suggest playful etymology: Shakespeare constantly construes it so that we are aware of its elements, *ad-*, "toward," and *facio*, "to make." One "affects" either some actual object or an image of an object, so that an "affection" (or "affectation") is a "tendency toward" or "likeness of." Again we are faced with that deepest of Shakespearean perceptions of love, that it is an orientation toward some object which is originally an identification with that object. The preposition "to" is often used to suggest motion toward:

> My King is tangled in affection to
> A creature of the Queen's, Lady Anne Bullen.
>
>   (*H.VIII* III.ii.35–36)

I dare pawn down my life for him that he hath wrote this to feel my affection to your honour and to no further pretense of danger.

(Lear I.ii.92–95)

We have seen that "affection" can suggest planetary motion, as when Valentine describes his love for Silvia, who is consistently likened to the moon:

Val. In conclusion, I stand affected to her.
Spe. I would you were set, so your affection would cease. (*TGV* II.i.80–81)

One of the many figures behind Leontes' madness speech is cosmological: "Affection! thy intention stabs the centre." "Centre" is here not only the center of the "affected" person—whether Leontes, Hermione, or Polixenes—but also the center of the universe—whether sun or earth. Later Leontes will swear:

> No: if I mistake
> In those foundations which I build upon,
> The centre is not big enough to bear
> A school-boy's top. Away with her to prison!

(II.i.100–3)

And Hermione will respond:

> There's some ill planet reigns:
> I must be patient till the heavens look
> With an aspect more favourable.

(II.i.105–7)

Swearing that Lysander is true to her, Hermia makes the same kind of reference to cosmic order in *A Midsummer Night's Dream;*

> The sun was not so true unto the day
> As he to me. Would he have stol'n away
> From sleeping Hermia? I'll believe as soon
> This whole earth may be bor'd, and that the moon
> May through the centre creep, and so displease
> Her brother's noon-tide with th' Antipodes.

(*MND* III.ii.50–55)

"Displace" yields to "displease" for the sake of the rhyme: Hermia's figure is of Artemis the moon piercing through the earth and confronting her brother Apollo the sun on the other side. Polonius uses a similar hyperbole:

> I will find
> Where truth is hid, though it were hid indeed
> Within the centre.
>
> (*Hamlet* II.ii.157–59)

We find then that Shakespeare often appeals to cosmic order as a model for human behavior, especially erotic behavior. The most complete statement of this principle is Ulysses' speech on degree in *Troilus and Cressida:*

> The heavens themselves, the planets, and this centre
> Observe degree, priority, and place,
> Insisture, course, proportion, season, form,
> Office, and custom, in all line of order.
> And therefore is the glorious planet Sol
> In noble eminence enthron'd and spher'd
> Amidst the other; whose med'cinable eye
> Corrects the influence of evil planets,
> And posts like the commandment of a king,
> Sans check, to good and bad. But when the planets
> In evil mixture to disorder wander,
> What plagues and what portents, what mutiny,
> What raging of the sea, shaking of earth,
> Commotion in the winds, frights, changes, horrors,
> Divert and crack, rend and deracinate
> The unity and married calm of states
> Quite from their fixure.
>
> (*TC* I.iii.85–101)

He also considers that concepts can lose the words normally attached to them, and that those bipolar oppositions which give language meaning can break down, when, under the influence of wandering planets, men confound themselves:

> Force should be right—or rather, right and wrong,
> Between whose endless jar justice resides,
> Should lose their names, and so should justice too.
>
> (*TC* I.iii.116–118)

Ulysses' speech has been claimed for evidence that Shakespeare accepted Copernican theory, but even here it is clear that "this centre"
is not the sun but the earth,[7] that Shakespeare sees the sun as a planet
"wandering" with the other planets in the heavens about the earth.
He even plays on the sense of "planet" as "wanderer": "But when the
planets/ In evil mixture to disorder wander."[8] If the earth is the center, is the center holding? Shakespeare's philosophy of affection, as
applied both cosmologically and psychologically, would seem to deny
it: there is no secure reference point in man or nature. Nor, it would
seem, is there any secure reference between them. Though Ulysses argues for order and degree in human affairs on the basis of order and
degree among the planets—the sun is the king—he admits that planets
wander, thus causing chaos in human affairs. Edmund, in *Lear*, ridicules even this:

This is the excellent foppery of the world, that when we are sick in fortune—
often the surfeit of our own behaviour—we make guilty of our disasters the
sun, the moon, and the stars, as if we were villains by necessity, fools by
heavenly compulsion. (*Lear* I.ii.128–33)

Even though we find in Shakespeare no proof of Copernican theory,
we cannot find there, either, proof that he continued to see in the universe the well-ordered system which medieval astronomers had taken
from Aristotle. No more did he see planets moving in predictable patterns than he saw all men behaving in the same way. "Affection" is
for Shakespeare very much what "appetite" is for Hobbes, an attractive force which acts on men and women as on planets, forcing them
into conjunction with each other, and each has his own peculiar appetite or affection. Again we should think of Foucault's distinction between the Renaissance episteme as a vast system of correspondences,
and the classical episteme as representation of representation—a kind
of phenomenalism or relativism—and should consider both Shakespeare and Hobbes under the latter rubric. In Shakespeare, as in
Hobbes, this insistence on perspective is closely tied to nominalism:
attaching words to things is what each man does to order his existence. They are not intrinsically connected, nor, indeed, is the existence of an abstract quality like Affection guaranteed by the use of the
word.

In the very opening lines of *The Winter's Tale*, Camillo describes the affection between Leontes and Polixenes as an almost physical force:

"Sicilia cannot show himself over-kind to Bohemia. They were trained together in their childhoods, and there rooted betwixt them then such an affection which cannot choose but branch now. Since their more mature dignities and royal necessities made separation of their society, their encounters, though not personal, have been royally attorneyed with interchange of gifts, letters, loving embassies, that they have seemed to be together, though absent; shook hands, as over a vast; and embraced, as it were, from the ends of opposed winds. The heavens continue their loves!" (I.i.21–32)

The basic figure is of two young trees planted next to each other, and bending toward each other. We soon hear from Polixenes himself that this affection was based on likeness:

> We were as twinn'd lambs that did frisk i' th' sun,
> And bleat the one at th' other: what we chang'd
> Was innocence for innocence: we knew not
> The doctrine of ill-doing, nor dream'd
> That any did.
>
>   (I.ii.67–71)

Here begins the "Garden of Eden" imagery that informs the rest of the play, that strange nostalgia men have for a time before women, when they were intimate with their male god and knew no difference, no need, no guilt. This is, of course, the projection onto universal history of each man's own primary experience of narcissism, that stage in his development when the mother is so available to him that she eclipses herself and his desire is then for himself rather than for her. Only thus can we account for the insistence of this vision on the woman as devil, a sure sign of man's irremediable division from his god and therefore from himself. Hermione, given the impossible task of reestablishing and maintaining the intimacy between Leontes and Polixenes, becomes that devil.

> Grace to boot!
> Of this make no conclusion, lest you say
> Your queen and I are devils.
>
>   (I.ii.80–82)

The oedipal mother is validated by the father as an object of desire for the son, but that desire is different from the original narcissistic desire the son has for himself. Leontes' love for Polixenes is that affection which attracts like to like, the child to the mirror, the ego to the ideal ego, the friend to the friend, but not the man to the woman.

So far we have seen that Leontes' use of "affection" in his madness speech suggests a physical force of attraction which draws planets to each other and, in the human realm, subjects to like objects. Leontes is thinking about Mamilius' likeness to himself, and seizes on Polixenes' likeness to himself. In thinking about Hermione giving birth to Mamilius, he seizes on the notion of creation and contemplates it abstractly with reference to words and things generally, and concretely with reference to Hermione and Polixenes:[9]

> Affection! thy intention stabs the centre:
> Thou dost make possible things not so held,
> Communicat'st with dreams;—how can this be?—
> With what's unreal thou coactive art,
> And fellow'st nothing: then 'tis very credent
> Thou may'st co-join with something; and thou dost,
> (And that beyond commission) and I find it,
> (And that to the infection of my brains
> And hard'ning of my brows).
>
> > (I.ii.138–46)

We have already noted the association Shakespeare makes between "affection" and "infection": something is catching here, something from one sphere is recreating itself in another; what Leontes thinks Polixenes and Hermione do in bed is happening in his head. "Intention" can signify both its "tendency" and its "intensity."

The language of this passage is compulsively erotic, focused on the scene of copulation. "Communicate" is usually used of people and means to hold intercourse with or converse (*OED*, 9); Shakespeare has personified the abstraction Affection and has made it a sexual agent. "Coactive" can suggest both the force of compulsion and concerted action. "Fellow" means both "to be a partner or share in," and "to produce a fellow to, to equal, to match." It is related to a specifically sexual term, found in fourteenth century texts, "fellowred," of the act of copulation. "Co-join" is used of marriage (*MAAN* IV.i.12) and sexual intercourse (*RJ* V.iv.31). "Commission," the fourth word in five lines with the "con-" prefix, suggests both the delegation of authority and sin. Hermione had used it earlier in speaking to Polixenes:

> Yet of your royal presence I'll adventure
> The borrow of a week. When at Bohemia
> You take my lord, I'll give him my commission
> To let him there a month behind the gest
> Prefix'd for's parting: yet, good deed, Leontes
> I love thee not a jar o' th' clock behind
> What lady she her lord. You'll stay?

(I.ii.38–44)

Hermione's only actual commission had been to convince Polixenes to extend his visit; here she imagines circumstances under which she would give Leontes her commission to extend a visit with Polixenes; Leontes imagines an act beyond any commission, an act of adultery. The preparation for this is the confusion of friends and lovers:

Leon.   Is he won yet?
Her. He'll stay, my lord.
Leon.   At my request he would not.
   Hermione, my dearest, thou never spok'st
   To better purpose.
Her.   Never?
Leon.   Never but once.
Her. What! have I twice said well? when was't before? (I.ii.86–90)

Leon.   Why, that was when
   Three crabbed months had sour'd themselves to death,
   Ere I could make thee open thy white hand,
   And clap thyself my love; then didst thou utter
   'I am yours for ever.'
Her.   'Tis Grace indeed.
   Why lo you now; I have spoke to th' purpose twice:
   The one, for ever earn'd a royal husband;
   Th' other, for some while a friend.
Leon.   Too hot, too hot!
   To mingle friendship far, is mingling bloods. (I.ii.101–9)

"Friend" can, of course, mean "lover" (*OED*, 4), as it does at *Love's Labor's Lost* V.ii.404, and at *Measure for Measure* I.iv.29. In going beyond her commission from Leontes to keep Polixenes with them, she has created in his mind the scene of adultery. We have seen that a

major theme of the play is the likeness of Leontes and Polixenes; now
we see that in Leontes' mind she pushes his friendship with Polixenes
to the point of physical intimacy, "mingling bloods," so that not only
can Leontes and Polixenes change places because of their likeness, but
Hermione can change places with Leontes, take Leontes' place in his
attraction to Polixenes. This answers our question about whose affection Leontes apostrophizes: it is that whole force field of fears and desires which holds these three together.

This all suggests the standard psychoanalytic explanation for Leontes'
madness, that Leontes imagines Hermione fulfilling his own desire to
have sexual intercourse with Polixenes.[10] (One readily compares Hamlet's madness: he cannot kill Claudio because he sees himself in Claudio, Claudio having killed Hamlet's father and taken his place in
Hamlet's mother's bed.) Kahn deepens our understanding by stressing the narcissistic and nostalgic determinants of Leontes' relationship
with Polixenes:

Clearly, Polixenes is Leontes' double, one of the same sex and age who only
mirrors him; loving Polixenes is depicted as guiltless, Edenic, and asexual, as
opposed to loving a woman.[11]

The way Kahn lines up her epithets suggests the distinction between
pre-oedipal and oedipal orientation of desire. Freud originally defined
narcissism as the libidinal investment of the ego, but he was reasoning
backward from his major concern with the male child's later oedipal
desire for the mother. Some qualification of the general priciple of infantile sexuality is necessary: desire for the self is not the same as desire for the mother or any other—at least in its nostalgic recollection.
For some reason the male child remembers symbiosis with the mother
as himself complete, and he blames the oedipal mother for his conflict
with the oedipal father: the phantom of the sexually insatiable woman
is, as we have seen in several of the earlier comedies, an amalgam of
the void from which the pre-oedipal child fantasizes himself springing
and the oedipal mother who demands both father and son.

While "affection" is both likeness and attraction, both identity and
desire, it is also imagination. There are close parallels between Leontes'
analysis of the workings of his own mind and Theseus' analysis of the
minds of the lunatic, the lover, and the poet:

> Lovers and madmen have such seething brains,
> Such shaping fantasies, that apprehend
> More than cool reason ever comprehends.
> The lunatic, the lover and the poet
> Are of imagination all compact.
>
> (*MND* V.i.4–8)

Leontes knows what is happening to him; he is making something out
of nothing. It is his own peculiar fears and desires of which he makes
the personified abstraction Affection, but so completely does he confuse both Polixenes and Hermione with himself, so completely does
he project his fears and desires upon them, that Affection becomes the
active scene of adultery between his friend and his wife. His own peculiar fears and desires have taken control of him, and like sexual
creatures communicate with dreams. We know that the dream which
the young lovers in *A Midsummer Night's Dream* are implicated in is
Oberon's dream of a sexually insatiable Titania; Theseus himself must
allay such fears on his wedding night. These are the fears which Hermione activates with her bawdy wit:

> I prithee tell me: cram's with praise, and make's
> A fat as tame things: one good deed, dying tongueless,
> Slaughters a thousand, waiting upon that.
> Our praises are our wages. You may ride's
> With one soft kiss a thousand furlongs ere
> With spur we heat an acre.
>
> (I.ii.91–96)

We have noted the double bind in which men catch women: they lock
them up, keep them "dully sluggardis'd at home," and then fantasize
them filling their empty hours with sexual longings. Fathers like Brabantio fear this of their daughters, and husbands like Leontes fear this
of their wives.

Lovers' and madmen's brains seethe with fantasies; Leontes' brain
is infected. We know, then, that there is a double determination to all
this, a phylogenetic as well as an ontogenetic explanation: all men are
misogynistic because of their particular experience of their own mothers, but there are also the myths, the culturally transferred archetypes
of female sexuality: Klytemnestra, Medea, Cressida.[12] The dreams are
collective, then, and individual men communicate with them through

art and literature, so that a hermeneutic circle is completed which has reference to nothing actual in mature men's experience.[13]

Hermione connects language, dreams, and Leontes' royal authority:

> Sir,
> You speak a language that I understand not:
> My life stands in the level of your dreams,
> Which I'll lay down.
>
> (III.ii.79–82)

Neeley remarks: "Henceforth in the play Leontes employs reason, language and tyranny to eradicate Hermione, and replace her with an abstraction whose 'actions' are in his 'dreams.' "[14] Leontes has taken his dream, which he constructed of his own infantile experience, and of the universal and culturally specific myths of female sexuality, and has hypostatized it as an abstract, a Form or Idea, to which he now makes reference, rather than to actual events and the real Hermione. He is more tenacious of this construct because he is a king, and he is the complete perversion of the gracious king we see in Theseus.[15] He tells his attendants precisely his method of reaching truth:

> Why, what need we
> Commune with you of this, but rather follow
> Our forceful instigation? Our prerogative
> Calls not your counsels, but our natural goodness
> Imparts this; which if you, or stupified,
> Or seeming so, in skill, cannot or will not
> Relish a truth, like us, inform yourselves
> We need no more of your advice: the matter,
> The loss, the gain, the ord'ring on't, is all
> Properly ours.
>
> (II.i.161–69)

This extraordinary independence—he distances himself from his advisors just as he distances himself from actual events: he communes only with preconceived Forms—this absolute self-reference, is, epistemologically, the equivalent of his erotic orientation. He makes of himself a pattern of truth and then refuses to refer to any actual contradictions. Something has come of nothing, and though when it was actually happening—when he first saw Affection couple with nothing and produce something—he knew that, like impregnation, it was a mystery and a paradox, he can no longer trace that path of reasoning, and he refuses to admit that something has come of nothing:

> Is whispering nothing?
> Is leaning cheek to cheek? is meeting noses?
> Kissing with inside lip? stopping the career
> Of laughter with a sigh (a note infallible
> Of breaking honesty)? horsing foot on foot?
> Skulking in corners? wishing clocks more swift?
> Hours, minutes? noon, midnight? and all eyes
> Blind with the pin and web, but theirs; theirs only.
> That would unseen be wicked? is this nothing?
> Why then the world, and all that's in 't, is nothing,
> The covering sky is nothing, Bohemia nothing,
> My wife is nothing, nor nothing have these nothings,
> If this be nothing.
>
> (I.ii.284–96)

Now that he has this knowledge, everything has come of nothing. Like a cloud it blocks out all else, obscures his perception. He sees and knows the guilt of sexual desire:

> How blest am I
> In my just censure! in my true opinion!
> Alack, for lesser knowledge! how accurs'd
> In being so blest! There may be in the cup
> A spider steep'd, and one may drink, depart,
> And yet partake no venom (for his knowledge
> Is not infected); but if one present
> Th' abhorr'd ingredient to his eye, make known
> How he hath drunk, he cracks his gorge, his sides,
> With violent hefts. I have drunk, and seen the spider.
>
> (II.i.36–45)

Spiders and snakes are among the most frequent symbols in myths and dreams for the mature female.[16] Hermione has become associated with the snake in the garden and now with the spider in the cup. Shakespeare forces us to see the evolution of sexual knowledge, to see it overwhelm reality. The sexual act as fantasized by the child—the nothing which his parents do together, from which something (he himself) comes—is the pattern for all perception.

This first part of the play, in posing this problem, also suggests a solution: grace. The situation is originally one of gracious hospitality, Leontes' lavish reception of Polixenes. In the opening scene Camillo states the paradox of grace to Archidamus, who fears that Polixenes will not be able to reciprocate fully: "You pay a great deal too dear for what's given freely" (I.i.18). Why is it that what is freely given in friendship is carefully measured in love? When Hermione begins to banter with Polixenes and Leontes on the difference between their relations with each other and their relations with their wives, she invokes the Christian sense of "grace," but as a corrective to the sin which they both seem to see in her and not in themselves. Hermione's response to Polixenes' suggestion that she and Polixenes' wife have tempted their husbands to sin—which they had not experienced before in their youthful, mutual innocence—is "Grace to boot!" (I.ii.80), which must mean, "I call on God's grace to save me from this imputation," and not simply "Grace in addition," as the Arden editor would have it. "Boot" in this sense occurs four other times in the play, as both noun and verb: thrice in Autolycus' exchange of clothes with Florizel (IV.iv.638, 674–76), but once in Hermione's own response to the accusation of adultery:

> Since what I am to say, must be but that
> Which contradicts my accusation, and
> The testimony on my part, no other
> But what comes from myself, it shall scarce boot me
> To say 'not guilty':
>
>   (III.ii.22–26)

In the bantering scene, she follows up the exclamation "Grace to boot!" with the figure of speaking well being a woman who might have a sister: "O, would her name were Grace!" (I.ii.99). Leontes has said that she is speaking well now in begging Polixenes to stay, and that she spoke well once before, in accepting him as her husband. We have seen how ripe her response is with sexual suggestion—"cram's with praise, and make's/ As fat as tame things . . . You may ride's/ With one soft kiss"—and how this comparison of two speeches, one to Polixenes and one to Leontes, further identifies in Leontes' mind the two men in Hermione's mind. Why should the first speech be called "Grace"? When Leontes explains himself, she says,

'Tis Grace indeed.
Why lo you now; I have spoke to th' purpose twice:
The one, for ever earn'd a royal husband;
Th' other, for some while a friend.

(I.ii.105–8)

Leontes immediately interprets her:

Too hot, too hot!
To mingle friendship far, is mingling bloods.

(I.ii.108–9)

Grace is then simultaneously God's forgiveness for sexual appetite in men and women and that quality peculiar to kings among mortals of giving and forgiving without expectation of recompense, as in "grace and favor."

What does grace have to do with speaking? It seems this is not just an idle jest; rather the woman in the play who is responsible for the central mystery in the play, Paulina, is characterized by speaking too much, and indeed without grace. Cleomenes complains, just after the arrival of Florizel and Perdita in Sicily, that Paulina did not need to remind Leontes, as she has repeatedly over the intervening sixteen years, of his responsibility for Hermione's death:

You might have spoken a thousand things that would
Have done the time more benefit and grac'd
Your kindness better.

(V.i.21–23)

As in *Othello,* then, and elsewhere in the corpus, we find Shakespeare associating men's suspicion of women's insatiable sexuality with their speech.[17] Paulina is to Hermione what Emilia is to Desdemona. Paulina would be a man so that she could champion Hermione's cause (II.iii.59–61), just as Beatrice would for Hero. The constant contrast is between the tyranny of Leontes and the grace of Hermione:

Fear you his tyrannous power more, alas,
Than the queen's life? a gracious innocent soul,

(II.iii.28–29)

Unlike Othello, Leontes does not require the "ocular proof":

>   Camillo's flight,
>   Added to their familiarity,
>   (Which was as gross as ever touch'd conjecture,
>   That lack'd sight only, nought for approbation
>   But only seeing, all other circumstances
>   Made up to th' deed) doth push on this proceeding.

(II.i.174–79)

Grace, then, is what is required to be innocent and to see innocence, and tyranny is the projection of evil. Hermione says she will answer the charges against her: "This action that I now go on/ Is for my better grace" (II.i.121–22), and she reminds Leontes of their previous relations:

>   I appeal
>   To your own conscience, sir, before Polixenes
>   Came to your court, how I was in your grace,
>   How merited to be so.

(III.ii.45–48)

With reference to Maxmilius, she is "his gracious dam" (III.ii.198). How does this complex pattern of associations between language and sexuality, the fact of innocence and the phantom of guilt, the active imagining of the man and the passive being of the woman, which is worked mostly in the first half of the play, related to more narrowly class-specific uses of the term in the second half?

Perdita, Time explains, is "now grown in grace" (IV.i.24). Polixenes says Florizel is not gracious for wooing beneath him (IV.ii.27–28), but Perdita calls Florizel, "My gracious lord" (IV.iv.5) and "The gracious mark o' th' land" (IV.iv.8). She worries, though, that his father will not approve, and uses epithets we know from the erotic context of *A Midsummer Night's Dream*:

>   How would he look, to see his work, so noble,
>   Vilely bound up?

(IV.iv.21–22)

She wonders, then, as Miranda does, at the truth and beauty of her young lover, and attributes all his virtues to his birth; indeed, the famous debate on flowers begins with the gift of grace. Perdita speaks to the disguised Polixenes and Camillo, offering them rosemary and rue: "Grace and remembrance be to you both" (IV.iv.76). The Arden editor comments: "Rosemary and rue signified respectively remembrance (friendship) and grace (repentance). Rue is known as 'herb grace.' " Perdita calls crossbred flowers "bastards" (IV.iv.83), and we recall that Leontes had insisted she was a bastard (II.iii.153–62). In appendix IV the Arden editor refers to Kermode's reading of *The Tempest* ("Nature and Nurture") and even cites a passage from Montaigne's "Of Cannibals." Is it possible to express the complexity of Shakespeare's thinking about the related structures of love, art, and reality? It would seem that he insists, against Montaigne, on the actual immanence of truth in things seen, as opposed to words heard and fantasies of the mind, in lineage and in nature. Perdita is not a bastard, but a princess, and therefore she is "gracious." Florizel loves her because he sees grace in her, which proves both his lineage and hers. We feel the conventions of comedy closing in upon us, shutting Shakespeare off from that total phenomenal freedom we would like to attribute to him, a complete egalitarianism of class and race and sex.

I think now we must also examine the theme of age. Grace is what young people shed upon each other and see in each other, and Shakespeare says it is actually there. Polixenes is as tyrannically wrong about Perdita as Leontes had been about Hermione. The old must yield to the young because the young, with their erotic energy, can reshape the world. The old are tired and will be absorbed by the world, which is death in many modes, as Hobbes shows:

Felicity is a continual progress of the desire, from one object to another, the attaining of the former being still but the way to the latter. . . . I put for a general inclination of all mankind, a perpetual and restless desire of power after power, that ceaseth only in death (*Leviathan* XI).

If this is the central concern of *The Winter's Tale* and all the other late romances, how do we read the end of *The Winter's Tale*? Shakespeare's greatest change in his primary source, Greene's *Pandosto*, is the resurrection of Hermione. Does her statue coming to life answer any of our questions about art and sexuality, seeing and being?

Strangely enough, the philosophical and ethical concerns of *The Winter's Tale*—grace as the redemption of reality—and the peculiar feature of the beloved as statue, also appear in Euripides' *Alcestis*. There

are many other similarities between the two plays. In the *Alcestis* Apollo
has granted Admetos, who received the god hospitably when he was
being punished by Zeus—there is a reference to this episode in *The
Winter's Tale:* Florizel compares himself to Apollo, disguised as "a poor
humble swain" (IV.iv.30)—the opportunity to live beyond the day fated
for his death, if he can find someone to die in his place. His wife Alcestis agrees, Admetos finds that his life has lost meaning when she is
gone, and Herakles, whom Admetos has received kindly even though
he is in mourning, brings Alcestis back from the underworld and restores her to Admetos. Admetos' great virtue is *charis*,[18] that aristocratic trait of giving with no expectation of return, the Greek equivalent of grace, and, in the argument of the play, a feature of friendship
between men (or men and gods), whereas *dikē*, or justice, which requires even exchange, characterizes the relations between men and
women. (We look back in the Shakespearean corpus to *The Two
Gentlemen of Verona*, and forward to *The Two Noble Kinsmen*.) There
is a strong statement of sexual orientation in Euripides' play, just as
there is in *The Winter's Tale*, and in both plays it expresses the fear by
the male protagonist of the mature female and the desire for a peren-
ially young woman, a woman who will not age and change but who
will always respond perfectly to his ideal image of an object of desire.
This ideal image is fixed in a male companion whom we recognize as
the lover's own narcissistic image of himself.

Admetos' father accuses him of having found a way of infinitely de-
laying the day of his death, seeking out always some young woman to
die for him. When Herakles brings Alcestis back from the dead, she
is veiled, and without identifying her, Herakles insists, in a parody of
the Greek betrothal ceremony, that Admetos take this young woman
(*nea gynē*) into his house. Since *nea gynē* can also mean "new wife,"
Euripides insists that we see that Admetos has taken a replacement for
Alcestis on the very day of her death, thus fulfilling his father Pheres'
"curse." As Alcestis lay dying, Admetos had promised never to re-
marry, that he would have a statue made of Alcestis and would pay
his devotions to it in his bedchamber. Even before that, in the myth
but not in the play—though one might argue that Euripides implies
this previous action with his constant reference to the marriage bed—
Admetos, on his wedding night, had come into the chamber to meet

his bride and found a knot of vipers in the bed. He required the help of Apollo to deal with this threat. If we read *The Winter's Tale*, Genesis, and *Alcestis* against each other we can identify the snake in the garden with the spider in the cup, the devil which Leontes and Adam and Admetos all face: it is the mature female, arousing memory traces of the sexually insatiable oedipal mother, against whom the only protection is regression to that stage of undifferentiation figured in myth by intimacy with a male god or companion.

Hermione dies and returns as a statue at the same time that Leontes is reunited with his daughter, a young and beautiful image of her mother, whom Leontes is attracted to. Paulina, who has kept Hermione secretly alive all those years since her husband brought false accusation against her, scolds him:

Paul.   Sir, my liege,
  Your eye hath too much youth in 't; not a month
  'Fore your queen died, she was worth more such gazes
  Than what you look on now.
Leon.   I thought of her,
  Even as these looks I made. (V.i.223–27)

Salangar has shown that this situation is frequent in classical and medieval romance:[19] the man promises his dying wife that he will never love another woman except the perfect image of her, which turns out to be their daughter. This is a version of the Persephone pattern, whose details and basic significance are determined by its male perspective. The man fears and distrusts the mature woman, wishes her dead, and replaces her in fancy with an unthreatening, unaging, unchanging (i.e., not fickle) ideal object which resembles her; Persephone returns every year as *kore*, "the maiden." We note, of course, in Shakespeare's late romances that this replacement is the daughter and therefore also an image of the father. This pattern we easily relate to that of the twins in the earlier comedies, especially Sebastian and Viola in *Twelfth Night:* it is a kind of narcissistic choice of object. Perdita appeals to her prototype Persephone in Proserpina (IV.iv.116), and the whole movement of *The Winter's Tale* is toward the rejuvenation of spring. Leontes is at first disappointed that Hermione's statue is "so much wrinkled" (V.iii.28), because he remembers her "as tender/ As infancy and grace" (V.iii.26–27).

The Winter's Tale leaves us then with thoughts on love as a perspective, a way of looking at life, like art: it is said of Julio Romano, the sculptor, that he "could put breath into his work, would beguile Nature of her custom, so perfectly he is her ape" (V.ii.97–99). He sounds like Pygmalion, who sculpted his ideal object of desire and then brought her to life with a prayer to Venus (Ovid, *Met.* X. 243–97). Pygmalion resorted to this method of fulfilling his desire because he was so disgusted by the sexual excess of "natural" women:

> One man, Pygmalion, who had seen these women
> Leading their shameful lives, shocked at the vices
> Nature has given the female disposition
> Only too often, chose to live alone,
> To have no woman in his bed. But meanwhile
> He made, with marvelous art, an ivory statue,
> As white as snow, and gave it greater beauty
> Than any girl could have, and fell in love
> With his own workmanship. The image seemed
> That of a virgin, truly, almost living,
> And willing, save that modesty prevented,
> To take on movement. The best art, they say,
> Is that which conceals art, and so Pygmalion
> Marvels, and loves the body he has fashioned.[20]

Clearly Shakespeare is resolving the paradox proposed by Montaigne and other sixteenth-century intellectuals who concerned themselves with the relation between art and nature by simply equating art and nature: Perdita *is* a princess and the statue of Hermione *is* the living Hermione. The obvious comparison to make with these revelations is the dream in *A Midsummer Night's Dream*. There we decided that Bottom's dream, which is the action in the forest we have seen on stage, is to a lesser extent Oberon's dream, and even Theseus': their male fears of the sexual insatiability of women are projected upon Titania and cause her to love an ass. We see a similar projection in the early scenes of *The Winter's Tale*. Leontes begins to meditate on Hermione's sexuality and convinces himself that she is an adultress; he wishes her dead; he realizes his error, but she is already dead; sixteen years later he wants to marry again, and falls in love with his own daughter; Paulina convinces him that this young girl is not so beautiful as his wife was when she died and produces the statue; the statue is aged and changed, but Leontes loves it, kisses it, and it comes to life. His dream is then extended past the fear of female sexuality, and the choice of a young girl to awaken his old love, to the final point where Shakespeare leads all his lovers: to accept age and change in their objects of desire.

This is grace, of course, and *The Winter's Tale* best illustrates Shakespeare's insistence that it is a human capacity. He identifies art with nature by identifying human perception with divine omnipotence. Hermione appeals to the gods to bless Perdita:

> You gods, look down,
> And from your sacred vials pour your graces
> Upon my daughter's head:
>
> (V.iii.121–23)

But Paulina has set the stage for her revelation in such a way that all present see Hermione herself as a goddess who can bless:

> Please you interpose, fair maiden, kneel
> And pray your mother's blessing.
>
> (V.iii.119–20)

Shakespeare's philosophies of art and love and life then come together under this rubric. The forces of the comic tradition, his own deep perception of the dynamics of desire, and the climate of intellectual change in his own time determine this pronouncement of the power of human eyes to see and human minds to conceive. With Menander he insists:

What a thing of grace is man, if only he be human.[21]

VI

SUMMARY

I. Comedy is concerned with social, political, and philosophical issues, but its primary concern is individual identity.

  1. Shakespearean comedy represents the world seen through the eyes of one character, usually a young male lover.

  2. As he sees himself in love, so he sees the world: the extent to which he can allow change and difference in the object of his desire is a measure of his openness to new and different experience.

  3. Shakespeare forces his young lovers to dispense with idealization in the objects of desire and with abstraction in their thinking about life, i.e., the courtly love tradition and medieval Platonism.

  4. Shakespeare restores to the comic tradition the concreteness and narcissistic orientation of Greek Old and Middle Comedy.

  5. Shakespeare restores to the Neoplatonic patterns of courtly love on which his comedies are drawn the homoerotic or autoerotic patterns of Plato's original philosophy.

II. The identity of an individual is a function of his orientation in the world: to which objects is he attracted and from which objects is he repelled?

  1. Among all objects of attraction and repulsion the most important objects are the erotic objects: comedy seeks the fulfillment of individual desires.

2. Shakespeare depicts an erotic world in which men can be attracted to women disguised as men.

   a. In the early comedies young men must choose between young male friends and female lovers *(CE, TGV, LLL)*.

   b. In the mature comedies young men must choose between older male friends and female lovers *(MV, TN)*.

   c. The two patterns are strangely combined in *WT*, a late romance.

3. The standard sequence of a young man's orientation of desire in Shakespearean comedy is first, an image of himself in a twin or friend; then, a young girl transvestized as a young boy; and finally, a young girl who fully reveals herself.

4. Shakespearean comedy is an accurate representation of male adolescent sexuality, which is characterized by:

   a. Fascination with the penis.

   b. Self-centered erotism.

   c. Lack of differentiation in the sex of the desired object.

   d. Pseudodifferentiation under social pressure: the pretension of a veteran's experience in the war of love.

   e. Lack of clear comprehension of sexual roles.

5. Since adolescent sexuality is a recapitulation of primary narcissism, Shakespearean comedy is also an accurate representation of primary narcissism.

   a. Freud: "The child has originally two objects of desire—himself and the woman who tends him."

   b. Fear of the mother is as pronounced a feature of the narcissistic stage as self-love.

III. Young lovers in Shakespearean comedy seek themselves and flee mature women.

   1. They seek themselves in twins, friends, and young women transvestized as young men.

   2. They express their fear of mature women by:

      a. Choosing debased women—whores, servants—as objects of desire: these they can control.

      b. Idealizing women to make them desirable: this is also an attempt to control.

      c. Being afraid of the liberated young women whom they

release from bondage to their father's sexual control, even though comic patterns traditionally depict this process.

IV. For Shakespeare's young male lovers, the choice of objects like themselves is a confirmation of themselves, while women pose a threat to their identity.

  1. They fantasize mature women as sexually insatiable: Titania loves an ass.

  2. Young women transvestized as young men reflect their male lovers' idealized images of themselves as younger and more beautiful.

  3. The young page in Shakespearean comedy is bold, beautiful, and witty; he seems to have the potential to do and to be anything.

  4. Young men turn finally to young women and away from other young men because young women lack that insistent aggression which so characterizes young men.

V. As each Shakespearean comedy follows stages in a young lover's development of his capacity to love, so Shakespeare's whole comic oeuvre follows the same stages, and this makes it a recapitulation of the stages of comic development.

  1. The early comedies focus on young men who are still mirroring themselves in male friends, before they can securely choose female lovers.

  2. The mature comedies deal with more mature lovers, but they must fight against preconceived notions of female sexuality, and yield, in some cases, the lead in love to the lady.

  3. In the late romances Shakespeare insists again on the erotic bond between fathers and daughters, and reveals that it, too, is narcissistic: Prospero, in giving up Miranda, relinquishes his hold on life.

VI. Shakespeare's lovers confuse male friends and female lovers, but whereas they allow mutuality in their relations with men, they insist on possessing and controlling women.

  1. Fathers think of daughters as gold in the bank or parts of themselves; Shylock is both robbed and castrated by Jessica's elopement.

2. Men imprint themselves upon women, like dies on metal:
women are material, men are form.

3. Men think of themselves as spirit and of women as flesh: women
are responsible for men's fall from grace with their gods, who
are men's own self-images.

VII. Shakespeare traces developmental stages in the orientation of desire, but does not allow for complete transcendence.

1. Men are never satisfied in their relations with women and always look back nostalgically to that time of innocence and bliss
when the world only mirrored them in their gods and friends.

2. Shakespeare traces developmental stages in erotic relations which
are also changes in philosophical perspective.

a. He validates phenomenal apprehension of difference in
specific objects against metaphysical speculation on absolutes.

b. Men must learn to accept age and change in the object of
their desire.

3. Shakespeare does not finally show a mature, transcendental
perfect love.

a. Having defined love as the appreciation of difference, he
validates finally only the initial stages of love, when the
conflicts between self and other are most intense. The relation between Beatrice and Benedick in *MAAN* is his fullest statement of love as tension; the love of Leontes and
Hermione as the end of *WT* is more the yielding of man to
nature, like Prospero's in *T*.

b. Just as Shakespeare's definition of love is a dynamic tension between two subjects who must see themselves in their
objects, but allow their objects to be as much subjects as
objects, so his philosophy is of man both shaping and being
shaped by nature.

1. Men must dispense with the idols of myth, religion, and
traditional wisdom and think of the world inductively.

2. Men must also create the world in their own images, bring
order to its chaos, beauty to its plainness.

3. In his cycle of phenomenal apprehension and projection, there is constant progress and growth, because there

is reference to no absolutes, no Forms, no perfect ladies, no patterns of human virtues, no God.

4. While Shakespeare frees men from the bondage which medieval deference to deduced patterns of perfection imposed on men in love and in life generally, he also obliges them to shape their experience fantastically, to make of all objects something rich and fine.

5. Shakespeare gives to men the shaping grace and creative energy which earlier poets and philosophers had attributed to God.

6. There are precedents for this kind of "humanism" in his classical, medieval, and Renaissance predecessors—in the comic tradition and in intelledctual history—but his statement of it is unique.

7. The lover's grace is to accept age and change in the object of his desire; the grace of every man is to impress himself upon his world while he has the energy to do so, and then to relinquish it to others.

8. Death is the end of desire; the end of desire is death.

NOTES

I. INTRODUCTION

1. See IV.2, for a discussion of the similarities between these two episodes. Shakespeare returned to this scene of the bride falsely seen false at the end of his career, in the lost *Cardenio*. L. Abel, *Metatheater* (New York: Hill and Wang, 1963) makes suggestive comparisons between Shakespeare and Cervantes: their characters take control of their own fictions, and through this new kind of irony, illusion and reality are inverted. M. Foucault, *Les mots et les choses* (Paris: Editions Gallimard, 1966), distinguishes the classical episteme from the Renaissance by noting that, beginning with such figures as Velasquez and Cervantes, artists were no longer concerned to show the relations between different orders of things, as in "the great chain of being," but rather concentrated on the representation of representation—the painter painting and the poet making. This kind of creative self-consciousness is what I claim as Shakespeare's essential aesthetic: he says nothing about the order of the world, knowing that there is none, but everything about the imagination, the shaping fantasy of poets, lovers, and madmen.

2. This is also one of the most difficult and misunderstood aspects of Freud's psychology. He felt that he had to accommodate to his own experiential model of the mind something of Jung's "collective unconscious," which is, in Jung, an article of faith, part of the human mysteries one is initiated into almost, it seems, genetically. The cusp between individual and universal experience is, then, in Freud, a place of defining tension; one experiences the harshness and cruelty of the father in the primal horde even if one's own father is weak and ineffective. The best description of the dynamics of these relations—individual and universal, present and past, actual and fantasized, self and other—is Lacan's proposition of *le nom du Père*. See "On a question preliminary to any

possible treatment of psychosis," *Ecrits*, A. Sheridan, tr. (New York: Norton, 1977), pp. 179–225. On the subject of women, then, we need to see the fears and desires of Shakespeare's young lovers in the context of the literary and philosophical tradition and as patterns of behavior recognizable as structures rooted in the infantile experience the male child has of the mother. Whether we approach the latter problem from Shakespeare's own experience—on which there is scanty evidence—or from the experience of each individual reader, the basic claim must be that men generally fear women because their first experience of women is of the all-powerful mother. Misogyny is, in this perspective, universal and inevitable; its guises are legion, and Shakespeare gives us an extraordinarily complete catalogue.

3. H. Fränkel, *Early Greek Poetry and Philosophy*, M. Hadas and J. Willis, tr. (New York: Harcourt Brace Javanovich, 1975), p. xi.

4. I paraphrase a summary of the positions taken by Cassirer in *The Logic of the Humanities, The Myth of the State*, and *The Individual and the Cosmos in Renaissance Philosophy*, offered by M. Domandi as introduction to his translation of the last of these (Oxford: Blackwell, 1963), pp. viii–ix.

5. J. F. Danby, *Shakespeare's Doctrine of Nature* (London: Faber and Faber, 1949).

6. I think, then, that Shakespeare is misread if he is read either as a final statement of late medieval and early Renaissance order—e.g., E. M. W. Tillyard, *The Elizabethan World Picture* (London: Chatto and Windus, 1956)—or as a prestatement of men's unity in reason. I do not know of any critics who admit they do the latter, but there is too much of the Enlightenment in the Shakespeare of most critics from the opening of that period itself down to the middle of this century. The necessary correction to both these views is made by such contemporary critics as Young, Kermode, and Carroll (see III.3 and IV.1). Finding unity in Shakespeare from an Enlightenment perspective is like finding unity in the pre-Socratics from Aristotle's perspective, a misreading which H. Cherniss corrected in *Aristotle's Criticism of Pre-Socratic Philosophy* (Baltimore: Johns Hopkins University Press, 1935). I think the most important philosophical statement ever made was Protagoras' "Man is the measure of all things." We know he meant that *each man* interprets his experience according to his own fears and desires; if we ask of every subsequent thinker whether he believes this proposition, and if not, what he believes instead, then we know where to place him along the phenomenological-metaphysical axis which is the history of Western thought.

7. I would like just to suggest here another dimension to this discussion which I shall explore in a bit more detail later. E. H. Gombrich, in *Art and Illusion* (New York: Pantheon, 1960), distinguishes between conceptual art and visual art and attributes to the Greeks of the early classical period the great breakthrough: Egyptian and other pre-Greek artists depicted in their work a schema, with reference to an ideal pattern, but Greek artists in the late sixth century began to depict a specific, even nonrepeatable moment in reality. They

thus introduced into plastic art the kind of narrative scope which so characterizes the Homeric epics, that quality which Auerbach distinguishes from biblical narrative in *Mimesis* (Princeton: Princeton University Press, 1953). The Greek artist, through his technical mastery of such problems as perspective, "qualifies" reality; a figure can be shown in profile and we do not worry where its other eye is, because we do not think of this figure as something in the world, or as a complete and perfect talisman, but only as the representation of a particular person or thing at a particular moment, seen from a particular angle. This kind of depiction ("visual") is then related to the other kind ("conceptual") as Homeric narrative is to myth (cf., biblical narrative as a system of *figurae*, moments which have reference to other moments, and only thereby have meaning). I think that what happened in Greece between Homer and Phidias happened again in Western Europe at about the turn of the seventeenth century. The result is what Foucault calls the classical episteme, when poets and artists began to concentrate on their own function in art, "to represent representation." I see Shakespeare as a prediction of this.

Gombrich notes Plato's annoyance with this development in Greek art; he preferred Egyptian art with its iconographic orientation, its suggestion of a Form beyond the object it presents. The Greek artist asks, "What if there is no Form of Table, but only this specific table, and others, all different?" And, "What if I depict not the Idea of Table, but this table as I see it, now, from this angle, with two legs hidden?" Shakespeare asks similar questions about men in love with women: "What do they see in particular women, in particular circumstances?" not, "What is the Idea or ideal Form of Woman?"

It will soon become clear that what I think Shakespearean lovers see in their beloveds is a mirror image of themselves. This image must be adjusted as it is reflected from twins, friends, transvestized young women, and young women fully revealed as young women. In the process the lover himself changes, so that there is a mutual phenomenology, with the original object of desire becoming as much subject as object. I attribute the "Greek miracle" to a similar worldview: men look in nature not for its secrets, but for themselves, and in their art, then, they seek another kind of mirror, a mirror held up to themselves rather than to nature, a mirror held up to themselves in nature, which is a kind of representation of representation. It is like Hegelian dialectic, which restores the lost positive: one looks for oneself in nature, and in art one looks for oneself looking for oneself. Art, thus elevating our self-consciousness, should make us aware of the way we see ourselves in nature. Shakespeare does this with his young lovers: they become aware of themselves loving, and we become aware of them seeking themselves in others.

II.1 THE PSYCHOANALYTIC TRADITION

1. C. R. Lyons, *Shakespeare and the Ambiguity of Love's Triumph* (Paris, The Hague: Mouton, 1971), p. 16.

2. C. L. Barber, *Shakespeare's Festive Comedy* (Princeton: Princeton University Press, 1959).

3. C. L. Barber, " 'Thou shalt beget'st him that did thee beget': Transformation in *Pericles* and *The Winter's Tale*," *Shakespeare Survey* (1969), 22:59–68.

4. L. Salangar, *Shakespeare and the Traditions of Comedy* (Cambridge: Cambridge University Press, 1974), p. 17.

5. R. Wheeler, *Shakespeare's Development and the Problem Comedies* (Berkeley: University of California Press, 1981), p. 14.

6. C. Kahn, *Man's Estate: Masculine Identity in Shakespeare* (Berkeley: University of California Press, 1981), p. 207.

7. S. Freud, *The Standard Edition of the Complete Psychological Works of Sigmund Freud (SE)*, 24 vols., J. Strachey, ed. and tr. (London: Hogarth Press, 1953–74), 14:87–88.

8. *Ibid.*, 14:98.

9. D. W. Winnicott, *Playing and Reality* (London: Tavistock, 1971), p. 45.

10. M. Klein, *Envy and Gratitude* (London: Tindall and Cox, 1948). O. Kernberg, *Object Relations Theory and Clinical Psychoanalysis* (New York: Aronson, 1976).

11. S. Freud, *SE*, 18:15, note 1.

12. A. Ehrlich argues this in *Hamlet's Absent Father* (Princeton: Princeton University Press, 1979); he does not, however, consider the pre-oedipal elements in Hamlet's malaise.

13. In Freud the death drive is a desire to restore previous stages of pleasure, reaching ultimately that equilibrium which was the child's first experience of the mother. We know now that that experience is one of symbiosis, when the child feels the mother to be an extension of himself, so that the two of them make up a closed system in which all the child's needs are met. See M. Mahler, *On Human Symbiosis and the Vicissitudes of Individuation* (New York: International Universities Press, 1968). The paradox I am trying to articulate—which I see clearly expressed in Shakespearean comedy—is that the mother is not always already there in a child's experience; she has to be constituted by oedipal conflict. First there is the void from which desire springs, expressed by Shakespearean characters as a feeling of being swallowed up in the ocean. Then there is the struggle to gain a sense of self, figured in Shakespeare by the search for a lost twin or the dependence upon a friend. I associate the melancholy of Shakespeare's lovers with the death drive: they have lost their sense of self in their love for unobtainable objects and their desire then is for an end of desire, a restitution of that equilibrium before desire was felt. See J. La Planche, *Life and Death in Psychoanalysis*, J. Mehlman, tr. (Baltimore: The Johns Hopkins University Press, 1976).

14. The philosophical statement of the death drive is the desire for the nonbeing of the self through nondifferentiation from the other, and the Platonic statement is absorption by the Forms. Everything would return to its

origin in unity. The erotic and ontogenetic origin for this philosophical nostalgia is clearly the child's desire to restore symbiosis with the mother.

15. J. Lacan, *Ecrits*, A. Sheridan tr. (New York: Norton, 1977), p. 4.

16. *Ibid.*, p. 2.

17. *Ibid.*, p. 55.

18. Freud, *SE*, 18:42.

19. N. Holland, *Psychoanalysis and Shakespeare* (New York: McGraw-Hill, 1966), pp. 130–31, 338–39.

20. Freud, *SE*, 14:94.

21. Lacan, p. 22.

22. *Ibid.*, p. 6.

23. See the forthcoming study of this play by R. Abrams in J. Redmond, ed., *Themes in Drama*, vol. 7, *Drama, Sex, and Politics*, (Cambridge: Cambridge University Press, 1985). This paper is but one part of a complete reading of the play by Abrams, which will help us appreciate how it recapitulates all the erotic concerns of the early and middle comedies and the late romances. Not only is there a pair of male friends who compete for a lady,—but there is also a pair of female friends, whose erotic attachment to each other mirrors with bewildering complexity the attachment of the male friends to each other.

24. The death drive was early on compared to the second law of thermodynamics: "a closed system suffers entropy." This comparison has been disparaged, e.g., F. Sulloway, *Freud: Biologist of the Mind* (London: Burnett Books, 1979), pp. 406, 414, but I still find it helpful. If we think of the psychic energy necessary for the child's coming into being deriving from his relation with his mother, whom he does not recognize as other, then we can think of his identity running down if he does not deflect some of that attention from himself onto another—first the mother herself, and then others like her, but different from himself. If we are uncomfortable with such an elaborate theory, then we need only consider the pitiful reality: infants deprived of adequate "mothering", such as those who spend their early months in hospitals, are known to have a high mortality rate, even when their physical needs are met. Their desires are not stimulated, and thus their potential for life is exhausted.

II.2 THE COMIC TRADITION

1. N. Frye, "The Myth of Comedy," *English Institute Essays—1948* (New York: Columbia University Press, 1949), p. 50.

2. N. Frye, *Anatomy of Criticism* (Princeton: Princeton University Press, 1957), p. 167.

3. H. Bergson, "Laughter," in *Comedy*, W. Sypher, ed. (New York: Doubleday, 1956).

4. C. Kahn, *Man's Estate: Masculine Identity in Shakespeare* (Berkeley: University of California Press, 1981), pp. 49–54.

5. Frye, *Anatomy of Criticism*, p. 182.

6. A. Watson, *The Law of the Ancient Romans* (Dallas: Southern Methodist University Press, 1971), pp. 37–38. It is interesting how the severities of Roman law become the motives of modern comedy. (See below, IV.3, note 5, on the "pound of flesh" in the Twelve Tables.) The culmination of this tradition seems to have been the *Gesta Romanorum,* a compilation made in the thirteenth century, and the pivotal point between ancient history and late medieval romance.

7. Kahn, *Man's Estate*, p. 224, but pp. 193–225 *in toto.*

8. *Ibid.,* pp. 95–96.

9. *Ibid.,* pp. 140–41.

10. *Ibid.,* p. 129.

11. S. Freud, "Character and Anal Erotism," *The Standard Edition of the Complete Psychological Works of Sigmund Freud (SE),* J. Strachey, ed. and tr. (London: Hogarth Press, 1953–74), 9:170 ff. E. Jones, "Anal-Erotic Character Traits," in *Papers in Psychoanalysis* (Boston: Beacon Press, 1961), p. 430.

12. On the equation between the gold and the girl generally, cf. F. Scott Fitzgerald, *The Great Gatsby:*

> " 'Her voice is full of money,' he said suddenly. That was it. I'd never understood before. It was full of money—that was the inexhaustible charm that rose and fell in it, the jingle of it, the cymbals' song of it . . . High in a white palace, the king's daughter, the golden girl."

Also, in George Eliot's *Silas Marner* the old miser returns from searching for his stolen money to find the child Effie asleep in front of his fireplace; he confuses her golden curls for his gold. On the relations between the Plautine and Menandrean misers, see W. T. MacCary, "Menander's Old men," *Transactions of the American Philological Association* (1971), 102:303–25.

13. L. Fiedler, *The Stranger in Shakespeare* (New York: Stein and Day, 1972), pp. 111–17.

14. See P. Pucci, *Hesiod and the Language of Poetry* (Baltimore: The Johns Hopkins University Press, 1977), pp. 82–115, on this same double paradox of sexual and material need in Hesiod's *Works and Days:* women fill a need which did not preexist them, and wealth is something which should be kept safe at home but can only be increased if it is invested abroad. Women and money are both necessary in the postlapsarian world, but when man was intimate with his god, they were so superfluous as to be unimaginable. Nostalgia therefore makes them evil.

15. See Hesiod on good and bad giving, *Works and Days,* ll. 354–59, and Wheeler, *Shakespeare's Development,* pp. 17–18, on misogyny in *Timon.* The connection between narcissism and nobility is inescapable. One might try to trace class-specific patterns of childrearing, but I prefer to think that we simply allow to our betters those perfect patterns of desire we deny to ourselves.

16. Greek mythology presents us with a clear statement of this pattern,

particularly close to the example in *Othello*. King Nisos' citadel is besieged by King Minos; Nisos' daughter Skylla sees Minos from the parapets and falls in love with him; she cuts from her father's head the purple lock of hair on which his life depends; his citadel falls, he is killed and Skylla throws herself at Minos' feet; he spurns her on the argument that a woman who could betray her father could betray her husband; she is metamorphosed into a seabird, who skims over the waves in pursuit of her beloved's ship (Ovid, *Metamorphoses* VIII.4–151).

17. Translated by H. G. Evelyn-White, in *Hesiod, Homeric Hymns, and Homerica*, "The Loeb Classical Library," (Cambridge: Harvard University Press, 1954).

18. Persephone is identified with wealth by the association of planting seed and burying treasure. The *Hymn to Demeter* ends:

> "But when the bright goddess had taught them all [the initiates], they [Demeter and Persephone] went to Olympos to the gathering of the other gods. And there they dwell beside Zeus who delights in thunder, awful and reverend goddesses. Right blessed is he among men on earth whom they freely love: soon they do send Ploutos as guest to his great house, Ploutos who gives wealth to mortal men."

Ploutos is variously another name for Hades and a son of Demeter by the Titan Iasios.

19. The Persephone pattern persists beyond Shakespeare in both cult ritual and drama. The initiates at Eleusis celebrated the cyclical nature of her experience, the alternation of rape and release, death and rebirth, barrenness and fertility, investment and return. In Mozart's *Magic Flute*, which dramatizes the Masons' basic beliefs, we first meet with a young man who is frightened by three witches. A young girl's mother then presents herself and laments that her daughter has been stolen from her and is being held in bondage by a satanic priest in the underworld. When the young man descends to rescue the girl, his whole perspective changes, for he discovers that the priest is the young girl's father, that he is a serene and gracious, though demanding, figure, and that he (the young man), who is now in love with the young girl, can marry her if he shows himself worthy by being initiated into the priest-father's cult. In Shakespearean terms this is Ferdinand carrying wood for Prospero. In both Shakespeare and Mozart, the most arduous ordeal for the young lovers is the postponement of their union. We are asked to believe that there is something intrinsically evil and chaos-producing in the spontaneous gratification of desire—this is particularly pronounced in *The Winter's Tale*, where Hermione is a devil, an intruder, and corrupter of Leontes' union with Polixenes. In this view desire must be regulated and validated by delays imposed from above: parental, social, political, and religious authorities—indeed all those structures of civilization which produce discontent, but which are, in Freud's final analysis, all that civilization is, i.e., libidinal energy displaced

and transformed. We come almost to believe that desire is created by such authorites, somewhat in the manner described by Girard, who sees behind and beyond the triangulation of desire in the oedipal moment a persistent confrontation of the self with the other, which is, of course, other versions of the self.

See R. Girard, *Desire, Deceit, and the Novel*, Y. Frecero, tr. (Baltimore: Johns Hopkins University Press, 1965), whose whole critical model seems derived from Lacan; see above, I, note 2, p. 22.

In Wagner's *Meistersinger* the young man's passion is literally modulated in the form of his song, the offering he makes to the guild in presenting himself as an apprentice. Ungoverned by the rules of the guild, his art is chaotic, and he is unworthy of marriage with the old singer's young ward, whom the old singer himself has contemplated marrying. This basic Persephone pattern, then, when elaborated from one particular perspective, shows us the channeling of young love, perhaps even the stimulation of young love, by parental prohibition. This variation on the Pyramus and Thisbe situation is certainly implicit in *Romeo and Juliet:* the course of true love never did run smooth because love demands delays and obstacles for its stimulation. A large segment of the comic population learn to love through their elders' example: Jessica and Juliet and Silvia are all immured by their fathers, and are therefore attractive to their lovers.

In *The Magic Flute* even after all the complex issues of mutiple authorship and revision are faced—see B. Brophy, *Mozart the Dramatist* (New York: Harcourt, Brace, 1964), pp. 121–212—one is left with a disturbingly sexist statement, and one wonders whether this is what the Persephone pattern—in myth, ritual, and drama—is all about. Sarastro, the father, responds to Pamina, his daughter, when she hearkens to her mother's voice:

"Und ein stolzes Weib!
Ein Mann muss eure Herzen leiten,
denn ohne ihn pflegt jedes Weib
aus sinem Wirkungskreis zu schreiten.

She is an arrogant woman!
A man must guide your heart,
for without that, every woman tends
to overstep her natural sphere."

The father gives his daughter to the young man of his choosing, and this whole structure of consignment perpetuates male control of female sexuality, as if, unrestrained, it would destroy the world. (See Wheeler, *Shakespeare's Development*, pp. 80–84; 90–91; and Kahn, *Man's Estate*, pp. 220–224.)

20. King Akrisios, hearing from an oracle that the son to be born of his daughter Danaë will kill him and take his place on the throne, buries her alive in an iron box, but Zeus penetrates in a shower of gold, and she has a son Perseus, who does indeed kill his grandfather. In an intervening adventure,

mother and son are cast adrift on the sea in a wooden box (Ovid, *Metamorphoses* IV:611–V:249).

21. See, however, *Much Ado About Nothing* (IV.2) and *The Winter's Tale* (V) for Shakespearean husbands' belief that women, living like caged beasts, have nothing to think about but sex, so that "tamed" (i.e. "domesticated") takes on the significance of "luxurious, licentious, depraved."

22. These two ideas are easily associated, as in the myth of Aegeus. When he goes to Delphi to question the god on his failure to produce children, the god's advice is, "Don't loosen the wine-skin until you return home." This means, of course, he should not sow his seed abroad, but he goes straight to Troezen and begets Theseus on Aithra (Plutarch, *Theseus*, 3).

23. G. K. Hunter, *John Lyly* (London: Routledge and Kegan Paul, 1962), pp. 299–348.

24. Mozart uses the same device in *The Escape from the Seraglio:* the guard of the harem, Osmin, is immoral and offensive to the young woman, but Pasha Selim himself is a paragon of virtue and finally releases her to marry her young lover.

25. Cf. D. M. McDowell, *Aristophanes: Wasps* (Oxford: Oxford University Press, 1971), p. 11, note 2.

26. This is a controversial point; see my "Philokleon *Ithyphallos*," *Transactions of the American Philological Association* (1979), 109:137–47.

27. This and all following translations of the *Wasps* are D. Parker's, from *Aristophanes: Three Comedies* (Ann Arbor: University of Michigan Press, 1969).

28. S. Freud, "On Transformation of Instinct as Exemplified in Anal Erotism," *SE*, 17:125ff. See also "Character and Anal Erotism," *SE*, 9:170ff.

29. See my "Menander's Old Men," *Transactions of the American Philological Association* (1971) 102:303–25.

30. N. Frye, *Anatomy of Criticism*, p. 171.

31. K. J. Dover, "Classical Greek Attitudes to Sexual Behavior," *Arethusa* (1973) 6:59.

32. T. B. L. Webster, *Studies in Later Greek Comedy*, 2d ed. (Manchester: Manchester University Press, 1970), pp. 37–97.

33. See my "Comic Tradition and Comic Structure in Diphilos' *Kleroumenoi*," *Hermes* (1973) 102:194–208.

34. See *Menandri Reliquiae Selectae*, F. H. Sandbach, ed. (Oxford: Oxford University Press, 1977), pp. 339–40, for a list of these titles.

35. Greenblatt, *Renaissance Self-Fashioning* (Chicago: University of Chicago Press, 1981), argues that a distinguishing feature of Elizabethan poets and statesmen was their ability to project themselves into strange circumstances, to assume a variety of roles. One readily compares Abel's argument that Shakespearean characters take control of their own plays. This kind of imagination is certainly the key to what Foucault sees happening in Cervantes and Velasquez: the representation of representation. One sees oneself in nature, or sees oneself seeing nature, rather than looking at nature as though it

were a constant truth presenting itself fully to all men. Admittedly fifth-century Athenians were more politically defined; Socrates could not imagine himself outside of Athens. In the fourth century this all changes and we trace the beginnings of cosmopolitanism. Though Greenblatt's claims are culture-specific to an important degree, I think that they can be used to describe adventurous aristocrats in almost any age and that he is essentially talking about narcissism. Alcibiades is easily compared with Sidney and Raleigh and Essex.

II.3 THE PHILOSOPHICAL TRADITION

1. P. Zweig, *The Heresy of Self-Love* (Princeton: Princeton University Press, 1968), pp. 23–36.

2. Plato, *Symposium* 208 c–209 c, M. Joyce, tr., in *Plato: Collected .Dialogues*, E. Hamilton and H. Cairns, eds. (Princeton: Princeton University Press, 1961), pp. 560–61.

3. G. Vlastos, "Love in Plato," in *Platonic Studies* (Princeton: Princeton University Press, 1973), pp. 3–42, stresses that there is nothing "altruistic" about Platonic love; the *erōmenos* is just a foil for the *erastēs'* self-recognition. We should recognize a similar pattern in the *Sonnets*, where the Poet simply sees in the Fair Youth a reflection of his own former beauty, so to claim that his love is "charity" is to miss the point entirely:

> "The love is, in the end, so simply and entirely love that our cadres are thrown away and we cease to ask what kind. However it might have been with Shakespeare in his daily life, the greatest of the sonnets are written from a region in which love abandons all claims and flowers into charity: after that it makes little odds what the root was like." (*Shakespeare: Sonnets*, J. D. Wilson, ed. [Cambridge: Cambridge University Press, 1967]).

In the *Sonnets* and in all his other works, both lyric and dramatic, Shakespeare never allows that such a flowering can take place. He insists that the radical nature of love is the search for the self in another like the self, or, perhaps, in mature love, another different from the self, but love is always a reflexive, a mirroring process, a validation of one's own existence. Shakespeare is neither Platonist nor Neoplatonist in that he never speaks of love in the abstract, never allows idealized objects to satisfy.

4. Plato, *Phaidros* 255 b–c, in R. Hackworth, tr., *Plato: Collected Dialogues* (Princeton: Princeton University Press, 1961), p. 501. I have altered the translation slightly because Hackworth uses "lover" where the Greek has no *erastēs.*

5. Cf. C. R. Lyons, *Shakespeare and the Ambiguity of Love's Triumph* (Paris, The Hague: Mouton, 1971). I suppose this distinction comes ultimately from D. de Rougement, *Love in the Western World*, M. Belgion, tr. (Princeton: Princeton University Press, 1983), first French edition, 1940. The antithesis is between love as *passion* and love in marriage: "Passionate love at once shared

and fought against, anxious for a happiness it rejects, and magnified in its own disaster—*unhappy mutual love*. . . . They love one another, but each loves the other *from the standpoint of self and not from the other's standpoint* . . . a twin naricissism" (p. 52). I do not see Shakespeare as part of this tradition; mutuality in erotic relations, unhappy or not, is not his concern; rather there is always a particular point of view in his comedies and lyrics, one lover with whom we are asked to identify. Perhaps only in *Romeo and Juliet* among the plays do we find the kind of "unhappy mutual love" de Rougement traces in the West, where two people feed on each other and tempt each other into ever higher flights of dangerous passion. The definitive lyric statement is, of course, "The Phoenix and the Turtle."

6. G. K. Hunter, *John Lyly* (London: Routledge and Kegan Paul, 1962).

7. S. Davies, *Renaissance Views of Man* (Manchester: Manchester University Press, 1978), p. 28.

8. L. Jardine, *Still Harping on Daughters: Women and Drama in the Age of Shakespeare* (Brighton: The Harvester Press, 1983).

9. *Ibid.*, p. 18, note 21: M. Delcourt, *Hermaphroditea: Recherches sur l'être double promoteur de la fertilité dans le monde classique* (Brussels, 1960), pp. 65–66 (Jardine's translation).

10. *Ibid.*, p. 20.

11. G. Devereux, "Greek Homosexuality and the Greek Miracle," *Symbolae Osloenses* (1968), 42:69–92.

12. This was taken by Oscar Wilde to be "The Portrait of Mr. W.H.," the Fair Youth of the *Sonnets*. It is difficult not to associate this miniature with the portraits of Italian youths of the early sixteenth century, especially those of Michelangelo, Botticelli, and, later, Bronzino. Their arrogant posturing and the way they seem to exist only to be looked at—or at least to have been painted that way—give specificity to the definition of narcissism. It is not their effeminacy which fascinates us; it is their brazenness, their consciousness of their own beauty and of their superiority over and insularity from others.

13. K. J. Dover, *Greek Homosexuality* (Cambridge; Harvard University Press, 1979). For the medieval period there is now J. Boswell's study, *Christianity, Social Tolerance, and Homosexuality* (Chicago: University of Chicago Press, 1980).

14. A. L. Rowse, *Sex and Society in Shakespeare's Age* (New York: Scribner's, 1974), p. 3. J. Kott usefully speculates on the wholesale transfer of the Florentine culture of the late fifteenth and early sixteenth centuries to London at the end of the sixteenth century, including the almost institutionalized *eros Socraticus;* see "Shakespeare's Bitter Arcadia," in *Shakespeare Our Contemporary* (London: Methuen, 1967), pp. 191–236. We should be encouraged to attempt a whole new definition of humanism, which will take account of the seemingly determinative component of narcissism.

15. W. T. MacCary, *Childlike Achilles: Ontogeny and Phylogeny in the Iliad* (New York: Columbia University Press, 1982).

16. This sequence is still recognizable, at least to Italians. In the recent film

Ernesto, directed by S. Samperi and based on the novel by U. Saba, a young
Jewish boy who has no father, but a strong, protective mother, is first, in adolescence, taken as a beloved by an older man. There is much talk of who
should do what to whom, and the older man insists that in such cases the
older man is always the active lover, the young boy the passive beloved. This
suits Ernesto for a while, but then he insists on trying the other way; the older
man relents and offers himself, but Ernesto loses interest and walks away. He
then pays a female prostitute, who takes the active role herself, masturbating
him *per vaginam.* Soon he meets a beautiful, young, aristocratic boy and agrees
to become his music master. As they are embracing each other one day, the
boy's twin sister enters the room. Ernesto is fascinated. The twins play at
transvestism to amuse him. Finally, Ernesto marries the girl, to the boy's great
chagrin. On the way to his engagement party he tosses his old male lover a
coin. The analogies of this beautiful, natural, and totally nonjudgmental film
with both the Greek and Shakespearean material should be obvious. Certainly
we see the two Antonios in the forsaken old lover. The psychological significance of all three patterns should be equally obvious. What are the figures of
twins and the device of transvestism for, if not to mark the easy stages in a
young man's transition from narcissism to a satisfying relationship with a young
woman?

III. THE EARLY COMEDIES

1. C. L. Barber, *Shakespeare's Festive Comedy* (Princeton: Princeton University Press, 1959), p. 106.
2. R. Wheeler, *Shakespeare's Development and the Problem Comedies* (Berkeley: University of California Press, 1981), p. 48.
3. *Ibid.,* p. 49.
4. *Ibid.,* p. 49.
5. *Ibid.,* p. 50.
6. *Ibid.,* p. 51.
7. M. S. Bergman, "On the Intrapsychic Function of Falling in Love,"
Psychoanalytic Quarterly (1980), 49:56–77. Cf. O. Kernberg, "Barriers to Falling and Remaining in Love," *Journal of the American Psychoanalytic Association* (1974), 22:486–511; "Mature Love: Prerequisites and Characteristics,"
Journal of the American Psychoanalytic Association (1974), 22:743–68; "Boundaries and Structure in Love Relations," *Journal of the American Psychoanalytic
Association* (1977), 25:81–114.
8. J. Vyvyan, *Shakespeare and the Rose of Love* (London: Chatto, 1960),
pp. 98–135; and *Shakespeare and Platonic Beauty* (London: Chatto, 1961), pp.
68–73.
9. See R. David, *The Arden Shakespeare: Love's Labor's Lost* (London: Methuen, 1956), pp. xxxii–xlii; and Sir Arthur Quiller-Couch and J. D. Wilson,

The Works of Shakespeare: Love's Labor's Lost (Cambridge: Cambridge University Press, 1923), pp. vii–xxxix.

10. P. Zweig, *The Heresy of Self-Love* (Princeton: Princeton University Press, 1968), pp. 23–36.

11. B. Morris, *The Arden Shakespeare: The Taming of the Shrew* (London: Methuen, 1981), pp. 136–49.

12. *Ibid.*, p. 146.

13. C. Kahn, *Man's Estate: Masculine Identity in Shakespeare* (Berkeley: University of California Press, 1981), p. 117.

14. On Shakespeare's misogyny generally, see L. Fiedler, *The Stranger in Shakespeare* (New York: Stein and Day, 1972), pp. 43–84.

15. Cf. the metamorphosis of the Erinyes into the Eumenides in Aeschylus' *Oresteia*, and F. Zeitlin, "The Dynamics of Misogyny: Myth and Myth-making in the *Oresteia*," *Arethusa* (1978), 11:149–84.

16. Kernberg, "Boundaries and Structure," p. 82.

17. O. Kernberg, *Borderline Conditions and Pathological Narcissism* (New York: Aronson, 1975), pp. 3–44.

18. The question arises in Shakespearean comedy and in erotic life—indeed in all aspects of life generally—whether one ever moves through one stage of development completely to another. We must think dialectically, and like Hegel rather than like Plato. We must appreciate that nothing is ever lost from the dialectic of our development. No matter how successfully we negotiate the developmental stages in our relations with others, the stages are never completely transcended. We negate certain modes of seeing others by adopting those modes and finding them wanting; indeed we negate our need for others by assimilating others into ourselves. Nevertheless Shakespeare and contemporary psychoanalysts do lay out definite stages in the development of satisfying erotic relations; they agree on these stages; they also agree that to skip a stage distorts our erotic perspective and makes every relation thereafter unsatisfying.

The same thing, of course, happens in the history of consciousness. Indeed my largest critical claim is that intellectual history is a vast projection of individual development—phylogeny recapitulates ontogeny—and since the energy for individual development is erotic, I look for derivatives of this in intellectual history. Vico showed how man makes his institutions and then his institutions remake man, so that there is a spiral of change in human nature. Recognizing that human nature is a function of change, rather than a static universal quality, is comparable to recognizing change in individual development: in either case, if we lose sight of our origins, or the stages of our development, we misread ourselves. If we have patience to consider one more polarity between Shakespearean tragedy and Shakespearean comedy—with the problem comedies and romances in between—it might be that men more grossly misread themselves in tragedy than in comedy, since men in tragedy see themselves and their world as constant, whereas men in comedy must accept change in themselves and their world.

19. Kernberg, *Borderline Conditions*, p. 325.

20. E. H. Gombrich, *Art and Illusion* (New York: Pantheon, 1960), cites the *Alcestis* of Euripides as an appreciation of the "Greek revolution" in the theory and practice of art. Admetos will have a statue made of his dead wife Alcestis and place it in their bedchamber; he will know it is a statue, but "dream" it as real: "What Admetos seeks is not a spell, not even assurance, only a dream for those who are awake, in other words, precisely that state of mind to which Plato, the stern seeker after truth objected. . . . The picture conjured up by art is unreliable and incomplete, it appeals to the lower part of the soul, to our imagination rather than to our reason, and must therefore be banished as a corrupting influence" (pp. 126–27).

Gombrich refers to the more "primitive" attitude toward art, where the art object "participates" in the true form of the real object, as "Pygmalion's power of making." (We might compare the rhetorical distinction between metaphor and metonomy, or the critical distinction between allegory and symbol.) Erotically, of course, there is also a distinction: does a man love a particular woman for her own sake, or the reflection in her of the Idea of Woman? J. Ferrante has shown this to be the great problem posed in the courtly love tradition: "We have seen historical and fictional women treated as abstractions and abstractions personified as women. In courtly literature we find a confusion of the two—a setting of courtship or marriage which would seem to demand a real woman, but more often yields a symbol." *Woman as Image in Medieval Literature* (New York: Columbia University Press, 1975), p. 64.

In speaking of all objects of desire as if they were statues, of course, we are playing a game similar to Plato's, when, in the parable of the cave (*Republic* VII), he speaks of all real objects as if they were shadows. I think only Lacan has addressed this problem in its original erotic dimension: *le petit objet a* is not imaginary but real; nevertheless it is impossible, a figure of the self as other. Shakespeare investigates the complexity of this dilemma through such devices as transvestism and petrifaction.

III.1 THE COMEDY OF ERRORS

1. A. Legatt, *Shakespeare's Comedy of Love* (London: Methuen, 1974), p. 9.

2. D. Palmer and M. Bradbury, *Shakespearean Comedy* (New York: Crane, Russak, 1972), pp. 7–8.

3. W. T. MacCary, "*The Comedy of Errors*: A Different Kind of Comedy," *New Literary History* (1978), 9:525–36.

4. J. R. Brown, "The Presentation of Comedy: The First Ten Plays," in D. Palmer and M. Bradbury, eds. *Shakespeareaen Comedy* (New York: Crane, Russak, 1972), p. 9.

5. *Ibid.*, p. 10.

6. O. Kernberg, "Boundaries and Structures in Love Relations," *Journal of the American Psychoanalytic Association* (1977), 25:99. The reference to Freud is to the opening of *Civilization and Its Discontents.*

7. S. Freud, *The Interpretation of Dreams*, in J. Strachey, ed. and tr., *The Standard Edition of the Complete Psychological Works of Sigmund Freud* (London: Hogarth Press, 1953–74), 5:399–401.

8. Antipholus of Syracuse was only eighteen when he began his search (I.i.125), and is twenty-three when the action of the play takes place (I.i.132). The twins should then be played as young men, and not middle-aged, as they often are. In Plautus' *Menaechmi* they are technically termed *adulescentes;* of course, comedy notoriously polarizes its male characters between *adulescens* and *senex* to accentuate the difference in the effects of love upon them.

9. Kernberg, "Boundaries and Structure," p. 108.

III.2 THE TWO GENTLEMEN OF VERONA

1. J. Athos, *Shakespeare: The Early Writings* (London: 1972), p. 161.

2. I.-S. Ewbank, " 'Were man but constant, he were perfect': Constancy and Consistency in *The Two Gentlemen of Verona*," in *Shakespearean Comedy* (= *Stratford-Upon-Avon Studies*) (London: Arnold, 1972), 14:51.

3. A. Legatt, *Shakespeare's Comedy of Love* (London: Methuen, 1974), p. 40.

4. See J. Vyvyan, *Shakespeare and the Rose of Love* (London: Chatto, 1960). I agree that the play is a consideration of Neoplatonic love, but not that Shakespeare validates this doctrine.

5. G. Devereux, "Greek Homosexuality and the Greek Miracle," *Symbolae Osloenses* (1968), 42:69–92.

6. Boccaccio, *Decameron*, G. H. McWilliam, tr. (London: Penguin, 1972), p. 778.

7. R. Girard, *Desire, Deceit, and the Novel*, Y. Frecero, tr. (Baltimore: Johns Hopkins University Press, 1965); and "Myth and Ritual in Shakespeare's *A Midsummer Night's Dream*," in *Textual Strategies*, J. Harari, ed. (Ithaca: Cornell University Press, 1979), pp. 189–212.

8. Boccaccio, *Decameron*, p. 780.

9. G. Bullough, *Narrative and Dramatic Sources of Shakespeare* (London: Routledge and Kegan Paul, 1957), 1:203–66.

10. Celia is taken from *caelum;* Delia is the adjective based on Delos, the island birthplace of Artemis and Apollo, twin offspring of Leto by Zeus. Artemis was known to the Romans as Diana, and Ephesus, the location of *The Comedy of Errors*, was the cult center for Diana in the Roman period, and Emilia is her priestess. We have already seen that there is a play on light and dark, suggesting the contrasting phases of the moon, in the names Adriana and Luciana in *The Comedy of Errors*. Phoebe is another of these appellations,

a feminine form of Phoebus, an adjective derived from *phaos* ("light") and traditional of Artemis, just as the masculine form is of Apollo; Cynthia is the feminine adjective from Cynthos, the name of a mountain on Delos, and therefore an epithet of Artemis. Shakespeare might have chosen Silvia for his moon-goddess character in *The Two Gentlemen of Verona* because she ends up in the forest. Just as *The Two Gentlemen of Verona* is the first of Shakespeare's transvestite comedies, so it is the first of his "green-world" comedies. She is, nevertheless, easily recognized as belonging to that company of Celia, Delia, Phoebe, Diana, and Cynthia.

11. In Greek myth and cult there is a paradox in Artemis' nature. She is both the virgin huntress and the maternal protectress of wild, young things, but remains essentially hermaphroditic, i.e., a woman with a man's virtues. Shakespeare captures this aspect in the transvestized Julia, and later in Portia, Nerissa, Rosalind, Viola, and Imogen. In the eclectic tradition of later Roman worship Diana becomes assimilated with the various eastern mother goddesses, as if in anticipation of the hold Monica and her eastern equivalents will have on Christian minds.

12. Wheeler *Shakespeare's Development and the Problem Comedies* (Berkeley: University of California Press, 1981); p. 50.

13. Just as we need Ovid (*Metamorphoses* III.341–510) to gloss Shakespeare's and Freud's texts on Narcissus, so we need Keats to gloss Shakespeare's and Lyly's texts on Endymion:

"I was distracted; madly did I kiss
The wooing arms which held me, and did give
My eyes at once to death: but 'twas to live,
To take in draughts of life from the gold fount
Of kind and passionate looks; to count, and count
The moments, by some greedy help that seem'd
A second self, that each might be redeem'd
And plunder'd of its load of blessedness." (*Endymion* I.653–60)

In "Bright Star," one of his last poems, Keats clearly equates the sleep of Endymion with death, or rather with the nonbeing consequent upon a failure in the child to differentiate himself from his mother, the failure of the lover to overcome that oceanic feeling of oneness with the beloved. It is a meditation then on love and death and childhood, but also on the young Shakespeare: Keats inscribed "Bright Star" opposite "A Lover's Complaint" in his volume of Shakespeare's poems as he sailed to Italy on September 28, 1820, where he died five months later.

"Bright Star! Would I were steadfast as thou art—
   Not in lone splendour hung aloft the night,
And watching with eternal lids apart,
   Like Nature's patient sleepless Eremite,

The moving waters at their priestlike task
  Of pure ablution round earth's human shores,
Or gazing on the new soft fallen mask
  Of snow upon the mountains and the moors—
No—yet still steadfast, still unchangeable,
  Pillow'd upon my fair lover's ripening breast,
To feel forever its soft fall and swell,
  Awake forever in a sweet unrest,
Still, still to hear her tender-taken breath,
And so live ever—or else swoon to death."

Endymion's sleep is the sleep of the child satiated at his mother's breast:

"O he had swoon'd
Drunken from pleasure's nipple." (*Endymion* II.868–9).

The affects are of dependence, rhythm, permanence—all those qualities we associate with the Neoplatonic lady. C. Spurgeon provides a photograph of the page on which Keats wrote "Bright Star'" in *Keats' Shakespeare* (Oxford: Oxford University Press, 1928) plate 17, opp. p. 42.

14. Shakespeare is certainly aware of the moon's influence on earthly life (e.g. *MND*, II.1.103–5), and since he seems generally to think of the sun orbiting the earth, then perhaps here he thinks the moon can "affect" the sun. Compare the extravagant image of the moon penetrating the earth and upsetting the sun (MND III. ii.52–55). To "rise" and to "set" is also, of course, to achieve and to lose erection, as is also to "stand" and to cease affection.

15. It should be noted that Julia's male persona is Sebastian (IV.iv.40), a name found in none of Shakespeare's sources. There is some consistency in his naming of these transvestized heroines. Rosalind is Ganymede, a figure recognized from antiquity through the Middle Ages as the younger male beloved of an older male lover; see J. Boswell, *Christianity, Social Tolerance, and Homosexuality* (Chicago: University of Chicago Press, 1980) pp. 243–66. I suggest that Shakespeare took the name Sebastian for Julia here, and for Viola's brother in *TN*, from St. Sebastian, whose matyrdom by arrows is much depicted by fifteenth- and sixteenth-century Italian and Flemish artists: he is always young and beautiful and nude. A useful study of the material is I. Zupnick, "The Representation of Saint Sebastian in Renaissance Art," Ph.D. diss., Columbia, University, 1958. There is nothing in the life of the saint to suggest youth at the time of martyrdom. Among the depictions there is something pathic in the saint's posture, and phallic in the arrows' penetration. At some point he became the patron saint of homosexuals, and remains so today. E. Waugh took the names of his two beautiful aristocrats in *Brideshead Revisited* from *TGV;* his hero falls in love first with Sebastian and then with his sister Julia. The young husband in T. Williams' *Suddenly Last Summer* is Sebastian: he loves even younger boys, and seems finally to be penetrated by their tin whistles.

16. O. Kernberg, "Boundaries and Structure in Love Relations," *Journal of the American Psychoanalytic Association* (1977), 25:81–114.

17. *Ibid.*, p. 88.

III.3 LOVE'S LABOR'S LOST

1. Berowne's wit elicits both praise and blame from Rosaline at II.i.64–76 and V.ii.833–46, respectively.

2. The notion of women as signs is one of the most controversial of our time. It began (or began again) with Lévi-Strauss, who concludes his *Elementary Structures of Kinship* with the speculation that women were the original objects of exchange between men, and exogamy the first currency. He cannot, however, accept his own conclusion:

> "But woman could never become a sign and only a sign, since, in a world of men, she is nevertheless a person, and since, in so far as she is defined as a sign, one is obliged to recognize her as a producer of signs. In the matrimonial dialogue of men, a woman is never purely that of which she speaks, since . . . each woman maintains a particular value, which depends upon her maintaining her part in a dual relationship, both before and after marriage. In opposition to the word, which has totally become a sign, woman has remained both a sign and a value at the same time. Thus is explained, no doubt, how the relations between the sexes have been able to preserve that reflective richness, that fervor and that mystery, which probably filled the whole universe of human conversation originally" (J. H. Bell and J. R. von Sturmer, trs., and R. Neehlam, ed. [Boston: Beacon Press, 1969], p. 496).

The most astute appreciation of the erotic significance of fetishism—its original significance being religious so that the derivation and double significance of "idol" is parallel—is Krafft-Ebings's:

> "Analogies with religious fetishism are always discernible; for, under certain circumstances, in the latter, the most insignificant objects (bones, nails, hair, etc.) become fetiches, and are associated with pleasurable feelings which may reach the intensity of ecstasy. . . . Thus it is understood why lovers are not understood by their unaffected fellow men; and why they deify their idols, develop a true cult of devotion, and invest them with attributes which objectively they do not possess. . . . In the ecstatic love of a man mentally normal, a handkerchief or shoe, a glove or letter, the flower "she gave," or a lock of hair, etc., may become the object of worship, but only because they represent a mnemonic symbol of the beloved person—absent or dead—whose whole personality is reproduced by them. The pathological fetichist has no such relations. The fetich constitutes the entire content of his idea. When he is possessed by it, sexual excitement occurs, and the fetich manifests itself" (*Psychopathia Sexualis*, C. G. Chaddoch, tr. [Philadelphia: Davis, 1920], pp. 17–18, 154).

We would call this a confusion of the signifier and the signified, but what would we be saying? Why did the God of the Old Testament want no graven images of himself made by man? Is it not because man is completely anthropomorphic and makes god in his own image? So, the unregenerate Shakespearean lover: he must stop mirroring himself in his beloved and allow her to manifest her difference. The same problem is examined by Shakespeare in language; on this topic Carroll quotes Wordsworth naively wondering: "If words be not (recurring to a metaphor before used) an incarnation of the thought, but only a clothing for it, then surely they prove an ill gift"(W. C. Carroll, *The Great Feast of Language in "Love's Labor's Lost"* [Princeton: Princeton University Press, 1977], p. 189).

　3. Carroll, *The Great Feast of Language.*

　4. *Ibid.*, p. 69, quoting M. Mack, "Engagement and Detachment in Shakespeare's Plays," in R. Hoskey, ed., *Essays on Shakespeare and Elizabethan Drama in Honor of H. Craig,* (Columbia: University of Missouri Press, 1967), p. 289.

　5. *Ibid.*, p. 257 note, referring to J. C. Calderwood, *"Love's Labor's Lost:* Awakening with Words," *SEL* (1965), 5:317–32.

　6. *Ibid.*, p. 161.

　7. *Ibid.*, where he quotes Berowne: "Behold the window of my heart, mine eye" (V.ii.830). What does Rosaline see when she looks in Berowne's eye? His "heart," which we might take as his love for her, or her own reflection? Is there at that point in the action a difference? Each previous use of that conceit has had the male lover looking in the lady's eyes and seeing himself, so, again, the women become active and assume prerogatives previously male.

Désir is a function of the difference between actual (somatic) need and *demande,* the verbal expression of that need. (The subject can never adequately express himself in language since language is the structure of the other.) As the child enters the mirror stage he begins to ask the mother for an image of himself; her return of his look (*le regard*) constitutes his first object (*le petit objet a*). As the child acquires language he enters the symbolic realm, which is also the realm of oedipal orientation: he takes as his object of desire the father's object of desire, the mother. Though his desire continues to be for an image of himself, he expresses that desire as a demand for the mother. Oedipal dissatisfaction, then, only veils narcissistic dissatisfaction. Shakespearean comedy captures all this. The lovers move through the stages, but they never find what they seek: in the early comedies they still choose self-images; in the mature comedies they achieve marriage; in the late romances they see themselves in their daughters, but then relinquish their daughters and face death. Desire is always for the self, and death is the only end of desire. Idealization of the oedipal object is simply a displacement into the symbolic realm of the primary narcissistic image. These are the statues and pictures of women in Shakespeare, the signs and idols.

　8. *Ibid.*, p. 199.

9. *Ibid.*, pp. 97–101.

10. *Ibid.*, p. 97.

11. *Ibid.*, p. 97.

12. C. L. Barber, *Shakespeare's Festive Comedy* (Princeton: Princeton University Press, 1959), p. 223.

13. Carroll, *The Great Feast of Language*, pp. 99–100.

14. D. de Rougement, *Love in the Western World*, M. Belgion, tr. (Princeton: Princeton University Press, 1983), p. 60.

15. The essential study here is J. Ferrante, *Woman as Image in Medieval Literature* (New York: Columbia University Press, 1975). Among many astute observations, she says, "The ideals of male and female beauty in the high Middle Ages seem to have been quite similar" (p. 4). Like so much else, Shakespeare shares with the troubadours an interest in sexual ambivalence and ambiguity.

III.4 THE TAMING OF THE SHREW

1. B. Morris, *The Arden Shakespeare: The Taming of the Shrew* (London: Methuen, 1981), pp. 12–87, 299–305.

2. G. Williams, *Person and Persona* (Cardiff: University of Wales Press, 1981), p. 28.

3. *Ibid.*

4. P. Slater, *The Glory of Hera* (Boston: Beacon Press, 1968).

5. A. Ehrlich, *Hamlet's Absent Father* (Princeton: Princeton University Press, 1979).

6. O. Kernberg, *Borderline Conditions and Pathological Narcissism* (New York: Aronson, 1975), p. 17.

IV. THE MATURE COMEDIES

1. The distinction between Platonic and Aristotelian currents in Renaissance philosophy is notoriously difficult; the leading authority, P. Kristeller, reproduces the humanists' elusiveness in his own text, *Renaissance Thought and Its Sources* (New York: Columbia University Press, 1979), pp. 17–81, 191–210.

2. I take Bacon's "notions" to be "formal," like the *ragioni* of the Italian Neoplatonists; see E. Cassirer, "The Subject-Object Problem in the Philosophy of the Renaissance," *The Individual and the Cosmos in Renaissance Philosophy*, M. Domandi, tr. (Oxford: Blackwell, 1963), pp. 132–91.

3. The crucial study of the relations among Michelangelo's art, poetry, and philosophy of love and art is A. Blunt, "Michelangelo's Views on Art," in *Artistic Theory in Italy, 1450–1600* (Oxford: Oxford University Press, 1959). He traces three stages of development, which sound like stations in a Neoplatonic progress. Michelangelo's love for Tommaso de' Cavalieri is considered

in the second and third stages. R. Liebert has considered this material from a psychoanalytic perspective: *Michelangelo: A Psychoanalytic Study of His Life and Images* (New Haven: Yale University Press, 1983), pp. 270–311, but his approach is biographical rather than critical. We need a study to define the Artist-Fair Youth relationship; it is obviously neither culture-specific nor traceable to a peculiar set of biographical imperatives. Plato's *Symposium* and *Phaidros* should be taken as a model, against which the work of Michelangelo, Shakespeare, and Thomas Mann, among others, might be measured.

4. "I think that in discussions of physical problems we ought to begin not from the authority of scriptural passages, but from sense experience and necessary demonstrations; for the holy Bible and the phenomena of nature proceed alike from the divine Word, the former as the dictate of the Holy Ghost and the latter as the observant executrix of God's commands" (*Discoveries and Opinions of Galileo*, S. Drake, tr. [Garden City, N.Y.: Doubleday, 1957], p. 182).

5. D. Young provides a sampling of English sixteenth-century theory in *Something of Great Constancy: The Art of "A Midsummer Night's Dream"* (New Haven: Yale University Press, 1966), pp. 126–41. Kristeller considers the rhetorical tradition in *Renaissance Thought*, pp. 213–59.

6. Two literary documents which reveal the importance of transvestism for a woman's self-realization are Virginia Woolf's *Orlando*, and the memoirs of Vita Sackville-West, published by her son N. Nicolson, *Portrait of a Marriage* (New York: *Atheneum*, 1973). They are, of course, related; I discuss them briefly in "The Comic Significance of Transvestism," *Letterature Comparate: Problemi e Metodo—Studi in onore di Ettore Paratore* (Bologna: Patro Editore, 1981), 1:293–308.

IV.1   A MIDSUMMER NIGHT'S DREAM

1. P. Olson, "*A Midsummer Night's Dream* and the Meaning of Court Marriage," *ELH*, (1957), 24:107–11.

2. *Ibid.*, p. 99.

3. D. Young, *Something of Great Constancy: The Art of "A Midsummer Night's Dream"* (New Haven: Yale University Press, 1966), pp. 137–39.

4. S. Fender, *Shakespeare: A Midsummer Night's Dream* (London: Arnold, 1968), pp. 50–51.

5. R. Girard, "Myth and Ritual in Shakespeare's *A Midsummer Night's Dream*," in *Textual Strategies*, J. Harari, ed. (Ithaca: Cornell University Press, 1979), pp. 189–97.

6. F. Kermode, "The Mature Comedies," in *Early Shakespeare* (=*Stratford-Upon-Avon Studies 3*) (London: Arnold, 1961), 3:219.

7. G. Bullough, *Narrative and Dramatic Sources of Shakespeare* (New York· Columbia University Press, 1966), 1:398–400.

8. Apuleius, *Metamorphoses* X. 21–22:

"Illa vero, quotiens ei parens nates recellebam, accedens totiens nisu rabido spinam prehendens meam appliciore nexu inhaerebat, ut Hercule etiam deesse mihi aliquid ad supplendam eius libidinem crederem, nec Minotauri matrem frustra delectatam putarem adultero mugiente."

9. J. Kott also makes this association: *Shakespeare Our Contemporary* (London: Methuen, 1965), pp. 182–83.

10. Translation, with slight changes, by J. Lindsay, in his introduction to Apuleius, *The Golden Ass* (Bloomington: Indiana University Press, 1967).

11. Girard, "Myth and Ritual," p. 197.

12. "Amazon" means "breastless": these female warriors were said to cut off their breasts to improve their shooting of the bow. On their place in Greek mythology and the history of psychosexuality, see W. Tyrrell, *Amazons: A Study in Athenian Mythmaking* (Baltimore: Johns Hopkins University Press, 1984).

13. J. Boswell, "The Triumph of Ganymede," *Christianity, Social Tolerance, and Homosexuality* (Chicago: University of Chicago Press, 1980), pp. 243–66.

14. N. Holland, "Hermia's Dream," in C. Kahn and M. Schwartz, eds., *Representing Shakespeare* (Baltimore: Johns Hopkins University Press, 1980), p. 12.

15. M. Faber, "Hermia's Dream," *Literature and Psychology* (1972), 22:179–90.

16. Olson, *"A Midsummer Night's Dream,"* p. 112.

17. Young, *Something of Great Constancy*, p. 138ff.

18. Olson cites N. Coghill, "The Basis of Shakespeare's Comedy," *Essays and Studies* (London: 1950), pp. 1–28; Cognill sees in Shakespearean comedy a tripartite movement, not unlike that of Frye. First there is "order" (Act I), which is broken by "unbridled passion" (Acts II, III), and then order is restored through "charity" and "cohesive community morality." These terms are useful for suggesting the ordering principle of each man's own perspective: he sees himself simultaneously fearing and desiring women.

IV.2 MUCH ADO ABOUT NOTHING

1. I am not talking about "phallic symbols"; aggression against self-objects is primary, so it would be more accurate to call penises "martial symbols." Violence of the mirror type is originary and only later comes under the genital organization.

2. O. Kernberg, "Mature Love: Prerequisites and Characteristics," *Journal of the American Psychoanalytic Association* (1974), 22:752.

3. O. Kernberg, "Boundaries and Structure in Love Relations," *Journal of the American Psychoanalytic Association* (1977), 25:81–114.

4. Again, the comparison of a man with Hercules, in a context where man's

difference from and relations with, women are involved: cf. *TS* I.ii.255–56. Also see W. C. Carroll, *The Great Feast of Language in "Love's Labor's Lost"* (Princeton: Princeton University Press, 1977), pp. 236–42, on Hercules in *LLL*. On the theme of men only seeming to be men, cf. *AYLI* where Rosalind announces to Celia her intention to transvestize:

"We'll have a swashing and a martial outside,
As many other mannish cowards have
That do outface it with their semblance." (I.iii.116–18)

5. Othello ambiguously suggests that Desdemona, in a similar martial context, would be a man; he says of her response to his tales of war:

"She wished she had not heard it, yet she wished
That Heaven had made her such a man." (I.iii.162–63)

6. See G.K. Hunter, *John Lyly* (London: Routledge and Kegan Paul, 1962), pp. 299–348.
7. L. Salangar, *Shakespeare and the Traditions of Comedy* (Cambridge: Cambridge University Press, 1974), p. 172. "In the main plots of his romantic comedies, the initiative in disguise or witty improvisation has passed to his heroines, at the same time as the typical motive for intrigue has become the securing of love."
8. Kernberg, "Boundaries," p. 83.
9. A. Kirsch, *Shakespeare and the Experience of Love* (Cambridge: Cambridge University Press, 1981) p. 55: "In most respects Beatrice and Benedick are quite different from Claudio. Both are clearly indisposed to idealize an object of love. . . . Unlike Claudio, therefore, both Beatrice and Benedick 'have a good eye,' they can 'see a church by daylight' (II.i.69–70)."
10. R. Girard, "Myth and Ritual in Shakespeare's *A Midsummer Night's Dream*," in J. Harari, ed., *Textual Strategies* (Ithaca: Cornell University Press, 1979), pp. 189–212.
11. *Don Quixote*, I.27.

IV.3 THE MERCHANT OF VENICE

1. L. Fiedler, *The Stranger in Shakespeare* (New York: Stein and Day, 1972), pp. 109–17.
2. *Ibid.*, p. 119.
3. St. Paul, Romans 2:29: "But he is a Jew, which is one inwardly; and circumcision is that of the heart, in the spirit, and not in the letter; whose praise is not of men, but of God."
4. St. Paul, Romans 2:13–15: "For not the hearers of the law are just before God, but the doers of the law shall be justified. / For when the Gentiles, which have not the law, do by nature the things contained in the law, thus,

having not the law, are a law unto themselves: / which show the work of the law written in their heart, their conscience also bearing witness, and their thoughts the meanwhile accusing or else excusing one another."

5. Nietzsche refers to the Roman law on "the pound of flesh" in his discussion of the relation between *Schuld* and *Schulden*, guilt and debts:

"Above all, however, the creditor could inflict every kind of indignity and torture upon the body of the debtor; for example, cut from it as much as seemed commensurate with the size of the debt—and everywhere and from early times one had exact evaluations, legal evaluations, of the individual limbs and parts of the body from this point of view, some of them going into horrible and minute detail. I consider it as an advance, as evidence of a freer, more generous, *more Roman* conception of law when the Twelve Tables of Rome decreed it a matter of indifference how much or how little the creditor cut off in such cases: *si plus minusve secuerunt, ne fraude esto* ("If they cut off more or less, let that be no crime!)" *The Genealogy of Morals* W. Kaufmann, tr., II.5).

The ancient sources on the law are Aulus Gellius, *Noctes Atticae* 20.1.52; Dio Cassius frag. 17.8; Quintillian, *Institutiones Oratoriae* 3.6.84; Tertullian, *Apologeticum* 4.9. For discussion, see M. Raden, "Secare Partis," *American Journal of Philology*, vol. 43 (1922). (I am obliged to Miles McDonald for these references.)

6. G. Bullough, *Narrative and Dramatic Sources of Shakespeare* (London: Routledge and Kegan Paul, 1957), 1:463.

7. Characters named Antonio appear in four comedies: Proteus' father is Antonio in *The Two Gentlemen of Verona;* he is Hero's uncle in *Much Ado* Antonio is a father substitute to Bassanio in *The Merchant of Venice;* Sebastian's life is saved by Antonio in *Twelfth Night,* where the older man, who "idolizes" the younger man, mistakenly accuses him of ingratitude and refusing to return to him money he had given Sebastian, when he, Antonio, needs it. Perhaps one could trace a connection between all of these benevolent, protective older men and St. Antony, who gave up his wealth to live in the desert.

8. One is tempted here to make a biographical speculation. Brown points out in his discussion of usury (Arden, p. xliii): "Great Elizabethans like Sidney, Essex, Leicester and Southampton were each thousands of pounds in debt"—his reference is to R. H. Tawney, "Introduction," in Sir T. Wilson, *Disclosure Upon Usury* 1925 ed.), p. 36. Would Shakespeare not have been sensitive to this paradox, that the money these young lords he served spent so lavishly was borrowed? He certainly concerned himself with the relations between generosity and friendship, in the context of nobility, in *Timon of Athens.*

9. Freud clearly based his conception of the superego on Nietzsche's conception of *ressentiment* in *The Genealogy of Morals:* the ego becomes indebted to the superego just as the creditor is set up internally as guilt, *Schulden* be-

coming *Schuld.* Nietzsche traces the evolution of *ressentiment* from the Jews. It is interesting to see the Christian "gentles" in the play as Nietzsche's Greek heroes, with all their liberality and amorality, roaming the world freely like blond beasts of prey. They learn *ressentiment* first from Shylock, who teaches them about debts, and then from Portia, who locks them up.

IV.4 AS YOU LIKE IT

1. C. L. Barber, *Shakespeare's Festive Comedy* (Princeton: Princeton University Press, 1959), p. 232.

2. *Ibid.,* p. 223.

3. A. Latham, *The Arden Shakespeare: As You Like It* (London: Methuen, 1975), p. lxxii.

4. N. K. Hayles, "Disguise in *As You Like It* and *Twelfth Night,*" *Shakespeare Survey* (1979), 32:65: "In putting aside her disguise Rosalind insists that Orlando love her as real rather than ideal object."

5. I think all these ladies take their names from the courtly love tradition, where the lover must resist the temptations of the pool of Narcissus, to pursue his quest of the bower of the Virgin, which is of roses, as in *Roman de la Rose.*

6. I am again claiming for Shakespeare, in his delineation of lovers loving, a premonition of an important future philosophical development. It corresponds closely, however, to that development in art and literature which Foucault traces from Velasquez and Cervantes, and which we trace from Shakespeare: the representation of representation. The rationalist Descartes claims that self-consciousness only comes when the self is conscious of an external reference, the perfection of God. The phenomenologist Shakespeare, however, shows that love is valid only when it is experienced through an other who is easily identifiable with the self. This is Girard's triangulation of desire, but with two members consolidated into one, the self aware of itself. It is representation of representation in that both Rosalind and Orlando see themselves loving in Ganymede. Kernberg is now using a Cartesian definition of the self for the child who has completed the individuation process and has achieved self-awareness: "the awareness of the self being aware" (in an unpublished paper delivered to the American Psychoanalytic Association, New York, December 17, 1982).

IV.5 TWELFTH NIGHT

1. Sir Arthur Quiller-Couch and J. D. Wilson, *The New Shakespeare: Twelfth Night* (Cambridge: Cambridge University Press, 1949), pp. 1–2.

2. J. M. Lothian and T. W. Craik, *The Arden Shakespeare: Twelfth Night* (London: Methuen, 1975), pp. xlvii–1.

3. F. Kermode, "The Mature Comedies," in *Early Shakespeare* (=Stratford-Upon-Avon Studies 3) (London: Arnold, 1961), 3:224–27.

4. L. Salangar, "The Design of *Twelfth Night*," *Shakespeare Quarterly* (1958), 9:124: "Orsino's love for Olivia is self-destructive, subject to time and change. Although, or rather, because it is 'all as hungry as the sea', it is impossible to satisfy. And it seems almost without an object, or incommensurate with any object, a 'monstrosity' in the same sense as Troilus' love for Cressida, in its grasping after the infinite."

5. S. Freud, "Mourning and Melancholy," *The Standard Edition of the Complete Psychological Works of Sigmund Freud (SE)*, J. Strachey, ed. and tr. (London: Hogarth Press, 1953–74), 14:244.

6. *Ibid.*, p. 247.

7. O. Kernberg, *Object Relations Theory and Clinical Psychoanalysis* (New York: Aronson, 1976), p. 29: "Introjection . . . is the reproduction and fixation of an interaction with the environment by means of an organized cluster of memory traces implying at least three components: (i) the image of the object; (ii) the image of the self in interaction with the object, and (iii) the affective coloring of both the object-image and the self-image under the influence of the drive representations present at the time of the interaction."

8. Specifically, Orsino sees Olivia as Diana and himself as Actaeon, torn apart by his own dogs after being metamorphosed into a deer:

> "That instant was I turn'd into a hart,
> And my desires, like fell and cruel hounds,
> E'er since pursue me." (I.i.21–23)

We are in the company again, then, of a moon goddess, but here her cruelty is suggested, as well as her unapproachability.

On the general principle of masquerade in *Twelfth Night*, in other Elizabethan plays, and in court entertainment, and as a basic human need, Kott, *Shakespeare Our Contemporary* (London: Methuen, 1967), p. 215, cites Marlowe, *Edward II:*

> "Therefore I'll have Italian masks by night,
> Sweet speeches, comedies, and pleasing shows;
> And in the day, when he shall walk abroad,
> Like sylvan nymphs my pages shall be clad;
> My men, like satyrs grazing on the lawns,
> Shall with their goat-feet dance an antic hay;
> Sometime a lovely boy in Dian's shape,
> With hair that gilds the water as it glides,
> Crownets of pearl about his naked arms,
> And in his sportful hands an olive-tree,
> To hide those parts which men delight to see,
> Shall bathe him in a spring; and there, hard by,
> One like Actaeon, peeping through the grove,
> Shall by the angry goddess be transform'd,

And running in the likeness of a hart,
By yelping hounds pull'd down, shall seem to die:" (I.i)

Which parts do men delight to see? The actors are boys, but the impersonation is of a woman. Kott suggests that transvestism is, perhaps, the most satisfying form of masquerade. Certainly Marlowe, in this speech given by Gaveston, manages to combine in the pool where Diana bathes the pool where Narcissus gazes upon himself, and the pool where Salmacis and Hermaphroditus were combined. The myth of Actaeon is usually given an oedipal interpretation: Diana is seen as a maternal figure and the crime, then, is scopophilia. (The fate of Actaeon's cousin Pentheus is a graphic depiction of all this.) Diana is, however, herself sexually ambiguous, and if we can allow Marlowe to gloss Orsino's speech, then the narcissistic nature of his love for Olivia is revealed: he sees something of himself in her. Certainly, this is the nature of his subsequent attraction to Viola.

At the same time, of course, we cannot ignore the contrast between Olivia and Viola: Olivia is stately, mature, and aloof, while Viola is boyish and eager. Indeed the social argument of the play is as complicated as the erotic, and they sometimes seem to contradict each other. Why would Olivia only marry beneath herself? She has lost both father and brother in the past year. It seems that she would choose an older, socially superior man.

9. Freud, *SE*, 14:255.

10. L. Danson has recently argued ("Jonsonian Comedy and the Discovery of the Social Self," *PMLA* [1984], 99:179–93) that Shakespeare differs from Jonson in that he consolidates a sense of self for his characters in their familial relations: "In Shakespearean comedy the psychological self is grounded between two potentially stable coordinates, the nurturing prior family and the mature generative family" (p. 185). (He cites Kahn, among others, who have traced this movement.) He also sees the tendency for a strong character to take over a play which is weak in plot; speaking of Rosalind in *As You Like IT*, he theorizes: "Each play, in the absence of a strong plot, requires the intervention of a strong character who must use extraordinary means to bring an end to the theoretically endless proceedings" (p. 184). Orsino is such a strong character, and he brings *Twelfth Night* to its conclusion by accepting change in the object of his desire, from Olivia to Viola. We know nothing of his family before the action of the play; we have difficulty projecting his marriage with Viola into the future. We feel, though, to begin with, that he is alone and lost, without a sense of self, and that during the action of the play he manages to seize a self-image in Viola, simultaneously releasing himself from his idolatrous love of Olivia. This transition, which we have seen in so many of the other comedies, is then from the idealization of a lady to the acceptance of change in a lady, but it is also the dismissal of a love-object which is alien and unreal and its substitution by one that is deeply self-relevant. Kott compares Shakespeare to Leonardo, who throughout his career painted onto his

religious and classical figures his own face as a young man (*Shakespeare Our Contemporary*, p. 205). Orsino does this in choosing Viola, and some suggestion of his ambivalence about anaclitic and narcissistic choice of object might be contained in that early reference to Actaeon (see above, note 8).

11. O. Kernberg, "Boundaries and Structure in Love Relations," *Journal of the American Psychoanalytic Association* (1977), 25:83: "Normal love relationships include . . . the experience of sexual intercourse and orgasm with the expanded sexual eroticism derived from the integration of aggression and bisexuality (sublimatory homosexual identification) into the heterosexual erotic relationship."

12. On this point, cf. *The Rape of Lucrece*, ll. 1240–46:

"For men have marble, women waxen minds,
And therefore are they formed as marble will.
The week oppressed, the impression of strange kinds
Is formed in them by force, by fraud, or skill.
Then call them not the authors of their ill,
   No more than wax shall be accounted evil
   Wherein is stamped the semblance of a devil."

See IV.1 on *MND* I.i.30–32: "Thou hast . . . / . . . / Stol'n the impression of her fantasy."

13. Freud, *SE*, 14:249.

14. See III.2, note 15. If all the lovers are young and all the others are old, then the arrogance and insensitivity of the lovers to the others can be explained as the failure of youth to see in themselves the seeds of age's disappointments. Adolescent love of the narcissistic type is absolute in its demands; all else is compromise. *Romeo and Juliet* corrects all the comedies that end in marriage. Death is the only possible end to desire for the self.

15. B. Brophy, *Mozart the Dramatist* (New York: Harcourt, Brace, 1964).

16. Cf. *Venus and Adonis*, ll. 265–66:

"That had Narcissus seen her as she stood
Self-love had never drowned him in that flood."

This is a variant of Ovid's telling of the tale, where the youth is metamorphosed into a flower, i.e., while looking at the image of himself in the water from the bank, he becomes a flower on the bank reflecting itself in the water (*Met.* III.341–510); Ovid's way generally is to take the suffering consequent upon some erotic orientation and to fix it in some plant or animal form; cf. Dante, such "metamorphoses" as those of Paulo and Francesca, *Inferno*, Canto V. We associate the pool in which Narcissus drowns with the sea in which Antipholus of Syracuse thinks he has lost himself, the sea on which Antonio is tossed in *The Merchant of Venice*, and the sea of Orsino's bottomless love. Only desire for the self (or the lost image of the self) is endless, insatiable.

17. I have considered the outsider in Menandrean comedy, and his seeming

inability to be assimilated finally into comic society, in "Menander's Old Men," *Transactions of the American Philological Association* (1971) 102:303–25.

18. At the end of Billy Wilder's *Some Like It Hot*, the Jack Lemmon character, still transvestized, gives the Joe E. Brown character a list of reasons why they cannot marry, ending with, "But I'm not a woman," to which Joe E. Brown, unfazed, replies: "Nobody's perfect."

19. The play actually ends with a song which also traces stages in love corresponding to the ages of man: "When that I was a little, tiny boy." See the Arden editors' comments.

20. This actually happens at the end of Caryl Churchill's *Cloud Nine*. The play is in two parts, the first taking place in colonial Africa in 1880, the second in contemporary London: we are to think, however, of the people who are young in the first part as those who are mature in the second part. The same actor plays a young bride in the first part, and then a young male hustler in the second part. An actress plays the young bride of the first part matured in the second part, and she, a forty-five year old woman, makes an assignation with the young male hustler. The actor who plays the hustler meets her, however, as her own younger self, and they embrace, just to complete, indeed to give the basic figure for, all the various kinds of sexual pairings which have previously been presented in the play.

21. Kermode, "The Mature Comedies," pp. 224–27.

V. THE LATE ROMANCES

1. L. Salangar, *Shakespeare and the Traditions of Comedy* (Cambridge: Cambridge University Press, 1974), p. 172: "Whereas in Jonson, for example, the typical movement in a comedy is an advance towards moral truth by way of the unmasking of imposters, in Shakespeare it is an advance towards self-discovery by way of disguise and illusion." Jonson seems to me more conventional, almost medieval, in comparison with Shakespeare. Jonson believes in a "natural" ordering of the world, and ready access to truth, whereas for Shakespeare such order must be imposed by the individual, and the necessity for this process of imposition is the basic truth of human existence. See Danson's comparison, above, IV.5., note 10.

2. It is reassuring to note that my reading of the late romances with its emphasis on the fathers who see themselves in their daughters, is similar to the reading of them given by Joyce in *Ulysses*, which was obscured for many years by bad editing:

—Marina, Stephen said, a child of storm, Miranda, a wonder, Perdita, that which was lost. What was lost is given back to him: his daughter's child. *My dearest wife*, Pericles says, *was like this maid*. Will any man love the daughter if he has not loved the mother?

—The art of being a grandfather, Mr Best gan murmur. *L'art d'être grandp* . . .

—Will he not see reborn in her, with the memory of his own youth added, another image?

Do you know what you are talking about? Love, yes. Word known to all men. *Amor vero aliquid alicui bonum vult unde et ea quae concupiscimus* . . .

—His own image to a man with that queer thing genius is the standard of all experience, material and moral. Such an appeal will touch him. The images of other males of his blood will repel him. He will see in them grotesque attempts of nature to foretell or to repeat himself.

The benign forehead of the quaker librarian enkindled rosily with hope.

I quote from the edition of Hans Walter Gabler, *Ulysses, A Critical and Synoptic Edition*, forthcoming from Garland Press, as reprinted in *The New York Times*, June 7, 1984, p. C19. Though the Latin quotation is from Aquinas, *Summa Contra Gentiles* (I. 91), it is based on an original argument by Augustine, *The City of God*. His basic definition of love is Platonic: "What we love in ourselves is the very love by which we love whatever is good" (XI.28), but he goes on to argue: "The supreme human law is love and this law is best respected when men, who both desire and ought to live in harmony, so bind themselves by the bonds of social relationships that no man monopolizes more than one relationship, and many different relationships are distributed as widely as possible, so that a common social life of the greatest number may be fostered" (XV.16). The sequence he traces is from self-love, through incest to exogamy and beyond, precisely that sequence I have traced in individual Shakespearean comedies and in the entire Shakespearean comic sequence. Shakespeare, however, does not allow, as do Augustine and Aquinas—what Joyce does must be determined now on the basis of the revised edition—the complete transcendence of that originally narcissistic orientation of desire.

V.I THE WINTER'S TALE

1. The Arden edition of *MV* reads:

   for affection
   (Master of passion) sways it to the mood
   Of what it likes or loathes,—

2. See III.3 for discussion of this passage, and reference to W. Carroll, *The Great Feast of Language in "Love's Labor's Lost"* (Princeton: Princeton University Press, 1977), who compares Leontes' speech, pp. 97–101.

3. Cf. the definition "sudden mental seizure," in H. Smith, *Shakespeare Quarterly* (1963), 14:163–66.

4. See also the association between "affection" and "breeding" in a later description of Perdita: "the majesty of the creature in resemblance of the mother, the affection of nobleness which nature shows above her breeding" (V.ii.36–38). In the second half of the play Shakespeare breaks down the difference

between "breeding" in the sense of "begetting," and "breeding" in the sense of "character."

5. Carroll, *The Great Feast*, pp. 97–101.

6. An example of "affection" being used with the sense of "affectation" is *2H.IV* IV.v.173–4: "Did with the least affection of a welcome/Give entertainment to the might of it." Cf. also *KJ* I.i.85–86: "He hath a trick of Cour-de-Lion's face./ The accent of his tongue affecteth him." The significance of "assume the character of" is noted for "affect" (*OED*, V.i.5), but not for "affection."

7. C. Clark, *Shakespeare and Science* (Birmingham: Cornish Brothers, 1929), p. 31.

8. Among the major commentators on this passage are E. M. W. Tillyard and R. Girard:

"We can estimate the eminence of Elizabethan writers by the earnestness and the passion and the assurance with which they surveyed the range of the universe. By the same means we may find an unexpected kinship between writers too often dissociated. Using this criterion I find that the most eminent are Spenser Sidney Raleigh Hooker Shakespeare and Jonson, and that all these are united in holding with earnestness passion and assurance to the main outline of the medieval world picture as modified by the Tudor regime, although they all knew that the coherence of this picture had been threatened" (*The Elizabethan World Picture* [London: Chatto and Windus, 1956], p. 100).

"The word *degree*, from the Latin *gradus* (step, degree, measure of distance), means exactly what is meant here by difference. Culture is conceived not as a mere collection of unrelated objects, but as a totality, or, if we prefer, a structure, a system of people and institutions always related to one another in such a way that a single differentiating principle is at work. This social transference does not exist as an object, of course. That is why, as soon as an individual member, overcome by *hubris*, tries to usurp Degree, he finds imitators; more and more people are affected by the contagion of mimetic rivalry, and Degree collapses, being nothing more than the mysterious absence of such rivalry in a functional society. ("Myth and Ritual in Shakespeare," in J. Harari, ed., *Textual Strategies*, pp. 205–6 [Ithaca: Cornell University Press, 1979]).

The question both these commentators raise is whether order and degree are inherent in nature and society or imposed on both by man; and if by man, by all men in agreement, or by each individual man in his own way? and if by each individual man, with a constant or changing vision?

9. C. J. Neeley, "*The Winter's Tale*: The Triumph of Speech," *Studies in English Literature 1500–1900* (1975) 15:327: "If the passage is predominantly

'about' Leontes' imagination in the first half, it is predominantly 'about' Hermione's and Polixenes' lust in the second half."

10. For a brief summary of this discussion, see M. Schwartz, "Leontes' Jealousy in *The Winter's Tale*," *American Imago* (1973) 30:250–73. The original perception was J. M. Stewart's, *Character and Motive in Shakespeare* (London: Longmans, Green, 1949) pp. 30–39.

11. C. Kahn, *Man's Estate: Masculine Identity in Shakespeare* (Berkeley: University of California Press, 1979) p. 215.

12. One of the most evocative statements of the power of sexual fantasy to create sexual desire is the myth of Ixion. Zeus graciously received this mortal man at his banquets on Olympus, but Ixion was unable to bear his good fortune and determined to seduce Hera, an appallingly oedipal crime. Zeus fashioned a cloud in the form of Hera and named it Nephele, "Cloud," with which Ixion coupled. The product of this unholy union was Kentauros, a monster, who mated with the Magnesian mares to create the race of centarus, those half-man, half-horse creatures who rape nymphs (Ovid, *Met.* XIII.498–509).

13. Mamilius experiences that mythical changeableness of women in his mother which he will not live to experience in mature relations with women. At the opening of I.i, she first spurns him—"Take the boy to you. He so troubles me/ 'Tis past enduring"—and then teasingly attracts him to her—"What wisdom stirs amongst you? Come, sir, now/ I am for you again." M. Garber, *Coming of Age in Shakespeare* (New York: Methuen, 1981), p. 30, comments on the preternatural maturity of Shakespeare's children who are doomed to die young. One might compare Dickens' Dombey's son, and Henry James' Miles. In the latter case, of course, it is specifically sexual knowledge that children are credited with, and one wonders where they get it. They see things: scenes of sexual intercourse are revealed to them or reflected from them. What did Dora know and what did Freud read into her?

14. Neeley, "The Triumph of Speech," p. 327.

15. The indictment of Hermione recalls the arraignment of Anne Boleyn on the same charge. For the King's consort to commit adultery is a crime against the state and against nature.

"Hermione, Queen to the worthy Leontes, King of Sicilia, thou art arraigned of high treason, in committing adultery with Polixenes, King of Bohemia, and conspiring with Camillo to take away the life of our sovereign Lord the King, thy royal husband. The pretense whereof being by circumstances partly laid open, thou, Hermione, contrary to faith and allegiance of a true subject, didst counsel and aid them, for their better safety, to fly away by night" (III.ii.12–22).

The arraignment of Anne Boleyn at Greenwich, May 10, 1537: "The Said Queen and these other traitors . . . conspired the King's death and destruction. The Queen often saying she would marry one of them as soon as the King dies, and affirming that she would never love the King in her heart. And the King having a short time since become aware of the said abominable crimes and treasons against himself took such inward displeasure and heaviness, especially from the Queen's malice and adultery, that certain harms and perils have befallen his royal body."

16. See P. Slater, *The Glory of Hera* (Boston: Beacon Press, 1968), p. 87n.

17. In Euripides' *Alcestis*, which is so similar to *The Winter's Tale* in other respects, the wife, having died and been replaced by a statue, returns to life, but does not speak.

18. A. P. Burnett, "The Virtues of Admetos," *Classical Philology* (1965), 60:240–55.

19. L. Salangar, *Shakespeare and the Traditions of Comedy* (Cambridge: Cambridge University Press, 1974), pp. 42–43.

20. *Ovid: Metamorphoses*, R. Humphries, tr. (Bloomington: Indiana University Press, 1969).

> "Quas quia Pygmalion aeuum per crimen agentis
> uiderat, offensus uitiis, quae plurima menti
> femineae natura dedit, sine coniuge caelebs
> uiuebat thalamique diu consorte carebat.
> Interea niueum mira feliciter arte
> sculpsit ebur formamque dedit, qua femina nasci
> nulla potest, operisque sui concepit amorem.
> Uirginis est uerae facies, quam uiuere credas.
> Et, si non obstet reuerentia, uelle moueri:
> ars adeo latet arte sua. miratur et haurit
> pectore Pygmalion simulati corporis ignes"
> (X.243–53).

See Gombrich's comparison of Pygmalion to Admetos (III, note 20). In claiming that, since Admetos knows his statue of Alcestis is just an illusion, like a dream, whereas Pygmalion actually brings his statue to life, Admetos represents a more sophisticated attitude toward art, Gombrich suggests a different erotic orientation, and Ovid's account supports this: Pygmalion brings to life not just his own peculiar image of the perfect woman, but every man's. Pygmalion thus has reference to an ideal of women beyond actuality, but Admetos only to the example of that ideal in Alcestis, so that his statue is an imitation of an imitation.

We note, however, that Admetos projects his image not only upon the statue of Alcestis, but upon all the young girls his father Pheres expects he will exploit. Thus the statue represents a fetish which Admetos prefers to any aging and changing woman. In this respect all statue tales are alike, including *The Winter's Tale*: Leontes would replace Hermione with Perdita or a statue because he fears the sexuality of a real, mature woman.

21. ὡς χάριέν ἐστ' ἄνθρωπος, ἂν ἄνθρωπος ᾖ (fr. 484).

Index

Chaucer, G., 27, 49
Claudio, 150-52, 154-55
Comedy, 13-15, 28-54: Greek, 13-14, 30, 42, 47-54 (Old, 48-54; Middle, 53-54; New, 28, 48-54, 188); Roman, 13-14 Dionysos pattern, 29, 48; and epic, 61; love and friendship in, 18-19; marriage as the end of, 14, 45-54, 81-82, 94; narcissistic and anaclitic, 14, 82; Persephone pattern, 13, 28, 33, 37-40, 45-46, 215, 231n18, 231n19; the social argument of, 16-18; scapegoat pattern, 29; and tragedy, 17, 21, 61, 108-9
"Content," 83
Copernicus, N., 6-9, 10, 202
Corps morcelé, le, 24-25, 54
Courtly love tradition, 1-12, 14, 27, 44, 57-58, 66, 68, 101

Danaë, 232n20
Danby, J. F., 10-11, 226n5
Danson, L., 251n10
Darwin, C., 6-9, 21
Davies, S., 59-61, 235n7
Death, 12, 23, 67, 108-9
Debasement, 73
Demande et désir, 25, 243n7
Desdemona, 41, 146, 152, 198, 211
Devereux, G., 60, 63, 72, 235n11, 239n5
Diphilos, 28
Dover, K. J., 52, 63, 233n31, 235n13
Dyskolia 48-51

Egeus, 31-33
Elyot, Sir T., 97
Emilia *(CE)*, 88
Emilia *(Othello)*, 152-53, 198, 211
Endymion, 74, 89-90, 100-1, 102, 240n13
Erastēs and *erōmenos*, 56-57, 75, 147, 234n3
Erlich, A., 126-27, 228n12
Eros, 147, 186
Euclio, 35, 48
Euripides, 53, 61, 188: *Alcestis*, 213-15, 238n20, 257n17; *Sthenoboia*, 49

Faber, M., 148, 246n15
Falstaff, 28
"Fancy," "fantasy," 5, 11, 107

Fathers and daughters, 31-37, 43, 45, 67, 193-94
Fender, S., 137, 245n4
Ferdinand, 29, 231n19
Ferrante, J., 238n20, 244n15
Fetish, 106, 180, 199, 242n2
Fiedler, L., 36, 162-63, 230n13, 247nn1-2
Fort-Da, 22
Foucault, M., 158, 202, 225n1, 227n7, 233n35
Fränkel, H., 9, 226n3
Freud, S., 1, 6-9, 16-27, 41, 50, 58, 68, 72, 206, 228n7, 228n11, 228n13, 248n9: *Beyond the Pleasure Principle*, 22, 24; "Character and Anal Erotism," 230n11; *Civilization and Its Discontents*, 24, 231n19; "Introductory Lecture XVIII," 6; "Mourning and Melancholy," 178-91; "On Narcissism: An Introduction," 20-26, 178-91; "The Theme of the Three Caskets," 12
Frye, N., 28, 31, 52, 72, 229n1, 229n2

Galileo, 10, 132, 245n4
Ganymede, 58, 60, 147, 174-76
Genesis, 166, 215
Genital organization, 48, 78
Girard, R., 98, 138, 143, 231n19, 239n7, 245n5, 247n10, 249n6, 255n8
"The gold and the girl," 34-41, 230n12
Gombrich, E. H., 226n7, 238n20, 257n20
"Grace," 92, 110-20, 130-33, 137, 140, 186, 205-17
Greenblatt, S., 233n35

Hamlet, 16, 22-23, 179, 206
Hayles, N. K., 249n4
Hegel, G. W. F., 11, 227n7
Helena, 135
Herakles, 115, 126, 153, 214
Hermia, 31-33, 40, 135-36
Hermione, 39-40, 45, 195-217
Hero, 150, 154-55
Hesiod, 230nn14-15
Hilliard, N., 61
Hippolyta, 136, 143-44, 146
Hobbes, T., 2-3, 10-13, 67-68, 131, 158, 191, 202, 213